IRELAND, WHERE OUR ROOTS GO DEEP

IRELAND, WHERE OUR ROOTS GO DEEP

Pat Nevin

COLIN SMYTHE
Gerrards Cross, 1987

First published in 1987 by Colin Smythe Limited
Gerrards Cross, Buckinghamshire

British Library Cataloguing in Publication Data

Nevin, Pat
  Ireland where our roots go deep.
  1. Multyfarnham (Westmeath)—Social
  life and customs
  I. Title
  941.8'15   DA995.M/
  ISBN 0-86140-255-3
  ISBN 0-86140-259-6 Pbk

Produced in Great Britain
Set by Spire Print Services Ltd, Salisbury
and printed and bound by Billing & Sons Ltd., Worcester

Dedicated to
daughter Deirdre

CONTENTS

PART THREE:
THE SUPERNATURAL

PART FOUR:
IN RETIREMENT

PART FIVE:
THE DEEP AND RECENT PAST

PREFACE

This is a second offering from the versatile pen of Pat Nevin, or, to give him his full name, military rank and decoration, Squadron Leader Louis 'Pat' Nevin C.D., Royal Canadian Air Force (Retired). His first book, *Ireland, Where Time Stands Still*, won the acclaim of many, especially in the United States and Canada, where it awakened a latent nostalgia among Irish immigrants and their descendants, and where reviewers were laudatory. People of many other nationalities read the book with avid interest too, enthralled by the author's descriptive powers, his economy with words; and yet, at the same time, his twinkling, underlying sense of humor brings to life in a vivid way, and in native color, the trivial and the mundane. That book was based on reminiscences of a childhood full of adventure, the childhood of one whose life was made all the more interesting by the various 'odd' characters who bestride its pages from time to time – a varied amalgam indeed, such as Ireland has been famous for through the centuries.

This second book, *Ireland, Where Our Roots Go Deep*, is, thanks to the author's keen memory, a re-enactment of occurrences and events that were once part and parcel of the lore of his native village, more than sixty years ago. This book shows that the author has a very wide range of interests – going back over the centuries to pre-historic Ireland. Despite many years abroad, the author has obviously retained a great love for his native heath, and a keen appreciation of its people, especially those who inhabited his childhood and are now the source of so many beautiful, poignant memories. He has salted his narrative with local words and phrases still in use in his native village; expressions which have trickled down from the peasant ancestors of the locality and from the native langauge, Gaelic, that had been spoken by our people from time immemorial till a few hundred years ago. These words are now couched in a dull anglicized garb; only a native speaker of Gaelic can really grasp the full meaning of such words.

9

Mr. Nevin's new book gives a meticulously accurate and vivid account of the life of an ordinary peasant community, their habitations, their manner of daily activity, in one of the more beautiful valleys in the lake district of Co. Westmeath. It gives a pen picture of their interests, their pastimes, their forms of recreation and their innate wit, in addition to their foibles, their failings and their sorrows. Having spent many years living among the Canadian people, a life completely different in texture from what he had known in his childhood, the author became keenly aware of the special character of life in his native village.

This book describes intimately, lovingly, even delicately, in language 'racy of the soil', that village which the author left at the age of eighteen, only to return out of something like personal necessity, to make his home there again. He has here recorded memories that would otherwise be lost – and regrettably lost – to posterity. His book is a record of a society quickly fading from memory and is a welcome addition to the store of native Irish folklore and social history. Would that many others had likewise penned similar accounts. Those who are children of Ireland would be richer to have many contacts with an ancestral past such as is available in these pages. But readers of every heritage will welcome this fascinating record of a passing era and of the human community that is its central theme.

The Abbey   Pádraig O Gibealláin, O.F.M.
Multyfarnham
Co. Westmeath
Ireland

PART ONE:
A 'MULTY' BACKGROUND

1. MY NATIVE VILLAGE

This book is not intended to be an autobiography: in reality my personal life is neither important nor interesting enough to provide material worth recounting let alone recording. Actually it's Ireland and her people I'm endeavouring to write about — not about myself. In order to write *firsthand* about Ireland I'll have to creep personally into the account from time to time but will honestly try to maintain a low profile — which after all won't be difficult because the profile I reflect or project, is just that.

I was bred, born and reared in a little village close to the geographical centre of Ireland where I spent the first eighteen years of my life. I then emigrated to Canada where, with the exception of frequent trips home, I lived for thirty years. At the end of that thirty years, accompanied by my Canadian family — wife and six children — I returned to my native village with the intention of settling down permanently. We only stayed for three years and at the end of that period we all returned to Canada.

Nine years later my wife Eileen, two sons and myself returned for the second time to live in Ireland. After a couple of years of Irish schooling the boys considered they were able to fend for themselves and decided to return to Canada and join our three daughters there.

Now from time to time Eileen and myself spend our vacations in Canada; other times our children come to Ireland on holidays. So for the past eight years here in my native village and among my own people, Eileen and I have lived and loved every full day of my second retirement. She refers to it as *our* final and fulfilling retirement.

The result of my effort to write about my native country may read somewhat like pages pulled at random or culled from a diary that took two generations, or longer, to write. The net result — no plot, little continuity or sequence and certainly no conclusion — but isn't real life just like that!

If you don't run out of patience, maybe together we will ramble down the highways and byways *and* boreens of Ireland, and our rambles in Erin will, I trust, afford you an insight into our unique way of life.

Our beloved ex-President, Eamon de Valera, soldier, scholar and statesman who devoted an entire lifetime, ninety two years, to the service of Ireland, once remarked that loving one's village was a genuine basis for loving one's country.

Multyfarnham, my birthplace, is a small village in County Westmeath, one of the counties in the Irish Midlands. The village which boasts of, or apologizes for, a population of 201, is only about fifty miles from Dublin, and 100 miles from Cork City.

Ireland's coastline is so deeply indented, especially its west coast, that no part of the country is more than seventy miles from either the Irish Sea in the east or the Atlantic Ocean in the west. The main highway from Dublin to Sligo passes within a couple of miles of here, but the village is still a bit off the beaten track, if that is what you would call those parts of Ireland that travel brochures and related literature extol and recommend to their would-be clients. I'll admit that the brochures and pamphlets on tourism do give glowing factual write-ups on motoring, horse and pony riding, golfing, forest walks and especially boating, sailing, fishing, diving and swimming in the network of lakes and waterways with which Ireland as a whole is endowed. In fact, the Irish Midlands contain such a profusion and variety of lakes and rivers (including two canals) that it has been given the proud title of Lakelands. Nevertheless, the people in our area feel miffed that tourism blurbs include little or no information on the village itself. It is a safe bet that future tourist brochures will remedy that omission.

Multyfarnham, the full official name of the village, sounds to my ears somewhat prim and proper, especially when it's used among friends and acquaintances. Multyfarnham with its five syllables, to Irish ears has a pleasant enough sound; but when I hear someone say 'Multyfarnham', it invariably reminds me of times in my childhood when a Bishop or V.I.P. addressing me would give the impression of speaking down to me when he'd say, 'My boy, where are you from?', and giving every syllable its full value I'd answer, 'Multyfarnham', just as if in military parlance I'd be giving the little unimportant place its full rank, number, title and decorations. Anyway, the word 'Multy' to my mind sounds simple, warm and intimate; but then, 'everyone to their own taste', the woman said as she kissed the cow.

There was a period in my young life when I felt an immense pride, a pride shared by an amazing number of other equally simple-minded, naive fellow-villagers, that so many emigrants from our little village had made vast fortunes in the U.S.A. — I mean the extraordinary number of multi-millionaires. Which brings me to the strange but true fact that we did have a Multy millionaire in our own family. He was Jimmy Hand, born in Edgeworthstown, County Longford, my grandfather's half brother who emigrated to U.S.A. — it must be around eighty years ago — and eventually became a real live multi-millionaire in Brooklyn.

That lengthy name of our village is due to its Gaelic origin; but then almost all place names in Ireland are of Gaelic origin. The names still preserve their ancient forms, some plainly, others in disguise, and their pronunciation by those who speak naturally and unaffectedly is, in many cases, as Irish as when the language was still universal in Ireland.

You may ask, 'What is Multy and the surrounding country like?'. My answer: I could sing, or rather write about its wonders, or at least its most desirable features. But then understandably, I'm terribly biased. Maybe I am in love with the place, being born, bred and reared here. In fact I lived here until my eighteenth birthday when the spirit of adventure coupled with the age-old vision — or is it euphoria — of 'fields are green far away' goaded me on and I sailed for Canada. For the following thirty years I lived a full, productive and happy life in that wonderful country — a young country which provided me with a working lifetime that was challenging, fulfilling and remunerative. It also enabled us to rear and educate a good-sized family that wanted for nothing that money could buy. Incidentally, without trying to appear modest, I marvel at the variety and number of responsible positions that Canadians and the Canadian Government permitted me to hold. I'm sure they were influenced by the fact that Canadians in general have a warm spot in their hearts for 'The Irish', because you often hear them appreciatively and admiringly exclaim 'the luck of the Irish'. In all my years in Canada my attachment, almost preoccupation, with Ireland was kept alive and nurtured by my yearly visits to, and continuing correspondence with my people and my immediate family in Multy.

Without any argument, my years in Canada were 'the best years of my life'. But Ireland kept calling and in 1960, I finally answered the call and with our six Canadian-born children we returned to Multy and bought a house where we lived three wonderful and memorable years. The 'call' must have been little more than a whisper because within three years Canada beckoned again and I went back for nine further financially fruitful years.

But in the fullness of time — actually 1972 — memories and lessons learned from those three years in Ireland added up so favourably that my wife and I made the momentous decision to return to Ireland for 'keeps'. God willing we intend to spend the rest of our mortal days in Multy among my own people. I suppose this decision could be accepted as evidence of deep personal affection (shared by my wife) for the place I was born, a place which, like a powerful magnet, drew me back; back from a young, prosperous country with a way-of-life second to none, where our five children are all gainfully employed and each lives a full life. Incidentally, thirty years ago I felt honoured and immensely proud when I was accorded Canadian Citizenship.

I want to stress that Ireland was not the sole place that offered us a perfect haven. Actually, we decided to come back after much soul-searching, especially in relation to accepting the unpalatable fact that our children seemed committed to staying in Canada. We had already experienced the Irish climate and accepted it. Thanks to being generously recompensed for my years of service with the Canadian Government and being blessed with a practical, economical wife, coupled with both of us accepting a modest life-style, we were confident that we could live in comfort almost anywhere in the English-speaking world.

Now back to the village itself. How does Multy measure up to other villages in Ireland? Well, I suppose the best answer is to list our past and present standing in Bord Fáilte (the Irish Tourist Board) Tidy Towns annual competition. In 1975, our village came first in its class and in 1976, it was within one point of winning the national title. Actually, at that time it topped its category for villages with a population of between 200 and 500 and received high praise from the competition adjudicators for its dedication to architectural conservation and for its picturesque character. It was just two points behind Adare, County Limerick, which achieved the highest-ever score in the twenty year life of the competition. Then in the autumn of 1977, all our national and provisional newspapers vied with each other in singing the praises of

Multyfarnham, the Lakeland village winning the overall National Award in the 1977 Tidy Towns Competition organized by Bord Fáilte; and also making it a 'double' by winning the National Title of The Best Village in Ireland.

I believe that Bord Fáilte's assessors drew the perfect pen-picture of Multy when they wrote: 'The village has a garden-like quality and in fact is more like a well-kept private garden than a small country village where many routine activities take place — going to shop, going to pray, or just enjoying oneself.'

Like eggs in a nest, the little village of Multyfarnham nestles in the Valley of the Gaine. The valley, about three miles long and averaging about three quarters of a mile in width, is enfolded and guarded by gently sloping hills on three sides while the open end of the north is bounded by Lough Derravaragh, long associated with the most poignant of all Irish legendary romances, The Fate of the Children of Lir*. The word 'guarded' in relation to the hills is not accidental; the skyline as observed from any part of the valley proper is interspersed by earthen fortifications, old mounds, ring forts and burial sites all connected with pre-Christian Ireland.

Judging from the numerous ruins and remains of pre-Christian structures, this area must have been thickly populated long ages before Christianity came to Ireland. The concentration of both ancient and modern religious houses, including some Patrician and other fifth-century sites here in the geographically remote centre of Ireland, affords striking evidence of the reason that in the centuries succeeding St. Patrick, Ireland was given the proud title, 'Island of Saints and Scholars'.

Invariably the monastic settlements and other centres housing

*See Chapter 31

religious communities were sited close to streams, rivers or lakes. Obvious reason for the waterside sitings was the normal requirement of water for everyday use, including water for farm and domestic animals. Fish for food was an important item, hence most of the religious settlements and communities had eel-weirs and salmon traps on nearby streams or rivers. At a relatively later date many of the monasteries installed mills, powered by water, for grinding their corn and grain. In that era of inadequate roads, it is obvious that the country-wide network of inter-connected rivers and lakes facilitated water transportation of people and supplies.

For the moment, I'll mention three religious foundations in the valley. At the head, or southern end of the valley at Killamalish where the river Gaine has its origin, you can discern the remains of an ancient church, plus traces of a building complex and a still-used Christian graveyard. About a mile from Killamalish, on the eastern side of the valley, in the townland of Tyfarnham, you can still see traces of a monastic settlement. I found its location on a map of Monastic Ireland but the only information it gave was, 'Early Celtic Establishment: possibly no community after tenth-century'. Looking at the grass-covered, raised outline of the scattered ruins it is apparent that the buildings of this old monastic settlement covered an area of several acres. For the moment all I can find out about its history is that up to 140 years ago only unbaptized infants were interred in its graveyard. The third monastic establishment in the Valley of the Gaine is one I could speak about interminably; it would be a labour of love because the Friars and the Abbey of Multyfarnham are near and dear to all our hearts.

A few words on monasteries generally. In the middle ages the monasteries were the shelter of arts and learning. Not only Ireland but the rest of the civilized world owes a deep debt to the Irish monks who, during that period, were about the only representatives of learning and knowledge. A seventeenth-century chronicler wrote:

In the cloisters alone were to be found painting, sculpture, poetry, the love of antiquity. Witness the splendid buildings, the temples, chapels, and houses of prayer which they reared! — the monasteries, the abbeys, the priories which they founded and endowed — the bridges with which they spanned rivers — the hospitals and infirmaries which they threw open to the helpless sick! — the colleges and seminaries which they instituted! It was in them that civilization took refuge. Without the cloister, Europe would have grown and perhaps perished in barbarism. Every monk had his appointed situation. Some sowed the soil, cleared forests, and cultivated waste lands, stemmed torrents, taught and transmitted the principles of irrigation, cropping and agricultural science. Others were employed in transcribing and deciphering ancient charters, thus preserving the titles of our corporation liberties, or in annotating and translating the text of Greek and Latin authors; whilst ordinary scribes laboured with the patience of angels in illuminating the hymns and proses of the Church.[1]

The heavily meadowed, fertile Gaine Valley, roughly the shape of the letter Z, is bisected by the River Gaine which flows in a northward direction, cuts under the ancient stone-built bridge at the foot of the village of Multyfarnham, snakes past and through the nicely landscaped and well maintained grounds of the historic Franciscan Abbey and a mile further on empties into Lough Derravaragh and eventually its water joins the lordly Shannon and finally mingles with the broad Atlantic. From a military or engineering point of view, I would surmise that Multyfarnham village was built or had its origin at the only feasible place, within miles, where in those days a road could be constructed to cross the Gaine River. Strategically speaking such a river crossing demanded fortifications, watch towers or military structures appropriate to each particular period or fashion.

Irish history, legends, tales of love and war abound with accounts of battles, sieges, heroic deeds and romantic rides connected with or zeroing in on fords, bridges and mountain passes. Most of the old Irish tales are associated with fords, including a picture of ancient heroes (Cuchulain, Ferdia) locked in unyielding single combat. The stone-built bridge at the foot of the village is in existence only a few hundred years and it replaced other bridge-like structures which in turn evolved from the pre-historic ford. Recently I found a brief historical reference[2] which went:

On March 19, 1412 the king granted licence to Maurice, son of John Delemere, to construct a castle over the bridge of 'Mullyfernan', for his

---

[1]*Annals of Westmeath*
[2]Rev. Paul Walsh, *The Placenames of Westmeath*, Dublin Institute for Advanced Studies (1957) p. 102.

manor lay on the marches of 'O Fferrolles country, Irish enemies', and
to exact tolls and customs for all things passing by the said bridge
between the water of Low[gh] Erin and logh Dervaragh.

Not within living memory has there been any trace found of
the castle but there is still the bulk of another historic structure,
The Motte, within fifty yards of the bridge and half that distance
behind the main street of the village. This motte was part of a
fortress called motte-and-bailey castle, which was a military
installation quite common in England around the eleventh
century.

On the north end of the valley where the Gaine River flows
into Lough Derravaragh, fairly recent drainage operations
exposed previously buried crannoges and portions of a (still)
submerged causeway.

The crannogs were artificial islands constructed in what
normally were (approximately 1,000 years ago) impassable
swamps, or shallow areas of lakes or rivers. Dwellings were
built on those islands and as a further defensive measure, the
crannogs were usually connected to the mainland by circuitous
causeways or paths whose travelling surface was located
slightly below normal water level.

The causeway was no mean engineering feat when you
consider it is so old that it is unknown even in the folklore of
the district. None of the old maps or records give any clue to its
existence let alone its origin. To reach the other shore of the lake,
the causeway had to traverse almost half a mile of swamp, or
probably shallow water; therefore much of the construction had
to be carried out from boats or rafts. This work consisted of
driving timbers (up to a foot in diameter) down into the wet,
spongy, boggy soil. In fact, there is twenty feet of peat
overburden in the area of the causeway. The builders drove the
timbers or piles so as to form two parallel timber retaining walls
about fifteen feet apart, then they placed layer upon layer of
sticks and branches between the two rows of piles until they had
a reasonably dry, stable travelling surface.

The Bog Road is one of the six roads that radiate from the
village. It is but a mile long and its name is descriptive of the
country it passes through — bogland. The name of the
townland the bog road cuts through, aptly enough, is
Abbeyland, for the simple reason that it contains the Franciscan
Abbey and the Abbey grounds.

The Bog Road comes to an abrupt end within a hundred yards of the south end of the causeway; so close that it is logical to assume that originally they formed one road, but that assumption begs the question, 'To where did the causeway road lead?'. That old causeway cuts across the lake bottom in the general direction of County Longford and heads straight as an arrow towards a point on the horizon (six miles distant) marked by the prominent Motte of Granard. This motte which is situated in the town of Granard is one of the largest mottes in Ireland. It is noteworthy that in 1315 Edward Bruce attacked the town of Granard and partially wrecked the motte-and-bailey. I wonder did Edward Bruce and his army pass through our village and use that old causeway on their way to Granard!

2. THE HEARTH

An extraordinary percentage of Irish-born people permanently residing in other countries sorrowfully and resignedly call themselves exiles. Regardless of whether they left Ireland of their own free will, or in the spirit of adventure (as I did) or one jump ahead of the bailiff, they still believe they were the victims of cruel fate. It's beyond my ability to explain it, but I believe it is all tangled up with a feeling, real or imagined, of a romantic spiritual love and longing for Ireland, the island of their dreams. All of us in Ireland thank God for this 'bred in the bone' affection for the homeland and the Irish connection. Ask in any corner of Ireland 'What's your opinion of John F. Kennedy?' and right away you will find they all have a soft spot in their hearts for Irish-Americans; in fact for all Americans.

When I was in exile, most of the Irishmen I ran into — and that phrase has nothing whatsoever to do with driving any kind of vehicle — were good types. I never considered myself a 'good mixer', being inclined to wait for the other guy to make the first friendly — or otherwise — move, but it gave me real pleasure, or as an American lady so nicely expressed it, 'it did me proud' to observe the way the Canadians and Americans took the Irish, and yours truly to their collective hearts.

I noticed that sooner or later most of my new-found Irish friends, even when sober, had an urge that almost amounted to a compulsion to talk about Ireland and things Irish. In the ensuing conversation — or monologue — the phrase 'around the fire' would crop up again and again. Naturally I avoided arousing suspicion that I was trying to find out specifically what makes an Irishman tick; but the point that emerged loud and clear was that reminiscences relating to 'around the fire' surfaced more often when the other fellow was reared, had been in contact with, or was under the influence of the 'Irish fire on the hearth'.

Invariably those open hearth-triggered talks, especially if the talker had not been home for years, contained a cry of loneliness and homesickness; a poignant reaching-out to recapture, and in imagination relive, what they called the 'best years of their lives'. This fireplace fixation is not confined to exiles. It packs a stronger wallop when it hits the millions who stayed in Ireland. Millions who as they say 'never strayed a mile from a cow-dung in their entire lives.'

An astute advertiser of one of our best Irish dairy products (Kerrygold butter) uses a commercial slogan that goes right to all our hearts. It is given first in Irish and then in English. To the Irish audience the slogan in OUR own language strikes a responsive chord. It's 'Nil aon tinteán mar do tinteán féin'. The English translation is 'There's no hearthstone like your own hearthstone'. That slogan evokes the traditional fireplace around which the daily life of the Irish family revolves. It conjures up pictures not only of today's tightly-knit family around the fire, but the fireplace of our youth and the fireplace of generations of our family long departed.

Maybe I should make an effort to go back in time; back to when primitive man first acquired the necessary skill to make and maintain fire; a skill that made it possible for man to survive in the climatically benign parts of the earth and eventually travel to, and settle in less favourable climates — including Ireland. Without the aid of textbooks or delving into learned tomes it's safe to run through the more obvious stages or steps that our ancestors worked out and followed in the ascent from their first primitive shelters, whether those shelters were caves, natural hollows in the ground or the lee of cliffs.

It would be beyond my ability to trace primitive man's progress step-by-step but I think it's reasonable to give some thought to the domestic or communal fire which our ancestors huddled around for heat, tended for cooking, or hunkered around for mutual comfort and communication.

The first inhabitants of Ireland, probably more than ten thousand years ago, could have been fishermen or hunters, or both, and it is logical that they managed eventually to improvise some type of shelter or habitation, also that they built and maintained their domestic fires close to its entrance. Even the relatively small number who were fortunate in finding caves could have managed to build some type of fire inside or in the shelter of the cave. Next, our (assumed) Irish ancestors could have constructed houses or shelters inside of which domestic fires could be maintained. I believe records are available confirming that as recent as the eighteenth century there were domestic habitations here that had a fire in the centre of the floor and a single opening in the roof for the smoke to escape. This brings us to our next step: the Irish habitation with the fire on clay, earthen, or eventually, the flagged floor. But now this dwelling contains a chimney, maybe not as sophisticated a chimney as our modern type, but a chimney that worked, or 'drew'.

From the evidence of many of our centuries-old, still-standing ancient historical castles and mansions there is little doubt that their builders were versed in the design and construction of chimneys — chimneys as we know them today. But it is noteworthy that all those buildings which were built before the end of the eighteenth century, had open fireplaces.

Up to the start of the twentieth century most Irish farmhouses and country dwellings had 'the fire on the hearth'. Even today most of the rural activities connected with Irish family-life centre on the kitchen. In real life and on the stage, or screen, both story-wise and for commercials the Irish kitchen fulfills the functions of the American kitchen and living room combined.

The fireplace in the average Irish farmhouse formed part of the kitchen but was looked on as a separate entity. It resembled a small rectangular room or alcove about twelve feet wide, six feet deep and five feet high. In reality the space taken up by the open fireplace was formed by the first ten feet of the chimney proper. The end wall of the kitchen formed the back wall of the chimney, both sides being formed by two short stub walls built into and at right angles to the back wall of the kitchen. The front wall or breast of the chimney started about five feet above the level of the kitchen floor. This front wall was usually built on a massive oak beam whose ends were securely built into, and supported by the stub walls. This beam was thus parallel to the kitchen floor and permitted a head clearance of five feet. You can visualize this rectangular space of the fireplace as closed on three sides, the fourth is open to the kitchen — in fact, it's part of the kitchen.

At this point I though I'd about covered the building layout, then had the good fortune to mention hearthstones to a person born 'within the roar of an ass' from here: a man at the top of his profession, an Orthopaedic Surgeon with a list of degrees and letters as long as your arm. My heart warmed to him when he confided, 'Some of my most treasured memories are connected with the open hearth in our place. Many's the night I sat in the open chimney corner and looking up our square tapering chimney, like sighting through the barrel of a primitive telescope, saw that square patch of sky right above our house. You'd be surprised the amount of sky you could observe and how close an eye you could keep on the weather.' Following the Specialist's train of thought, I said, 'Maybe our first astronomers got the germ of an idea about our place in the vast universe as they peered through such an aperture at the moon and stars as those heavenly bodies out there in space moved with precision and conformity.'

Normally the fire was level with the kitchen floor, although in some houses the base of the fire was on a slab of stone or brick slightly higher — never more than three inches — than the floor level. In most open fireplaces, a slab of stone (flag) or a plateau of brick about three inches higher than the level of the floor was built as a base for the fire. A hollow or receptacle called the ash-pit was constructed close to either side of the slab. This ash-pit was functional and whether it evolved or was invented, it had the essence of genius. This type of ash-pit surely owes its existence to the fact that turf (peat) was and is the principal Irish fuel resource and has been used as domestic fuel for thousands of years.

A substantial layer of residue of ash forms on turf while it burns. In fact if a turf fire were permitted to burn without the interference of shaking, raking, poking or being subjected to a current of air, the turf would end up with a complete coating of ash. Hence the thicker the blanket of ash the slower the burning rate of the turf. This property of burning turf creating its own layer of insulation is the basis, the key, to our age-old custom of 'raking the fire'. This raking procedure took place when the kitchen activities ceased for the day; it was called 'putting out and raking the fire'. The object of raking the fire was to ensure that there would be sufficient live coals (*griósch*) to kindle a fire on the following morning. The raking was not an unimportant chore delegated to some inexperienced member of the household; it was a specialized duty or ritual usually restricted to the 'Man of the House' or his wife. Properly raking a fire is not something you could master in ten easy lessons because there are so many variables involved. First of all, it consists of building a base of partially burned sods of turf that are already lit, or smouldering. The next step is to pile the ideal amount of ashes on those partially lit sods. Ideal means taking into account that too much ash will suffocate the burning coals, while too little ash will allow the sods to burn through. You could also rake the coals in the ash-pit; in fact if the pit is large enough and has the correct amount of ashes in it you could keep smouldering coals alight for days. This is not as easy as it sounds. It will be a failure if you put too many live coals in the ash-pit, or do not make provision to permit the optimum quantity of oxygen to feed the smouldering coals.

Quite often you hear the word hob and I'm sure everyone knows its meaning: 'projecting ledge at the back or sides of a fireplace used for keeping a kettle, saucepan etc. warm.' It appears that those hobs were a later improvement or addition to our open fireplaces because in our locality there were very few of them. It is obvious that if you built a hob on one side or both of the open fireplace you would be sacrificing valuable seating and working space around the fire. Some of the more modern fireplaces had one small hob on their right hand side. This hob or projection sometimes formed a base for the crane.

Pretty soon if you wish to see one of those old Irish cranes you will have to visit a museum. The cranes in our country fireplaces were all made by local blacksmiths and each was different in detail and style. All the cranes I saw were surely intended to last. The vertical part or post was made from a two and a half inch square iron bar (almost as heavy as an axle of an ass's cart). This post was about five feet long and its bottom portion fitted loosely into a spud-stone securely set into the floor of the fireplace. The top end of the post rotated freely in an iron 'eye' which protruded from the side wall of the chimney. This eye, plumb in line with the spud-stone, was a heavy piece of iron also hand-forged and I suppose got its name from the shape of the oval aperture which, like the spud-stone below, permitted the post to rotate freely. I said the post was about five feet long: actually its length was dictated by the height from the floor of the oak beam that formed the lintel of the fireplace. The arm of the crane was designed to swing freely for a quarter of a full circle. This was so that a pot or some cooking utensil hanging on the arm of the crane could be swung out into the roomy kitchen clear of the fire and the fireplace.

Considering the intense heat that is generated by a roaring turf fire and the size and weight of some of the pots that swung from its extremity, it is obvious that the inventor of the crane was mechanically ahead of his time. The same inventiveness was shown in the variety and efficiency of the many types of hangers, chains and links that permitted the cooking utensils to be raised or lowered without risk to life and limb. You'll appreciate how sturdy the crane had to be when you realize it had to support the pig's pot which held about twenty five gallons (200 pounds) of pig's vittles.

The layer of ash which forms on burning turf calls for constant 'minding' the fire. Minding entails moving and rearranging individual smouldering sods to knock off accumulated ash and allow the fire to draw; hence the tongs was an important piece of fireside equipment.

Previous to the machine age people were inclined to invest inanimate objects with a will and a kind of a life of their own. Our tongs, that pincer-like instrument for lifting and handling hot coals, was such an object. It had been in our family for maybe a hundred years and like most handcrafted items of the period, it bore the image and stamp of its maker — in this case a local blacksmith long gone to his reward. Now, some tongs were quite easy to operate and when you took one in your hand you felt it was making an effort to cooperate whether you were lifting a big shapeless lump of burning turf out of the inferno on the hearth, or gingerly lifting a small, glowing red particle of 'clod' to deposit in the bowl of a ceilier's dudeen (short stem clay pipe). Personally I always imagined our tongs resembled the blacksmith who hammered them out, and pictured him as big, powerful, awkward and dogged. My grandmother often remarked, 'No matter how long or how carefully you handle that tongs the time will come when it will turn on you like a cur, and bite a lump out of the palm of your hand.' In our household, the smith who made that tongs was often remembered — but not prayerfully.

Unlike a modern fireplace, the Irish hearthstone was designed and located so as to make it easy for people to sit in comfort around the hearth and at the same time give ample room for

tending the fire and domestic cooking. I wish I could give you a
'feel' for our traditional fire on the hearth because it was an
integral part of our culture. The Irish fire on the hearth and the
quality of life connected with it was part of something that soon
will only be remembered in folklore.

I can tell you a true story of real *grá* (love, affection) for the
hearth. A family in County Galway decided to build a new
house but did not follow the usual practice of siting the modern
one some distance from the old house and using the latter for
farm buildings or sheds. They took great pains and spent
considerable money to build their new home on the site of the
old one. They first demolished the old structure, but in the
process preserved the complete hearthstone, chimney corner
and chimney of their ancestral home. Their explanation: 'Next to
the altar in church, that old fireplace means more to our family
past and present than any place on earth.'

As I let my mind wander across the long bridge of bygone
years I vividly see Brennan's living fireplace. That dim,
smoke-filled, cave-like recess could be a chapel of some ancient
cult — a sanctuary partially lit by the immense floor-level turf
fire around which a circle of fire worshippers sit or crouch. The
turf itself is hand-won peat, that took thousands of years to
reach its present form. Above the fire, like a medieval jibbet
looms the massive soot-encrusted crane from which blackened
pots and pans dangle, and presiding over, and dominating the
scene is the priestess — the Woman of the House — performing
the age-old rituals that include tending the fire and cooking.

That phrase 'hand-won peat' begs for an explanation. First of
all, peat is formed chiefly from grasses, heather and sedges; it
develops where cold, water-logged soils prevent bacterial
decay, as a result of which little or no disintegration of
vegetable matter takes place. Hence, layer after layer, season
after season, this mass of raw vegetable matter builds up until
eventually a great thickness of organic material results.

About six per cent of the surface of Ireland is covered with
bog, the greatest concentration of which occurs in the central
lowlands. Bogland is a series of small bogs, each several square
miles in area, which vary in depth from ten to thirty feet. Our
peat bogs have always been an important source of domestic
fuel; in fact in Ireland the cutting of turf dates back to
pre-history. Since the countryside was denuded of forest about

three centuries ago, peat has become the only Irish fuel of importance.

I don't really know the origin of 'hand-won' but it's a very appropriate description of how, before the introduction of peat digging and processing machines, the peat was dug and finally carted home to burn. By the way, we always call it turf. We cut the turf, rear it, and when it's reared, cart it home. Notice that expression 'reared'! We 'harvest' crops, 'save' hay, but 'rear' turf. Rearing turf invariably was and is a joint family effort. When the dry turf is finally carted home and built into a weather-proof 'rick', each sod — that's the usual name in Ireland for the brick-shaped lump of dry peat — has literally been handled at least a dozen times by members of the family. Unlike purchased fuel delivered at the house, we always feel different towards hand-won turf. When we see our own sods of turf 'put on the fire' each of us feels a personal, proprietory interest in every individual sod.

Many ancient customs and beliefs still survive among Celtic peoples. For instance, in Ireland we still religiously follow the old tradition or belief that a household is bound to get a run of bad luck — or worse — if they let the fire in the house die out. This custom of keeping the domestic fire perpetually burning is as old as the hills and undoubtedly was perpetuated — if not originated — by the Druids.

The inhabitants of Ireland were never faced with much difficulty in keeping their house fires continually alight, because their main domestic fuel — peat — was easily procured. In addition to being ideal for domestic heating and cooking, peat burns slowly because a coating of ash forms on it and appreciably slows and controls the burning.

In the past hundred years many of the old customs died out; but even the introduction of matches did not change the universal practice of raking the fire every night by covering the still burning remains of today's fire with ashes to ensure some coals are 'still alive' to start tomorrow's and successive tomorrows' fires.

In addition to raking the fire nightly, there is another old practice still followed. When a long established family moves to a new home, they invariably follow the old custom of 'bringing their fire with them'. This means that the last act they perform at the house they are vacating, is to bring a live coal from their last fire to start — or continue — the family fire in the new house. This practice is still followed in most parts of Ireland and includes instances where the 'newcomers' secretly follow the old ways: secretly because they fear their new neighbours might 'think we still follow primitive practices if they caught us at it'. Another poignant side of this practice occurs when the last surviving member of a family is at Death's door. Then an understanding neighbour co-operates with the last family representative to ensure that the latter's fire will not die out. He takes home a live coal from the final fire and 'rakes it' with his own rakings that same night. This ancient rite helps to perpetuate the dead family's fire and somehow entwines the spirit of both families.

This Celtic pre-occupation with fire, its place in our way of life and especially the immense volume of folklore surrounding it, intrigued me and it was my good fortune to have many a 'no howlts barred' discussion about it with my venerable friend John Brennan. John, who justifiably claimed 'My brain is still as sharp as a razor although I'm about to step over the century mark', appreciated and understood my interest in the subject. Many a time in an attempt to get at the root of some of the old ways and customs, I managed to draw him out.

In John's time there was much speculation as to how peat was created. He was extremely knowledgeable and in spite of his advanced age had an open, receptive mind. I remember how excited he was when I explained the latest theory of how peat was laid down. John said 'That makes sense; when you look at the face of a dry bog hole, especially one near thirty foot deep, you can make out thousands of layers like pages in a thick old book. In the top layers you see blades of grass, ferns, heather and the deeper down you go, the more squeezed and rotted vegetation is. Down at the very bottom, just before you come to bed-rock or marl the turf looks like mud; them's the layers we call stone turf. You remember from your own wheeling-turf days that if you cut the bottom layers and spread it out on the turf bank to dry it falls apart like a fistful of dry tea leaves.' When I mentioned archaeological evidence supporting the theory that people lived in our area continuously for at least the past eight thousand years, John was neither surprised nor impressed; all he said was 'Avic! My people and yours have been around here for a lot longer than that. That turf that's burning there in front of your shins on the hearth was cut only a couple of miles from here and well I remember my grandfather saying it would take more than famine, fire or flood to root us Brennans out': I said, 'The layers of bog were like pages in a book; maybe they *are* pages, each page stamped with a record of our breed, seed and generation'.

Six per cent of the surface of Ireland is bogland and because it is accepted that our country had been inhabited continuously for millenia, it is reasonable to suppose that each layer of peat — as it was laid down — contained, and still contains some trace or part of each generation of those early Irish people. Last year, only ten miles from here in this exact same type of bog, normal turf digging operations exposed a human habitation that contained evidence, supported by Carbon 14 dating, that its occupants were engaged in settled farming eight thousand years ago.

I asked John, 'What's behind this widespread custom of never letting a household fire go out?' He shook his head. 'I don't know except that continuity is an important part of life; maybe it is life, and sure there is plenty of connection between fire and life. It goes deeper than that — my father before me said it was part of a very old belief that came down to us from an ancient religion that had its roots in another planet. It's beyond me to put into words. Anyhow, when I sit here alone at the fire it gives comfort to my soul to know that my fire is the self-same fire that served my family when Adam was a whistling boy.'

My own mind tries to grapple with the enigma of the Irish eternal fire. I see it as a continuous and endless chain. A chain made up of alternate links; a link that blazed by day followed by a link that smouldered through the night. At midnight one day was ended, one night was always ahead. The smouldering fire on the hearth was the link between the two; the continuity could symbolize eternity.

In my heart I looked on John Brennan as an Irish patriarch and many's the memorable conversation we had in his snug fireplace about history, culture and the future of our race. Between us we worked out some of the meaning and significance of what John called 'the fire that was never quinched [quenched]'. Once, as if thinking aloud he remarked, 'I'll bet some of my ancestors, my own flesh and blood thousands of years ago walked through the heather and grasses that is now the very turf that we are burning on this hearthstone today.'

One night John and myself were threshing out the deep significance of fire on the hearth and I ventured to ask Mrs. Brennan how she felt about it. Her response was moving. She replied, 'Strange you should use the word "felt". I feel searc-grá (intense love) for the family fire. My own fire is part and parcel of me; and that goes for the family fire, past, present and future. If that fire could speak to you as it does to me it would tell many a tale — the odd sad tale but mostly happy ones.' She continued, 'The second I step into somebody else's kitchen and glance at their fire I usually size them up and get a fair idea of the nature of the Head of the House — whether generous or stingy. When I was only a slip of a girl and for the first time met this fire' and she gestured towards the hearth, 'that big fireplace with its huge turf fire, spoke one single word to me: Fáilte — welcome. And it spoke God's truth. From the day I came into this house to start my married life, this area around the fire was and is the equal of the Altar in the church. It was around it I nursed my babies, taught them their prayers and around this fire, at the end of every single day our entire household, like generations before us knelt with our bare knees on the warm clay floor to say the Rosary. When I sit here as I'm sitting now in this old sugán chair (hammock-like seat made of twisted straw) sure I wouldn't swap places with the Queen of England on her own golden throne.

'The odd time when I'm alone it's comforting to sit here idly watching the figaries (antics) of the flame devouring each sod of turf; that's when my thoughts drift back over the years, and they never stop at the time when I myself was only a child; no! they ramble back and back just like turning back the pages of a big, thick book, each page with a written account of a previous generation kneeling around this selfsame fire and speaking with the selfsame eternal God.'

I felt on the verge of a breakthrough, when in a mixture of modern English and ancient Irish, John once confided, 'Sitting here alone I sometimes feel a oneness with generations of my people stretching back in the mists of time; each one sitting at his fire; a fire that in essence was one fire; a fire that is all there in the fire I'm now looking into.' There with John Brennan, somehow it seemed clear to me that my roots like John's roots go down, down even deeper than the ten thousand year old, thirty foot layer of peat in our deepest bogs.

3. CHILDHOOD MEMORIES

Many memories of my early childhood seem like frames from old, half-remembered movies; bits of scenes without a beginning, lacking coherence and continuity and invariably without any logical ending. Sometimes semi-obliterated memories of yesteryears are mixed up with yesterday's day-dreams.

Did you ever notice how a memory of something long buried and completely forgotten suddenly becomes clear in your mind; and whatever evoked it does not seem to have any connection with it. It could have been a sound, smell, a word or even a phrase. The other day I heard a certain phrase and although I had met it hundreds of times before this time it rang a bell. The phrase was 'toe the line'. Everyone knows what 'toe the line' means. Just to make sure, I looked it up and the dictionary says: 'To stand or crouch with the toes touching the starting line of a race'. Peculiarly enough the 'bell' that had been rung had nothing whatsoever to do with a race — except, possibly the human race.

This is a portion of the memory which 'toe the line' evoked for me. I'm standing in the infants' class in Multy National School and with a dozen other gossoons [boys] am literally 'toeing the line'. In our school the teacher had the idea that he would have better control of a large class if his pupils were standing, unsupported, in a cleared area of the classroom. I suppose there is less chance of a student falling asleep if he is 'standing on his own two feet'. I am not suggesting that he might be standing on any other pupil's foot or feet and it has nothing whatsoever to do with anyone's scholastic standing in the class.

When a class was assembled, the teacher would take his stand in a bare corner of the classroom. I suppose the idea of the corner was developed to ensure that none of the children got behind the teacher's back or performed any flanking manoeuvres. The teacher would then produce a piece of white chalk and draw an arc on the floor. The ideal length of the chalk mark would be such that without undue crowding and without leaving big gaps, each individual pupil could toe that line. If some of the students' attention wandered, it would be difficult for the teacher to 'cop on', but if a child's feet wandered — even an inch — the teacher's keen eye immediately would detect the wanderer and take action. In my class and era it would be a stern 'toe the line', possibly accompanied by a 'crack of the cane' on some vulnerable portion of the offender's anatomy.

On this occasion, the teacher gave the order 'toe the line': we did. I looked down — to make sure that my toes were 'at' the line. The front part of my brogues would be well over the line because they did not exactly fit me like the proverbial glove. In fact they were several sizes too big for me. Now looking down at my extremities I suddenly suspected that something was amiss. First I thought 'I've my legs crossed!' Then the real horror of the situation struck me. I don't know my age at the time, but had reached the stage when I was able to put on my own shoes. Now to my embarrassment, I realized that in the morning's rush I had put my boots on the wrong feet. No! not on somebody else's feet — just the left boot on the right foot which in reality was the wrong foot.

My infant embarrassment was as big and monstrous as the offending boots appeared to my mortified eyes. I thought it must be only seconds before the teacher and the entire school would discover and expose me. I could have put up my hand in the time-honoured manner and asked for permission to go to the 'outdoor privy' so that I could interchange the 'cursed boots'. But that could entail standing in front of the teacher and if he were in a certain mood he would 'look me up and look me down' for telltale signs that I might be malingering. There was nothing in the world I could do but suffer in silence and wait interminable hours for lunch-time and home to right the situation.

They say 'open confession is good for the soul', so seeing that I am in the mood, I may as well get another embarrassing moment off my chest and relate a further childhood experience that is of a delicate and somewhat more traumatic nature. It concerns the 'Procession' which was part — and still is — of the observance of the Feast of Corpus Christi held annually at the Friary. Had better explain the Procession before I bare my soul.

The Procession was one of the most important events in the village, especially for us schoolchildren. After Mass in the

Abbey, the Blessed Sacrament was carried in solemn procession for about 300 yards along the Friary avenue to the football field where Benediction was celebrated at an open-air altar temporarily set up in the shade, or if it happened to rain, in the shelter of the giant horse chestnut trees. No one kept statistics on the number of times the weather 'let us down', but over the years we all agreed that no matter how bad the weather was in other places, on Corpus Christi day invariably the sun shone for us in Multy. Actually, I'd substitute 'The Blessed Virgin' in that sentence for 'weather', because the Mother of God was annually bombarded with prayers to 'intercede with Her Son' for good weather — even for two hours of sunshine — for the Procession.

Hours before going to the Friary for the Mass and other religious ceremonies leading up to the actual procession, the pupils of the parishes' three National schools assembled in their particular schoolhouses to be drilled for the ceremony at the Friary. The children were dressed in their Sunday best. Most of the girls wore their First Communion dresses and both boys and girls had broad red sashes draped over the right shoulder and pinned at the left hip.

Immediately after Mass the procession lined up outside the Friary. Girls with large baskets of flowers walked in front, strewing flowers and petals in the path of the Blessed Sacrament. Following after the flower girls the priests carried the Blessed Sacrament and walked under a moveable canopy carried by four males. Next came the schoolchildren, followed by the women. The men brought up the rear.

I have to mention the religious banners carried so proudly in the procession. Those huge, coloured banners with religious emblems beautifully painted on them were a sight for sore eyes. Each banner appeared to be as large as the sail of a small boat: on windy days they displayed the same antics. Every banner was mounted on a single pole carried by hand-picked, muscular, active men. Strong ribbons were secured to the lower corners of each banner. As the men carried the banners each one was flanked by two small boys who firmly clutched a ribbon to assist in holding the banner in an upright position.

Needless to say there was fierce competition among the men of the parish for the honour of carrying the banners; but it was child's play compared to the effort and prayers we children expended in order to win the honour of being ribbon carriers.

May God forgive my vanity, but I still tingle with pride and pleasure when I think of my supreme moment when I was considered big enough and important enough to march — strut would be more like it — as a ribbon-bearer.

The Benediction in the Friary football field, or any other religious ceremony in the open, invariably had a strong impact on all of us; it brought home the historical fact that it was not so long ago when our priests were, 'by the laws of the land' obliged to hold such religious ceremonies in the open, because they and their congregation then stood a better chance of escaping the English soldiers' wrath.

In those days the marching column was so long that the people singing the hymn at the front were hardly ever on the beat with the singers at the tail end; in fact, there were times when two separate hymns were being sung simultaneously — I honestly won't try to speculate how the musicians in the middle of the procession coped.

Apart from the possibility of spiritual joy which the participants may have received from the ceremony, there was a general feeling of pleasure somewhat like a less-than-usually boisterous Mardi Gras. They say 'everyone loves a parade'. We loved our parade: the peaceful setting deep in the heart of the quiet countryside; the movement of the crowds; the banners; the singing, and especially the flowers and their perfume. All my life, a whiff of perfume from a flower or combination of flowers has triggered memories of Corpus Christi Processions long past. It being a 'moveable feast', Corpus Christi falls around the beginning of June which is well into the growing season when Ireland's fields and hedges are alive with wild flowers and blossoms. It is the season when the whitethorn hedges that parcel Ireland into innumerable shapes and sizes of fields, are in full bloom. Individual perfumes are all there simultaneously, but never does one particular perfume predominate, not even the never-to-be-forgotten smell of the new-mown hay from the countless acres of surrounding farmland. Now the scent of the primroses mingles with that of the lilac coupled with the exquisite aroma of wild woodbine, wild roses, honeysuckle mixed with the heady perfume of hedge rose in full bloom. The wonder of it all was that the smell of the hawthorn blossoms did not smother all the other heavenly perfumes, because the whitethorn, one of its species, is the predominant bush that takes the place of barbed wire and creates impregnable fences.

On completion of the open-air ceremonies everyone returned to the Abbey and we all took our appointed places; younger schoolchildren like myself were consigned to kneeling around a long arc of the altar rails. It was at those altar rails that the most traumatic moment of my childhood — or even my entire life — took place.

As I already mentioned, we schoolchildren were dressed 'up to the nines' for the occasion. The standard dress for boys, in that era, even up to the age of sixteen, consisted of boots or shoes, long stockings turned down at the knee, knickers/short pants, ganzi/jersey and tie and I mustn't omit the skull cap. We were not warmly dressed; the entire ceremony was lengthy, and central or any kind of heating did not exist in the Abbey. The iron, ornamental altar rails were set in a foundation of marble, but for the ceremony the cold, hard marble surface was covered by a continuous series of cushions, each cushion encased in some type of scarlet-covered, silky material. I remember that the scarlet of the cushions contrasted vividly with the snow-whiteness of the Irish hand-embroidered linen altar cloth. That was before the present austere fashion of church furnishings arrived.

Due to the interminable length of the ceremony, cold climate, lack of warm clothes, coupled with the fact that I had been away from home for over two hours, I gradually became very uncomfortable. In those days it must have been taken for granted that children never had a 'call of nature' while attending (imprisoned by) religious ceremonies at the Abbey or any other church, because there were no public toilet facilities that I was aware of. In my case that 'call' amounted to a 'scream'.

Although only around six years old at the time I was cagey enough to pay attention to the material and construction of the cushions on which we were kneeling. The reason for my interest was not pure curiosity. I had two options. I could have walked or trotted outside to the relative privacy of the back ditch or the partial shelter of a wall or a tree. Then I had another choice — possibly I had already unconsciously made it. The church was full; I was right out there in full view of the congregation, as much, if not more exposed as the priest himself on the steps of the altar and myself like the other children with their backs to the people. You could 'feel' them staring at the back of your neck. The idea of turning around to face them, including the teacher, was unthinkable. I made the choice — you guessed it — I could not 'hold out' any longer. The chilly church, the very short pants, absence of underwear plus the hollow created by my knees in the yielding, and hopefully porous covering and the absorbent stuffing of the kneeler invited — and thank God received — the contents of a bladder distended well beyond its capacity.

Thank the Lord plastic coverings for kneelers had not yet been invented. I recall that even at that tender age I was cunning enough to perform the undercover, dewatering operation as slowly as possible so as not to stretch the absorbent capacity of the cushion beyond its absorption time limit. A miracle. There was no outward visible sign of my dereliction. This is the first time in my life I have summoned up courage enough to mention the harrowing experience. You are right; I feel better already for the belated confession.

4. GRAVEYARD ROW

One of the several county roads connecting our village of Multyfarnham with Mullingar (chief town of County Westmeath) passes about sixty feet in front of our little blue-roofed bungalow.

From our front door you have an excellent view of countless irregularly shaped fields with, as the song goes, 'Forty Shades of Green', stretching like a gigantic quilt to the western horizon. This illusion of a quilt is heightened by the hilly, folding pattern of the land which gently slopes upward in waves like a blanket undulating.

Geographically speaking, our 'place' is in the village proper, but the nearest abode is 100 yards distant, so we have plenty of elbow room which is a welcome change from many of the forty-foot frontage lots we lived on in Canada.

Portion of the two acres that comprise our house, yard, lawn, garden and small field is marked on the Survey Map as Ballindurrow. A Government survey of 1750 noted: 'Baile an Dore (town of the oak wood). It contains a fort in the centre. It also contains a great part of Multyfarnham village and St. Andrew's chapel in ruins, two stone pillars standing higher than a man, a Roman Catholic chapel and Sessions house. The local pronunciation now is Ballinderra.'

This past summer I watched with interest a bulldozer being used to carry out reclamation work on Kane's field, an open area across the road from our house. By the way, this field has one of the stone pillars still standing, but in 1750, the time of the survey, either the men were quite short, or the pillar since then has sunk at least a foot. When the operator came to clear and level an area along the wall of the old graveyard which borders Kane's field, I asked him if he would mind if, keeping a safe distance from his blade, I stayed close enough to keep an eye open for any material that the bulldozer blade might turn up, move and deposit. I explained that I was interested in what appeared to be a series of four foot high, irregular, grass-covered mounds, which were in reality the remains of five houses that are marked on a 1909 Ordnance Survey map I happen to have.

The bulldozer operator — a young man — said, 'You must be codding me; there couldn't be room for two, let alone five houses in that little area'. I would have liked to have exclaimed, 'Ten chances to one, your grandparents also lived in a house as tiny as one of these'. 'Let's see what your blade turns up', I replied casually.

Those green covered mounds have not changed one whit in my lifetime, but when I was a child, quite often I heard the area referred to as Churchyard Row. My childhood friend Bill Barden often spoke of the Row because he was born in one of those five houses. He and I never got around to talking about how the houses were constructed, but I do remember him bragging that their house was easily heated and proudly saying, 'The coldest night in winter — and them winters were a hell of a lot colder than the ones we are having now — a few sods of turf on the fire and with top and bottom of the half door closed, you'd be as snug as a bug in a rug'.

I assumed that Bill's house was a mud-wall cabin with a thatched roof and earthen floor, or possibly it was a more primitive type of building roofed with sods; I believe the latter type were called *clochán*. Now as I watched the bulldozer in action, my guess about it being a mud-wall structure was verified, because when the blade burst open the grassy mounds, very few building stones were in evidence. The stones that were unearthed turned out to be corner stones that originally strengthened and supported the walls which were built from a special type of clay. I suppose the fact that the building clay had to be mixed with water gave rise to the term mud-wall, i.e. built with *clóib* (plastic clay).

The blade exposed some flat stone flags that undoubtedly were stone thresholds. The centre or walked-on portions of those stone thresholds were worn down to a depth of four inches and I could not help wondering how great a passage of time and how many human feet it took to wear those solid thresholds almost hollow. We also found flat stone flags with one side worn smooth. They must have been sills of windows, but windows not any wider than fifteen inches. Later on I caught an odd glimpse of a stone fireplace, but no corresponding bricks or building stones which could have been part of a modern-type chimney. It is conceivable that the heating and ventilation was so primitive that smoke from the hearth had to find its way to escape through some kind of opening in the roof.

As the bulldozer relentlessly levelled the grass-covered stubs of the mud-wall dwelling, and unearthed, upended and smashed stone thresholds worn thin by generations of our people, I felt a sense of sadness. But that feeling became more poignant when the bulldozer blades bit into what was originally the fireplace, the chimney corner and the charred hearth-stone which a hundred years later again saw the light of day for a few moments before being crushed by the huge machine, broken into rubble and mixed with the dark layer of hard-packed earth — once the clay floor of a building that was 'hearth and home' to generations now buried in the ancient graveyard the other side of the nearby wall.

When I looked at the pile of detritus, my imagination endeavouring to separate it into the various components of the original houses, I thought, 'The roots of the Bardens, the Nolans, the Reillys, the Morans and the Daltons went deep and throve and grew in what is now but a level corner of a farmer's fertile field'. But to me and to the numerous descendents of those hardy, virile families who lived there until around the turn of the century, that level corner will always be Churchyard Row.

I've already written about the antiquity of the village of Multyfarnham. By present day practice the portion of the village in the area of The Row would be rated as an ideal residential district. It is a fair guess that Graveyard Row never was exactly 'the slums' of Multy because it occupies the highest ground and belongs to the most fertile part of a district famous for its rich farming land. The five families that lived in The Row have always been much to the fore in our neighbourhood and judging from the behaviour of their living descendents and the accounts people give of their antecedents they were all well respected by their neighbours.

In the village, the Barden family is accepted as Old Stock and I've even heard people refer to them as Old Residents. I can't put a time-span on how long a family has to live in one location in Ireland before they earn these titles: in our area it is not unknown for a family to be labelled Newcomers even if they have been around here for over two centuries. Although everyone knows that generations of the present Barden family lived in Churchyard Row, not even the Bardens themselves can hazard a guess as to when they first settled around Multy. Local tradition has it that originally they came as labourers. I don't know how true that claim is, but for generations few men of the Barden family ever turned their hands to anything but manual labour. Recently I heard an extremely old man say, 'With the Bardens it must have been bred in the bone, because at any kind of labour they were second to none, every single one of them, men and women had a taste for work and took a fierce pride in the job'.

My own family were on good terms with all the 'Row' people, but the Bardens had a special place in our lives. In my time and even in my grandfather's day some of the Bardens were invariably around the house doing odd jobs such as babysitting, cutting and rearing the turf, tilling the garden and so forth. They were specially welcome because the Barden girls were wonderful housekeepers and scrupulously clean (as my mother used to say); the men and women were tasty, dependable workers. They were — without exception — honest, and had a strong sense of loyalty to the members of our family.

Generally speaking, all the Bardens ran true to form; if you asked locally, 'Is there any outstanding trait common to the family?', the answer would be 'Lightheartedness'. If the Multy branch of the Barden family were asking for a motto, I'd suggest it be 'Never Complain'. The average one of them, the men anyway, was not exactly devil-may-care, but rather had a sunny, optimistic disposition, quick to see the funny side even of a situation which appeared humourless and even dismal to others.

No matter how far back my memory reaches, I remember only four of the Barden brothers: Kit, Jack, Pat and Bill. Bill, the youngest, was the only one of the brothers I got to know intimately.

Many a tale is told around the fires about the Bardens, because many of them were newsworthy and most of them were individuals — rugged individuals. Take Kit Barden. Bring the subject of laughter around and before you know where you are, someone will say, 'Do you remember Kit Barden's laugh?' Kit was gifted with an infectious laugh. Professional funny men or comics, whose business it is to make their audience laugh, would be out of work if they had to compete with someone endowed with Kit Barden's gift of laughter. He did not have to put on an act, tell a story or indulge in antics to get people laughing, all Kit had to do was laugh. Kit, like most of the males of his family, had a barrel chest and if the wind were right his laugh carried at least a mile. That is an explanation of Kit's range. But it was the quality, the clear, bell-like tone coupled with an indescribable something that caused — no, compelled, his listeners to join in the laughter. Even sour-pusses were known to unsuccessfully battle the urge to smile when within ear-shot of Kit when he 'did his thing'. It could be truthfully said, 'When Kit Barden laughed, no one ever laughed *at* him, everyone laughed *with* him.' I know it's wishful thinking because he died years ago; but if Kit's laugh had been electronically recorded or 'taped' it would have gladdened generations then unborn.

Pat Barden was the second youngest of the brothers. He was also the smallest of them, but people who knew him well swore that 'inch for inch and pound for pound, Pat Barden was as hardy a man as ever stepped in shoe leather'. When I returned home in 1960 and I was stuck for help building a rick of hay, the only 'expert help' I could find was Pat Barden. Pat was eighty three years old, diminutive and so much like a gnome that (out of ear-shot) one of my sons whispered to me, 'You remember the movie Snow White and the Seven Dwarfs; Mr. Barden looks exactly like Doc'. Pat did have a rather large nose and due to his advanced years his once wiry body had shrunk somewhat. But his indomitable will had not deteriorated. When out of deference to his age I suggested that once the rick got to a certain height he could stay on top and I'd pitch the hay up to him and he'd take it off my fork and build the rick, he became indignant at the idea of me asking him to do the lighter work. He complained, 'You're trying to treat me like I was an auld man'. Before many hours had gone by I was the one who felt like resting, but naturally could not admit that to Pat. I ask myself, 'What kind of a man must Pat have been sixty years ago?' In spite of my inexpert share of the work the finished rick was a masterpiece. Pat Barden was in his ninety-fourth year when he went — like a man I'm sure — to meet his Maker.

Jack, another of the Barden brothers, worked with a farmer

about a mile outside the village and always went by his nickname. If you asked anyone around, 'Do you know Jack Barden', they'd have to scratch their heads to place him, because Jack was known to everyone as the 'Weed' Barden. He got the name Weed when he was growing up, for the reason that he hardly seemed to grow at all. In his prime he was barely five foot tall and thin as a whip, but in the Weed's dwarf-like body there was prodigious strength. His favourite 'show off' was to take a length of half inch, brand new hempen rope, twist a length of it tightly around each fist and with his hands almost ten inches apart raise them to the front of his chest, exhale and stretch the rope, inhale slowly and pull his fists apart; then one strand after another slowly and reluctantly would break until the remainder of the rope burst assunder.

All the Bardens were good-natured and Jack was no exception. People who knew him claimed he'd be the last person in the world to get into a fight — especially a fight to the finish with a man like Pat Keefe.

When it came to fighting with fists or with an ash plant, Pat Keefe was universally dreaded. Pat was tough. He never asked for quarter or gave it. When the country was officially named The Irish Free State, our new government advertised for a hangman and 'me bould' Pat applied right away. He even enlisted my father's services to help him fill out the necessary application forms. Afterwards, Pat complained, 'I'm not going to like this government any better than the English one, they turned me down and me having my heart set on the job that I'd willingly do for half the salary.'

Pat was tall, wiry and agile. He won most of his pub and street fights by following his own number one rule of, 'get in that first clout and make sure it's a hay-maker'. One day a bunch of 'the boys' were tossing (pitch and toss) at the 'corner' opposite the parish church. An argument over a bet developed between the Weed and Pat Keefe and without so much as saying 'by your leave', swift as a snake strikes, Pat, who towered a foot and a half over the Weed, swung a wild roundhouse at the diminutive man's head. If our hero had not ducked in a flash, Keefe would have torn the Weed's head off. Both of them were standing less than two yards from the wall that forms the 'corner' and when Keefe's wild swing half rotated the upper part of his body, Barden ducked, quickly stepped behind Keefe, slightly bent his legs like a weight-lifter, threw his arms around Keefe's thighs just below the hips, violently heaved upwards, lifting the tall man's feet clear of the ground and like a telegraph post whose base is suddenly cut through, Keefe's long frame overbalanced, toppled, and crashed facedown to the sidewalk. On his way down, Keefe's skull struck a small projection in the stone wall and suddenly his body became strangely inert. Someone turned Pat over and said, 'By God he's snoring!'

Luckily for both Pat Keefe and the Weed, the doctor was — for a wonder — on the scene in minutes and he diagnosed Keefe as a bad case of concussion. The ambulance arrived within a half hour. They took Pat to the hospital and within a fortnight he was as right as rain, but as far as anyone knew, till his dying day he had lost his taste for fighting. Whether it was the shock of the injury, or the terrible disgrace for a fighting man of Keefe's calibre to be defeated by the Weed, we'll never know. Pat Keefe was over ninety when he died — peacefully, in bed.

The Weed was the best ballad singer in the Midlands, although 'begrudgers' said he sang through his nose like a Tinker ballad singer; that was before Country and Western music became popular. The remarkable thing about the Weed's singing was not the way he rendered the ballads, but the innumerable number of verses he had memorized letter-perfect.

Like many unfortunates of his era, he was illiterate; as they say, 'He wouldn't know a B from a bull's foot'. The Travelling People (new polite term for Tinkers) still sell ballad sheets at fairs, race meetings and other gatherings. When the Weed was in his prime the ballads sold for a half-penny each and you surely got your money's worth because some of those ballads were forty verses long. When they were recited or sung the chorus 'came in' after every verse, which meant that reciting or singing an entire ballad took longer than a long-playing record.

As I said, the Weed couldn't read, so when he saw ballads being peddled, in order to avoid buying one already in his vast repertoire, he'd ask the seller to read aloud the title and some of the contents of each ballad. Then when he purchased a ballad he'd bring the green sheet home (they were always printed on green paper) and when the day's work was finished the Weed would coax someone to read the entire ballad to him — once. Sure he only had to hear it once and ever after he could repeat it perfectly word-for-word.

Remember how I tried to explain about certain hereditary

traits and gifts and how we say 'it runs in the family'. Recently I happened to read about the Barden name in a book about Irish families: their names, arms and origins. It was no surprise to learn that O'Barden, Bardon, Bardane were listed as a bardic family in Co. Westmeath in Petty's census of 1659. The profession of the Bards normally was hereditary, but it was not automatic because the prime professional requirement was the ability to memorize thousands of songs, poems and tales. Personally I'm convinced that the Weed was a true Mac an Bhaird (son of the bard). When someone was marvelling about the Weed's repertoire, a neighbour summed it up in an old Irish saying, 'It's not off the grass the Weed licked it'.

We had come to where I was writing about the Weed's singing voice when my wife suggested, 'Why don't you mention Kathy's singing?' Kathy's ringing, joyous laugh gives everyone within earshot a lift; even if you were feeling low, her laugh would make you feel better. When Kathy sings at ten o'clock Mass every Sunday at the Friary, her voice sounds so flute-like and vibrant that instead of trying to join in the singing you just listen. So you see, I did mention Kathy; she happens to be a niece of the Weed.

5. THE FAIR

Actually I'm a bit ahead of myself talking at all about Bill, seeing I never clap't eyes on our hero until that famous incident we still talk about as if it were only yesterday — 'the fair day in Multy when the police lifted Bill Barden'.

But first I'd like to say a few words about Irish fairs. Up to fifteen years ago livestock fairs were held in the main streets of most towns and villages. In some places the fairs were held every fortnight which meant that by the time the debris and the cow dung were cleaned up it was fair day all over again. The holding of fairs in built-up areas was eventually abolished and it sure was high time, because the droves of cattle in the busy part of a town or village tied up traffic hopelessly and in addition left the area in a shambles.

Like many another one of our old customs, the traditional fairs of cattle, sheep, pigs, goats, horses, ponies and asses have almost disappeared or been replaced by the more orderly (and less entertaining) auction markets which are now held in most of our cities and larger towns. Fortunately for those who still relish the old customs and traditions, plenty of fairs are still held where the old order has not changed.

Attend one of our country fairs as an onlooker and you get the feeling that the clock has been turned back and you are now watching a scene from the nineteenth century. You will find the bargaining extremely interesting, even fascinating. Bargaining is a way of life down in the country. In some county towns, even in a modern shop or market you will still hear the odd farmer try to bargain for a commodity which already has a fixed price tag on it — the American 'fixed' sometimes could apply literally. Most of our bargaining is connected with farming and country life. I've a feeling that our bargaining ritual is a carry-over from the old barter system of exchanging goods or services without using money. Obviously bargaining had its heyday before coinage came into general use and one can imagine the number and complexity of the items and services a farmer (for instance)

47

would bargain for in exchange for a cow; or a cobbler would ask in exchange for a pair of brogues. My wife's reaction from watching and taking an 'inside' interest in our fairs is one of wonder and admiration. She says, referring to the 'cast' involved in 'striking a bargain', 'they all act as if they are on the stage of the Abbey Theatre'. She hit the nail on the head. The 'players' in the scenario, as ex-President Nixon would say, are not just confined to the seller and the buyer. The cast can be, and usually is, the relatives, friends, acquaintances of either of the two principals and even complete strangers or 'bilkers'. The latter horn into the bargaining with the hope of meeting the principals later on in the pub where all will 'quench their thirst' in the ancient ceremony of drinking the 'luck penny'.

There is also a 'character' connected with our bargaining who has almost disappeared from the Irish scene, but I believe that he is worth mentioning. That is the Tangler. His role — and he was a specialist — was helping to close a bargain. His services were availed of when there appeared to be an unbridgeable gap between the 'asking price' and the 'price offered'.

A factor that also comes into most of our bargaining is the Luck Penny. It has failed me — so far — to run down the origin of the Luck Penny and I'm extremely curious about it, because I'm sure it goes further back than the ancient Greek custom of placing a coin in the mouth of a corpse to pay Charon for ferrying the dead in his boat across the dark waters of the underworld (Styx). Each of the shades (spirits) was obliged to pay Charon an obol, which was placed in the mouth of the deceased at the time of burial. When payment is being tendered for something purchased, or for services rendered, the person receiving the cash payment immediately returns a portion of that cash to the purchaser. The cash thus returned is called Luck Penny. Quite often the amount of the Luck Penny is haggled about and finally agreed on, in the course of the bargaining.

You hardly ever hear the expression 'drive a bargain', but 'strike a bargain' is common. I wonder if the latter has a connection with another unique and intriguing custom related to our bargaining, namely the 'slapping of hands' or 'striking of palms'. To try and explain this strange procedure, I had better give a brief pen-picture of an ordinary country fair.

Suppose we become part of the crowd at a fair and discreetly follow a farmer and his boy (the 'boy' may be pushin' sixty) who have six bullocks for sale. They already have them safely 'penned in' awaiting an offer. Out of the corner of his eye the farmer sees the buyer approaching (buyers are also called 'dealers' or 'jobbers') so he 'stirs up the bastes' with a few taps of his stick which is usually a supple ash plant, to make sure that the animals don't look as if they are ready to collapse with the hunger or from sickness. The dealer very casually approaches and is careful not to seem too interested in the six cattle. He runs a shrewd and disparaging eye over them; unerringly picks out the 'poorest' one and gives it a tap of his stick with the muttered remark, 'I wonder if its alive at all, at all, maybe it a piner'. Then he feels its haunches or pinches the skin over its hips and mutters, 'Skin and bone'. Then a loud voice, "Good day to you Sir, how much for the six fine bastes?' Next follows a bit of skirmish bargaining with the jobber offering a ludicrously low price which is curtly refused and he moves away to make room for another jobber, who to all intents and purposes has never 'clap't eyes' on the first in his life. After a lengthy bargaining session this second dealer offers much less than his predecessor did. The seller just looks at him long and sorrowfully and half-turning away, over his shoulder retorts, 'Are you cudding'. Naturally the latest offer of a much smaller price makes the original bid seem more attractive and when the first dealer 'happens to be rambling by' the now 'softened-up' seller may have come down a bit in his asking price.

When the bidding gets into the final stage where the gap narrows between the asking price and the jobber's 'this is my very last offer', a knot of people mostly on the side of the seller butt into the bargaining session and one of them chimes in, 'Take an honest man's word and split the difference.' The 'difference' is this. After much bargaining both men now have reached a deadlock; the seller is asking one hundred pounds, while the buyer offers ninety pounds. The seller 'won't accept a penny less' and he is histrionically apt to implore the spectators, 'Don't stand there and see me robbed', while the jobber 'Would be damned if I can afford to think of advancing even a ha'-penny more'. When they finally settle on a satisfactory selling price, the buyer says to the seller, 'Hold out your hand like a daycent man'. The other stretches his hand out, palm upwards. Then the buyer spits on his own palm and noisily slaps it down on the other's palm. I'd dearly love to find the origin of this strange spit-sealed settlement which has been in fashion here from time immemorial.

I suppose it takes some imagination to tie in an Irish country fair with a 'western', but my first recollection of Bill Barden always reminds me of a scene from a western movie. It was a scene so dramatic and exciting that it became well-etched in my memory so that now, more than half a century later I can easily recall the entire scenario.

It was fair day in Multy and the village was humming with the sounds of the droves of cattle, sheep and pigs, plus the crowds of people involved in driving, selling and buying the animals. In those days a fair attracted the hawkers and peddlers selling their wares and of course, no fair was complete without at least one ballad singer. I suppose I was about ten at the time and was standing at our front door which faced out into the middle of the main street of Multy, enjoying the sights and sounds of the fair. Twenty feet away a ballad singer was singing at the top of his voice — he had to, to be heard over the high noise level of the fair. Then someone shouted, 'The police are arresting Bill Barden'.

I stepped out on the sidewalk to get a good view of the upper part of the street in front of Egan's pub — which is now Sean Weir's pub — because all eyes were focused on that area. Suddenly the singer was silent and the other noises subsided because Bill Barden was famous (with everyone but the Law) for resisting arrest. Didn't everyone read or have it read out to them, from the 'Westmeath Examiner' an account of Bill's prowess. It reported in part: 'A sergeant gave evidence; "Your Worship, from personal experience I can truthfully state that six constables using fair and reasonable physical force and without using their batons would not be able to subdue and arrest William Barden, if the said William Barden wanted seriously to resist".' Apart from Bill when 'his dander was up' enjoying a rough and tumble with the 'Peelers' it was extremely difficult for the 'inimy' as Bill called them, to secure a grip on his abnormally short and thick arms, legs or neck.

I have forgotten the reason the constables were arresting Bill. Neither Bill nor any of his brothers were rowdies; they were never known to attack anyone; on the other hand, they'd never turn their backs on a fight. In pubs and in the company of his peers, Bill was known on occasions to announce, 'I am the equal of any man standing in shoe leather.' I suppose he was a living challenge to many another 'hard man' and the clash of personalities could have often led to a clash of bodies.

A man beside me excitedly exclaimed, 'There's only two of them, they'll never take him, big and all as they are.' The policemen were well over six foot tall and compared to Bill they looked immense. What I first noticed was that each of the policemen had a strangle-hold on Bill's upper arms and was holding him with his feet almost clear of the ground and he violently swinging his legs and kicking the air. Still keeping Bill's feet clear of the ground they started down the street towards me on their way to the barracks, but anyone could see that they would tire long before they made the couple of hundred yards to the lock-up. Pretty soon they lowered Bill until his feet were on the ground and all three ploughed slowly forward because Bill's feet were like the coulter of a plough trying to dig into the surface of the sidewalk. By now there was a complete change in the battle and you could feel the wave of disappointment hit the spectators as in a horse race when the 'favourite' falls at the last jump. The big policemen were winning. Bill was actually going with them. Not exactly going; his short unwilling steps were matching his captors' and each step brought him closer to captivity and disgrace. Disgrace, because it was a question of pride with Bill that he'd never be taken without a fight, and here he was, 'making a public spectacle of himself' as one old lady remarked, and somewhat inappropriately added, 'going like a lamb to the slaughter'. Sure it was a terrible letdown, especially the size of the audience and the opportunity everyone had of seeing Bill in action, not against a small army of Peelers, but a 'paultry two', even if the smaller of the two towered head and shoulders over their prisoner. The police were arresting Bill at the widest part of the village street where three roads meet, and it was packed with people. It afforded Bill an arena to perform in and 'do his thing'. Instead, Bill's public felt a sense of loss, and anticlimax, because the big, red-faced Peelers were winning hands down. Now Bill was walking between them, not willingly, more like a trout on the end of a line, that a fisherman had about played out; he was still struggling but without a doubt the two big men were winning. Worse was to come. Gradually the minions of the law assumed control and the next thing we knew they had Bill walking between them so fast that with his short legs he appeared to be trotting. A woman made the Sign of the Cross and said, 'Mother of God, I don't believe the evidence of my eyes; they have Bill's spirit crushed and he's cooperating with them.' So he was. By now he was almost putting on a spurt as if he wanted to get away to the shelter of the lock-up and hide his humiliation from the crowd.

The policemen must have been elated and the crowd disgusted to see such an ignominious ending to what had promised to be a 'donneybrook'. By this tme they were bearing down on me, the two huge captors tearing towards me like men in a three-legged race. I realized now that Bill cooperated with his captors to obtain that burst of speed and he also managed to get his tormentors in step. In a flash Bill took a little 'spang' forward, spread his legs apart and with feet anchored solidly on the ground, in the same motion, with a heave of his shoulders combined with a powerful sweep of his arms, catapulted the policemen forward to trip awkwardly over Bill's feet. As Bill told it afterwards, 'I splathered them two big men on the sidewalk like a woman slapping a wet dishcloth on a table.' The pair of policemen had hardly hit the pavement before Bill spun around and ran 'hell for leather' through the droves of cattle, slipped into Moughty's yard, climbed the chapel wall and it was 'over the hills and far away' for Bill.

The discomfited, disgraced policemen unsuccessfully spent the rest of that day and half the same night hunting high up and low down for their man. The following morning at six, Bill, a man always up with the lark, loudly knocked at the front door of the Barracks. A surprised sergeant answered the door; Bill said, 'I hear you were looking for me.'

6. BUTCHERS

When we were youngsters, football was our favourite game; unfortunately we were well into our teens before any of us owned a real football. In those days you'd see hordes of youngsters kicking a rag ball around either in the playground or the fields around the village. Our patient mothers and cooperative sisters found time to keep us supplied with balls which they wound from ribbons of rags securely stitched. But no matter how well a rag ball was put together, its life was short and it had other obvious drawbacks. Yet us children had as much fun with rag balls as our modern counterparts have with their easily-procured inflatable ones.

In addition to the primitive rag ball we had another and much better kind, one made from a pig's or bullock's bladder. The bladder had a decided advantage over the rag ball because invariably we played football in our bare feet. Some of us improved on the bladder ball by covering it with an expanded portion of the leg of a lady's discarded stocking.

Although there were two butchers in business in the village it was difficult for us to procure an animal's bladder, because neither butcher had much patience with young people. Then again we must have made a nuisance of ourselves hanging around the slaughterhouse hoping to get the coveted bladders.

One of the village butchers was named Ernie, but behind his back everyone referred to him as The Huckster. Ernie got the name Huckster because although his main living came from butchering, he also sold odds and ends; it was still only a meagre living, for in those days butcher's meat was considered a luxury on account of the majority having very little ready money to spend, even on food.

None of us children ever became friendly with either of the two village butchers, but *all* of us had a dread of the Huckster. Our feelings towards him were mixed, compounded by the trade he followed — he did his own killing — and the fact that if you didn't keep on the good side of him he wouldn't save the next

53

bladder for you. To obtain that bladder you had to hang around
the slaughterhouse for hours and practically prostrate yourself
to secure that coveted bladder. For those bladders the Huckster
demanded a high price — abject humility from all of us, *all* the
time — and he somehow managed to keep us in a state of
apprehension. If one of us gave him the flimsiest excuse to find
fault it was good-bye bladder. Sometimes when our
expectations were at their highest and after standing around in
the cold watching the long-drawn-out 'slaughtering', Ernie,
literally from the bowels of the carcass would yell 'Be God! this
baste *never* had a bladder.' And the odd time just as he was
removing the bladder, with mock humility he would say 'Me
knife slipped, it cut the bladder in two' — he who was handier
with a knife than Stokes himself, the famous Dublin surgeon.

Our whole village knew when a slaughtering was going on
but I can't recall any public expression of revulsion or
compassion 'though the victim's squeals and screams were
audible from one end of the village to the other. You might hear
a casual remark like 'Animals have a sixth sense. No matter
how often the floor is washed they always smell the blood of the
slaughterhouse; the men must be having trouble driving the
beast in.' Our parents did not object to us children hanging
around watching every step of the bloody operation: the kill, the
paunching, the hanging up, the skinning and the cutting up
(dismantling). They were well aware that the bigger boys
sometimes gave a hand hauling on the thick tether that —
thanks to fresh applications of suet — ran freely across the
sturdy round beam, whose ends were set securely in opposite
walls high above the slaughterhouse floor.

You may wonder if such a spectacle had a brutalizing effect on
anyone connected with it. I know for sure that not a single one
of us youngsters would cause an animal — not even a rat —
unnecessary suffering. The common saying 'put it out of pain'
about summed it up. No one around was needlessly cruel to
animals. On the other hand few of us had an easy life and fewer
had any inclination to pamper animals. That was because most
of us lived off the land, and that included preying on any
animal, bird or fish we could make money or a meal out of. I
recall the public outcry when a local boy — he was twelve at the
time — was caught torturing frogs. He'd catch a frog, insert a
traneen (hollow grass stalk) in its rear end, inflate the animal,

withdraw the tube, throw the balloon-like frog into a pool and relish the futile efforts to dive and escape its tormentor.

From a safe distance a crowd of us kids would avidly follow the preparations for the kill and especially the actual dispatching of the unfortunate beast. It strikes me now that the stark name 'slaughterhouse' belongs to another era — an era that didn't use euphemisms like abattoir. The bullock usually weighed well over half a ton and it took several men to drive, beat and force it into the building — force that included twisting the unfortunate animal's tail. Once inside the building the stout door was secured and the men cornered the now terrified animal, put the noose end of a thick rope around its neck, just behind the ears at the back of its jaw and just behind the butt of its horns. Then the free end of the rope would be pushed through a stout iron ring which was securely affixed to an iron eye set in the stone wall about twenty inches above the stone cobbled floor. Cobblestones provided a less slippery surface than would a flagged floor.

Then the tug-of-war commenced; several strong men versus the doomed bullock. At no time was there any doubt of the outcome. The now beserk animal, frothing at the mouth, with bulging blood-shot eyes and hide bathed in 'cold sweat' was contesting every inch of the way. Its hoofs were slipping and slithering on the greasy cobblestones as by 'main strength and ignorance' it was inched to the iron ring. Finally the last bit of slack was taken up and the bullock's head anchored.

Now the butcher takes over in earnest. He is handed the adze. The butcher's adze is designed to do two jobs: to be used as an axe for chopping, and to stun an animal preparatory to killing it. The adze is somewhat like a woodsman's axe with a long wooden handle and a steel head. One end of the head forms an axe, the other end has a six inch protuberance. The latter, in reality part of the one-piece axe head, used to be a solid steel spike. About forty years ago the design of this spike was improved on and it is now shaped like a three-quarter inch diameter hollow pipe with the killing end sharp. This means that a violent blow with the improved adze cuts and caves in a circular section of the beast's skull. The solid spike used to crush a larger area of the skull and punch a jagged hole.

With his sleeves rolled up, the butcher hefts the adze, sets his feet firmly on the cobblestones and takes aim, meaning, placing the killing end of the adze at the exact place on the beast's forehead. He now rests the adze against the wall, wipes his hands on his apron, spits into his fists, takes up the adze again, takes aim and with a swift, smooth swing crushes the weapon through the skull into the brain of the victim. The beast collapses. Immediately the butcher has the killing knife behind the jugular, and cutting towards the windpipe severs the artery.

When the butcher considers the bullock has about bled its last drop he carries out what I think is the most barbarous act of all — the 'ramming'. He is handed a three foot length of pliable wood — somewhat like the cane the Master used to slap us with at school — inserts the stick into the hole he has punched in the skull and rams it into what he claims is the nerve centre of the spinal cord. This revolting act induces a convulsive, violent movement in every nerve of the apparently dead animal. The ramming was designed to bleed the final drop of blood out of the carcass and any butcher would assure you that 'mate won't keep if its badly bled'. Please keep in mind that I'm speaking of a time before Irish country butchers had facilities for refrigeration; when well-hung meat was a 'must'.

Back there when I tried to describe the one-sided tug-of-war, I said the outcome was never in doubt but I remember an unforgettable incident in that same slaughterhouse when the outcome was in doubt — or postponed. The other village butcher was ill and two butchers from the nearest town were hired to slaughter for him.

Afterwards it came to light that the pair were not professional butchers at all; they were what we call knackers. A knacker's job is usually confined to skinning animals that died of natural causes or accidental death. Many a time I heard accounts of how the two knackers in question would 'deliver' a bullock to a town butcher for slaughter — to be sold eventually over the counter as prime beef. The two 'boyos' always delivered the carcass to the slaughterhouse in the dead of night on a rubber-tired cart; but artists that they were, the noise of the horses and cart was muffled by the stamping and running of feet, 'wallops' of ash plants and exciting cries and comments of 'Stop that beast', 'Head him off' or 'Mind the wild bastard doesn't get away from us.'

Anyway, the knackers arrived in the village to do the job and a bigger than average crowd gathered to see 'how good the townies are'. For a start, the audience was not impressed because both the visiting butchers 'appeared a bit small to pole-axe a beast properly'. The operation was proceeding smoothly and the big moment came when the bullock's head was in the correct position for the 'stroke'. One knacker gripped the adze, took his stance and in approved style 'measured the bullock'. Then raising himself on 'tippy toes' to his full sixty four inches he swung the huge adze in an arc and down it came on the beast's head. A gasp arose from the onlookers. The little man's nerve must have forsaken him. Certainly the disparaging whispers of the crowd didn't help — somehow the adze had twisted in the unfortunate little fellow's sweaty hands and the chopping end of the blade came down full force on the bullock's forehead and severed the rope.

The bullock was not even stunned. Severely wounded, the maddened beast exploded out the door of the slaughterhouse and for two solid hours it rampaged around the village before a police marksman managed to put it out of its misery.

Needless to say the two knackers did not wait to collect their blood money; in fact the entire community was incensed at the bungled killing and that evening in the pubs there was serious discussion as to whether the botched job warranted lynching.

7. DOGS

When we start a sentence with 'God knows', the complete statement can convey several meanings. It can convey wonder, puzzlement, bafflement, admiration, enquiry, exasperation, helplessness, resignation and many others. If the true answer could prove incriminating, the 'God knows' is employed.

God knows how many dogs there are in Ireland. The Authorities, in this case either the office of the Minister of Taxes, or the Garda Síochána, could produce a figure giving the precise number of dogs licensed in the Republic; but in relation to the true dog census, that count would only be the tip of the iceberg.

Around 1922, when the long desired freedom from foreign domination was won, credit — and the blame — went to a pitifully small number of active patriots. The rest of us, I suppose you could call us armchair patriots, suddenly became articulate and loudly boasted how we won the fight for freedom, a boast that recalls the old saying, 'Victory has a thousand fathers; defeat is an orphan'.

Prior to the founding of our State we gloried in dodging payment of taxes to Britain. I remember one tax in particular that we resented bitterly. That was the tax on domestic dogs, which pinched the poor people both in pride and pocket. Anyone who kept a dog or several dogs and took the legal risk of not paying tax on them, felt he was striking a blow for freedom — in addition to saving the tax fee.

So we won our freedom and then our very own Government slapped a bigger dog tax on us — at present it's one Pound. In spite of not having the patriotic excuse any longer, we still consider it 'fair game' to do the Government out of the dog tax. So you see, only a judicious number of Irish dogs are taxed. I'm sure there are numerous ways to beat the dog tax, but the most common dodge if you own several dogs is to pay tax for one animal and never allow the others to appear in public. Up to a week ago the Missus and myself, like good citizens, paid the license for our collie, an animal who spends most of his time outside the house. He is an extremely friendly dog and almost knocks himself out trying to strike up friendship with people passing the house. The other day I was happy to see him positively fawning on a genuinely amiable young police constable who had stopped to pat him on the head. The following day, to my horror, I saw that our collie, not satisfied with making up to the Law, somehow had managed to introduce to the young man in uniform our toy Yorkshire terrier who is normally housebound. We are now in the unique position of being the only family around with two licensed dogs.

Villages, let alone towns or cities, would never have evolved or existed if their inhabitants had not learned to get along with each other; so I suppose it's natural and imperative that villagers remain on friendly terms. They say that fighting dogs have caused more bad blood between neighbours than any other single factor and it wouldn't at all surprise me if there is an Irish saying to the effect that 'Bad fences make bad neighbours; fighting dogs make battling neighbours'. To maintain peace in the village and keep on good terms with your neighbours, it was a cardinal rule that no matter how good a fighting dog you owned, you couldn't very well 'set him' on their dogs, or be detected promoting a dogfight. The exception to this was the odd time when gypsies or tinkers happened to pass through the village. These people were noted for the number and fighting ability of their dogs and it was to be expected that their canines were very well able to look after themselves, especially because they were fair game for every 'dog and devil' they encountered on all the highways and byways of Ireland.

A good ballad singer, a travelling fiddler, a harper, or a bag-piper invariably attracted a large crowd when they performed on the main street of the village but a dogfight drew a bigger crowd. By the same token, it would be unfair to use that as evidence that all the villagers preferred watching a dogfight to listening to our national airs being rendered by our traditional musicians.

Most of us who didn't own dogs, or whose pets were safe at home, gathered at those dogfights in the hope that there would be the added attraction of the owners of the dogs becoming embroiled. Nowadays there appear to be just as many dogs in the village as when I was a youngster. The other day I remarked that we seldom see a dogfight, and got my answer: 'These days dogs are better fed than Christians were in my time and they're too pampered to have any fight left in them'. There may be a lot of truth in that but I well remember four villagers — and I can't tell you the names of three of them because their people are still around — who kept ferocious dogs purposely for their fighting prowess. The fourth dog fancier was Paddy Blueman. In the pub on one occasion after he had a few pints in him, he was heard to brag, 'A dog of mine never was bet in a fight' and before the words were out of his mouth the man next to him cut in with, 'Sure you always do away with your dog if he gets the worst of it in a fight and then you comb the country for a murderous baste.'

Mention of Blueman's dog reminds me of something else. Looking back now, I wonder if in our childish ignorance — or innocence — our understanding of certain things was clearer than that of our parents and other adults who often appeared to be unaware of certain details, for instance the strange resemblance that existed between some dogs and their owners. We were convinced that certain traits such as bravery and cowardice, trust and suspicion, openness and slyness were often dominant in, and common to, both dog and owner. This seemed more apparent in those who 'made much' of their dogs — the ones who went to the extreme of investing their pets with qualities not only bordering on, but surpassing that of humans. Even physical characteristics were mirrored in some of the owner/dog relationships. For instance, Paddy Blueman was red-haired, long, lean, with a vulpine-shaped face, and he always kept a dog with lots of red in its coat. He never owned a small dog.

It's got nothing to do with dogs, but Paddy's hair was so unusual that I can't resist mentioning it. He was clean-shaven except for a red moustache and I have no idea how often he shaved. There wasn't a barber shop within seven miles of the village, so the haircutting was done by a few locals who had a taste for the job. Paddy Blueman only had his hair cut every three years. You are wrong! He did not wear his hair shoulder-length; in fact it was never longer than two inches and it took over three years for it to grow that long. I remember even when he was an old man he'd a good head of dark red hair which was composed of a mass of tiny, tight curls hugging his scalp.

My guess is that far, far back, Paddy Blueman's ancestors must have been warriors; fierce fellows who enjoyed going into battle, who gloried in hand-to-hand combat. Bill Barden summed it up: 'Paddy Blueman must have fighting blood in him; it escapes through his fighting dogs.' I'd have said that Paddy got a vicarious pleasure from his own personal dog doing the fighting. Maybe it is something like the way that we modern 'sportsmen' get our kicks from watching, instead of physically participating in, 'sports' where the players sometimes risk life and limb for the spectators' enjoyment. Personally I'd sooner play tiddlywinks than be a mere spectator watching a game from the safety of the sidelines, the comfort of a ringside seat, or the ultimate luxury of T.V. viewing.

As I've already explained, there were more dogs in our village than met the eye; but it took a dog fight to bring them into the open and it was as good as a circus once a genuine dogfight erupted. I mean a fight that developed past one of these snarl, snap, bite-and-run affairs. To anyone in the know, the stages of any of our dogfights were predictable. Usually the ruckus (fracas) would start by some small, snarly terrier or half Pom throwing its weight around by snapping at some smaller dog. Within seconds the genuine fighting hounds would appear on the scene and in a flash the Pom and the smaller opponent would 'skedaddle' for home and safety. They would flee, literally with their tails between their legs. I'm sure you know that when a dog — or bitch — adopts that defensive posture it is wisely using its tail to cover up and protect the most vulnerable part of its anatomy, thereby ensuring it will have offspring who will in turn recognize that precise moment when discretion is better than valour. Writing those lines I was toying with something that could be worked into some kind of doggerel poem, or into a corny epigram; something like 'If its sex activities were curtailed, its offspring couldn't be cur tailed'.

After the preliminary snarls, yelps and howls from the canine combatants, innumerable curs from all directions would zero in on the fray. Next the spectators would arrive. I got more fun out of watching the antics of the dog owners than excitement from the dogfight itself. No one would ever admit that he kept and trained dogs solely for fighting. But if you kept your eyes peeled you could usually identify the owner of individual dogs by the behaviour of their masters. Invariably you could pick out the owners, because each one of them would happen to have a stick casually carried as if to say, 'the auld rheumatism is killing me, I'm reduced to using a sthick.' You might also notice that if a dog was winning hands down its owner would never appear to be around; but let the battle go against his animal and it was remarkable how quickly he would appear on the scene. I once detected a dog owner ostentatiously pulling his victorious dog free from a three-dog fight but managing 'accidentally on purpose' with his hob-nailed boots to step on the feet of the two losers.

If one were writing a set of rules for owner behaviour during village dogfights here is the first suggested rule: be circumspect and diligent so that it does not appear as if you are egging on your dog or covertly assisting him in any way. Second: if your dog happens to be getting the worst of it, it is definitely dangerous to life and limb to clout the dog 'getting the best' of your animal because if the owner of that dog happens to be within striking distance, you may get the worst of it. Another: if your dog happens to be winning, please restrain yourself, try to keep your elation to yourself; it's bad form to cheer for a cur who happens to be top dog in a fight. Finally: it is not considered good form to allow your dog to savage an obviously out-classed canine opponent, even if the beaten dog bullies all the other dogs in the village and you happen to heartily dislike its owner.

Bill Barden always owned a dog. He said, 'I like dogs, I was never without a good hunting dog but it had to be a dog that would earn its keep.' To Bill 'keep' meant a provider or what he called a 'forager'. I suppose he unconsciously used that old military expression denoting to ravage; to spoil; to raid. The traits he desired, in fact demanded, in his hunting dogs were cleverness, speed for hunting and the ability to catch and kill hares and rabbits. As far as fighting dogs were concerned, he said, 'It is unnatural for a dog all the time wanting to fight — especially against its own kind; on the other hand I'd be ashamed to keep a dog if he couldn't give a good account of himself if another dog sticks in him.' Bill, if he wished, could literally 'live off the land' as we say in Canada when referring to Eskimos and Indians living solely by fishing, hunting and trapping. Here in Ireland rabbits are plentiful; in fact, until recently the rabbit was our most common mammal. About twenty years ago it was decided that there were too many rabbits in the country and that they were depriving our grazing cattle and sheep of a significant quantity of grass. So the rabbit population was decimated by the callous (I feel) introduction of the Myxamatosis virus. The rabbit population has recovered strongly and they now appear to be as numerous as ever.

When I was young, rabbits were almost the sole source of meat for middle-class families; in addition there was also a good market for the skins of rabbits. We had many ways of catching rabbits. In fact, in my youth I had a go at nearly every method hunters ever devised to catch rabbits; trapping, snaring, netting, ferreting, hunting and catching them with the aid of hunting dogs. I almost forgot to including shooting, but use of a gun to kill rabbits was then considered expensive and anyway, as a sport it was not very highly rated.

Looking back now I realize that there must have been a bit of cruelty — to the rabbits — in most of the methods we employed in catching them and other wild animals; but as Bill Barden would say, we were 'Teetotally unconscious of inflicting unnecessary pain'. I don't know whether it was just in our nature or it had been drummed into us but when hunting, if any of us caught a wild animal we immediately did our best to put it out of pain as humanely as possible. And like the Eskimo and Indian hunters who, as a way-of-life hunt for food, we never hunted solely for pleasure; maybe that is why we were never overly enthusiastic about 'the Gentry' fox-hunting.

When I was in my teens, Bill Barden often took me along when he went hunting rabbits. We travelled light; just his two dogs, an old potato sack to carry the spoils, and his hunting stick. The larger dog was Bill's current half-greyhound and the smaller one was the fox terrier used for 'beating' the thickets. Thickets are clumps of dense, prickly furze bushes, whitethorns and briars which normally provide a temporary haven for rabbits, hares and pheasants. Bill's hunting stick was a four foot long piece of well-seasoned young ash tree about the thickness of a broom handle. He used the stick to 'beat' clumps of bushes to dislodge the 'game', and was able to throw the hunting stick with such amazing accuracy that quite often he could 'bring down' a rabbit or hare up to a distance of twenty yards.

Irish rabbits live in the safety of their burrows which are usually holes or passages that form a labyrinth in the heart of the Irish ditches and earth mounds.

The terrier was about the size of a rabbit and when we were out hunting, his job was to run around the outside of a clump, both to try to locate a rabbit, and possibly confuse it; then he would suddenly make a dive into the thickest portion. In the meantime the half-greyhound would also be circling the clump and obviously working in concert with the terrier. Sometimes the terrier would pounce and kill the luckless rabbit in the thick briers, but most times he would 'bolt' the rabbit. The rabbit would run for the open field and then the half-greyhound would 'do his thing' and such was his speed that if the rabbit took for the open fields it was caught in a matter of yards.

On one occasion, Bill, the dogs and myself hunted for about four hours and in that time we must have walked a dozen miles and were so loaded with rabbits that Bill decided to call it a day. We had over twenty rabbits and to lighten the load Bill said, 'They are so full of grass I'll "panch" them.' I assumed that was his pronunciation of 'paunch'. In a modern dictionary I looked up the word that Bill used to describe removing the rabbits' distended stomach and intestines and found that nowadays the word does not appear to be used as a verb; but my century-old dictionary gives it: v.t. To pierce or rip the belly of; to eviscerate; to disembowel.

When we returned home I was bragging about his half-greyhound and mentioned that Bill didn't seem to show much affection or friendship for either of his dogs. 'Funny you noticing that', Bill said, 'I only loved one dog and when he was destroyed I made up my mind never to allow myself to get too fond of a dog again.' I muttered 'Yes, dogs have a very short life compared to ours.' He said, 'That's not the reason at all, I'll tell you about a rale dog.'

As Bill himself tells it: 'His name was Prince; he was a half-greyhound and his coat was black and always shiny as an otters's. He killed more rabbits and hares than any ten "poochin dogs" in Ireland and he not only kept the house in rabbits but many's the price of a pint he brought me when I'd sell the odd pair of rabbits he'd killed. Prince had another gift; plenty of dogs go hunting on their own account, but it's for diversion or because their bellies are empty and they kill the odd rabbit or even slaughter some unfortunate farmer's sheep or lambs, but our Prince used to go off hunting on his own accord, but then he'd do the same as a mother fox with cubs in the den would do — he'd bring home the kill.

'The first time it happened, Prince was missing for an hour and I happened to be looking towards Carrigy's hill and here was me bauld (sic) Prince coming towards me with a fine big rabbit in his mouth. You could'ave knocked me down with a feather I was so took back. I just talked quiet to him and into the house I went and stood beside me mother who was sitting at the fire and I whispered to her not to take any account of Prince. You could hear a pin drop in that kitchen; be God if Prince didn't walk right across that floor and lay the still-warm rabbit at me mother's feet!

'She just patted Prince on the head, didn't say a word, but got up and gave a full pint of fresh milk to him and you could tell by the look in Prince's eyes that he felt like a real hero. I said afterwards that it was only by accident that it was to me mother he gave that first rabbit because he was my dog and no man alive ever took him hunting since I rared him from a pup. Within a week Prince made a liar of me when he went through the whole kemares (performance) again, and who do you think he gave the rabbit to? — me mother of course.' As Bill continued speaking about Prince I understood how the dog was accepted and treated as 'one of the family', because it had now become a breadwinner. Prince was what we call a 'half-greyhound'. That is not to be taken literally of course. Full greyhound is the name we give to a pure-bred or registered greyhound; half-greyhound is a dog (or bitch), one of whose parents was a registered greyhound, while the other parent was of any breed, or a mixture of breeds. The half-greyhound was so named regardless of whether a registered greyhound happened to be its dam or sire.

As Bill wistfully recounted Prince's unique hunting ability it transpired that the hound had another gift. I never got to the bottom of whether this gift came naturally to the dog, or whether it was the result of training or coaching combined with a natural aptitude for bringing home the spoils; but to hear Bill tell it, Prince literally 'brought home the bacon'.

Before the era of cold storage, refrigerators, glass cases, etc. the village shopkeepers used to keep the day's requirements of bread, bacon, eggs and so forth, displayed on long counters, benches and tables. Some of them still do.

Bill would never steal, at least not from a friend; nevertheless, his attitude towards private property was quite liberal. Keep in mind that when Bill was a young man, the wage for a labourer was six pence a day and feed himself. He would say, 'When I was a young man and labouring for ten hard long hours a day I was often so famished with the hunger that I'd be glad of the chance to lift a couple of turnips of a farmer's field and hide in the shelter of the ditch while I'd be eating them.' Understandably, in our confidential talks I never brought up (our) Seventh Commandment, Thou Shalt Not Steal, but I'm dead certain that Bill had no qualms of conscience regarding Prince's activities. As if reading my mind, Bill, on one occasion when I was beating around the bush said, 'We never trained or sent Prince to steal; we would just let him loose and give him the run of his tooth.'

Bill said: 'Some dogs are smarter than people. Take Prince, he'd know what you were thinking. We were all round the fire one day; me mother was boiling a pair of rabbits for the dinner and she happened to say, "I'd give me two eyes for a bit of bacon to go with them two rabbits." Sure as I'm alive, if me bould Prince didn't get up from where he was supposed to be sleeping in a corner near the hob, stretched himself, walked to the doorway where the bottom of the half-door was shut and he lept over it like a flash. Me mother said, "What's got into Prince? I never saw him lep the half-door before." We gave no more thought of it but a while afterwards, Prince gave a little bark outside the door and when I went to let him in, be God if he didn't have the tail-end of a lovely, salty, flitch of bacon in his mouth.' I said, 'Bill where did he get it?'. He answered, 'When you are hungry you don't ask foolish questions' and he continued 'From then on Prince was the scourge of the shopkeepers. In a way they respected him and it became a battle of wits between the cagey dog and the shopkeepers because though they tried hard and tried every trick of the trade, they could never catch him red-handed.' Then as an afterthought he said, 'But it did make the shopkeepers attend to their business and keep a better eye on their groceries. Many a steaming-hot loaf Prince brought home from Tommy Gorman's and the odd time he was lucky enough to snaffle a bit of mate from either of the two butcher shops. I mind him dragging home a string of sausages that 'id make your teeth water that he'd lifted from the Huckster's shop at the bottom of the village.'

Remember! It was difficult for the shopkeepers to secure their wares from Prince because due to the absence of central, or any other kind of, heating in country stores, the door or doors were usually kept open. Even if the shop door was supposed to be closed after someone going in or out, inevitably it would be left open at least half the time. People here have a Thing about closing a door — I know. Hence the dog had plenty of opportunities to get in and out of a shop. Of course, the shopkeeper or his assistant was supposed to be in attendance and ever since Prince went on the warpath, surveillance by the shopkeepers was the order of the day. The snag, from the shopkeepers' point-of-view, was that Prince did not raid a shop every day or develop any predictable pattern of pilfering.

Most of the villagers with the exception of Prince's victims, took an active interest in what was now turning out to be a bizzare battle of wits between a bunch of intelligent people and a 'dumb baste'. Gambling instincts were aroused. But 'aroused' could be misleading to foreigners. I just read an article in our principal daily newspaper and discovered that one can't arouse Irish gambling instincts — because already they are rampant — if that is the correct word. The leader in my paper fulminates against '. . . the gambling mentality of the nation, a mentality that everyone sets out to foster . . .' It harps on gambling being a ruinous addiction. It goes on to take a wallop at church bingos; also at 'respectable' charities distributing their lotteries through National Schools. As a clincher it declares, 'The State has it's Prize Bonds'. Strangely the leader writer omitted to mention our biggest money spinner of all, the Irish Hospital Sweepstakes, which to our collective chagrin (mixed with suspicion of dirty work at the crossroads) Americans appear to have a monopoly on winning the Super Prize of — £250,000 pounds mind you, not dollars.

Pardon the small detour and back to Prince. As I was stating, or understating, gambling raised it's ugly head and many people took a 'flutter' by placing bets on the daily ups and downs of the contestants. Significant sums of money changed hands every time Prince 'made a hit', as Kojak would say: Some bettors cried 'foul' when it appeared that Tommy Gorman was covertly aiding and abetting Prince. Tommy Gorman, baker, poet and philosopher called Prince his steadiest non-paying customer. Tommy, who loved all things both great and small, was suspected of entering into the spirit of the game when he moved his loaded counter closer to the door of the shop.

A devotee of Prince said, 'There even was one in the Garden of Eden' and he wasn't referring to either of our (reputed) biblical First Parents; he was sniping at the Huckster because the latter was heard to threaten and brag, 'If I ever catch Barden's dog on my premises I'll let daylight into him'. If a village popularity vote were taken of Prince versus the Huckster, the dog would win in a trot. Do you know what the word huckster means? In Ireland? We ascribe only one meaning to it: 'A shopkeeper with little capital, a small range of merchandise and a smaller clientele; one who charges exorbitant prices.' People said, 'The Huckster has a mean, cruel streak in him and an odjus (odious) hatred of all the animals that God ever created' and he proved it by the unsporting tactics he used to get the better of Prince. He baited and set a badger's trap for Barden's dog and when the unfortunate animal was struggling to get free, he tried to finish the dog off with a big butcher knife. He almost succeeded.

I had better let Bill tell it in his own words. 'To me dying day I'll carry bitter memories of the evening Prince met his end. Outside our house a woman screamed, "Missus Barden, Missus Barden something terrible has happened!" We all ran out and Mary Ward shouted, "I was passing the Huckster's yard and heard an animal yelping with pain. Then your dog came hell-for-leather out of the yard and close behind him with his big butchers' knife in his fist was the Huckster. Your dog started up the street with a trap and a lump of chain dragging behind him and he leaving a trail of blood like a leaking bucket. By the time he was halfway up the street he was only staggering." Later on the family tawld me most of what Missus Ward shouted, but the minute she screamed for me mother I was out of the house and down the road where I saw Prince dragging himself towards me like a snail and he leaving a smare (smear) of blood on the road behind him and he so wake he was only managing to put one foot past another and he dragging a few feet of rusty chain tied to a big badger trap with it's teeth sunk into his badly smashed hind leg. With me bare hands I forced open the jaws of the trap, pitched it to one side, scooped Prince up in me arms and into the house where me mother had the table cleared and dragged to the middle of the flure. She said, "Put him down aisy on the table and stand back the rest of you."

'As well as a terrible bad hind leg, Prince had a hole in his side you could put your fist into; he wasn't bleeding much — he had already reddened the road home.

'Me mother was trying to get something into his mouth on a big spoon out of the bottle of brandy that we always complained you'd have to be close to death's dure before she would even let you take a whiff of the cork. I wasn't worried because wasn't me mother looking after him and Prince with the heart of a lion. The others stood back because she towld them to; but she let me stand beside her. There she sat at the table and though we all knew that Prince was my dog, wasn't it in me mother's hands he put his head. Me brother, Kit, said, "Be God he'll live; he's licking her hand" Before Kit had the words out of his mouth, she said "He's gone" and for the memory of a dog's soul me mother did a peculiar thing, she blessed herself.

'I lost me head then. I made for the door and she must have read me mind because she said, "Bill where are you off to?" "I'm going down to the village to 'do in' the Huckster and I'll strangle him with me bare hands."

'Herself and the three brothers were struggling trying to hold me back. Me brothers, big and all as they were, would never have held me because I was twenty years old and me dander was up. But me mother got down on her bended knees between me and the dure and said, "For the sake of the Blessed Virgin leave the Huckster to God. I know He will take care of him in His own good time." Of course, I gave in to me mother but for many a year I held in the black spite and every single night when the whole family would be on our knees and her giving out the Rosary and me supposed to be praying, I'd be cursing his sowl to hell and asking God to give the Huckster the short knock.

'It must have been twenty years before I was man enough to ask The Man Above — and I meant it — to forgive the Huckster. That change of heart came about when I heard, not that he was dead, but the way the Huckster died.'

It was no secret that the Huckster was a wife beater. His unfortunate wife Ellen was several years his senior and they were childless — which everyone said 'was just as well because Ernie says he can't abide children.' The beatings occurred so regularly that the neighbours almost got used to hearing the screams of Ellen and watching her inevitable flight from the house with the Huckster in her wake swinging his ash plant and the blood pouring down the poor woman's face. She always made for our house and sanctuary.

My earliest memories of Ellen are kind of vague; but there she'd be sitting on a chair in our kitchen and she moaning and crying and my mother and sisters fussing over and trying to comfort her while they washed and dressed the wounds on her face and scalp. My clearest memories are those of my father and brothers in the background, fuming and frustrated, because the unfortunate woman always refused to 'call in the law' and when the police tried to intervene she refused to press charges. To make matters worse, all the time she was taking shelter in our house — sometimes for two days at a time — her husband would stand a safe distance away shouting abuses and accusing us of harbouring his wife. The extraordinary part of it all was that while sheltering with us Ellen would groan, 'Poor Ernie, he's no good to cook for himself.' Usually after a day or two she would return to 'poor Ernie' when as she'd say 'He got over throwing his tantrums.' I don't know how many years or how many beatings the Huckster inflicted on his wife, but I was in my early teens when my brother Tommy 'put the kibosh on the Huckster'.

Tommy was one of the best — if not the best — athletes around and the time came that he determined to 'put a stop to the Huckster's gallop'. He did not have long to wait; there in broad daylight was unfortunate Ellen fleeing for her life and Ernie behind her with the ash plant in his fist. Close to our front door he overtook her, swung the stick and caught her behind the ear. She dropped like a log. Tommy shouted 'Carry her into the house; I'll fix Ernie,' Bare-handed he rushed at the Huckster, but the brute had a head start and made it to the safety of his shop. Then he appeared in the doorway with the big meat cleaver and yelled 'Be God just put one foot on my doorstep and I'll split your head down the middle like I'd split a turnip.' Tommy made a strategic retreat, but his blood was up. He lined up two big men to go to the front of the Huckster's shop and act as if they were about to take on Ernie and told them to 'Keep him engaged at the front; I'll go around the back in my bare feet and take him from behind'. So there was the Huckster standing in his doorway furiously brandishing the cleaver and daring the two men to 'Come and fight'. Like a cyclone Tommy burst on him and the Huckster never stood a chance. Once my brother had wrenched the cleaver out of his hand, Ernie turned into the craven coward he was and kept begging for mercy while Tommy 'gave him something to remember'. He did remember — all the days of his life — because never after did he raise a hand in anger to his wife. Everyone said, 'It's a pity no one was man enough to lambaste the dirty brute thirty years sooner.'

After Ernie, as the Canadian might say, 'got his comeuppance', he and his wife lived in peace, although I heard it said that there was no love lost between them. Ellen predeceased him by several years and from then on he drew into his shell and had little contact with the neighbours. I was out of the country when Ernie died. His was not a happy death. Neighbours reported to the Garda that he had not been seen around for several days. The police tried both front and back doors and discovered both were securely locked and bolted from the inside. They forced open a window on the ground floor, failed to find Ernie, went upstairs, came up against a bedroom — his bedroom — and were unable to open the stout door. Finally they put a ladder on the sidewalk and one of them forced open the bedroom window, pushed in the heavy wooden shutters that were a security feature of most old houses, and saw a macabre sight.

The bed was pushed tightly against the door which had already been secured by two big iron bolts. The policeman yelled down that Ernie's feet were sticking out from under the bed but that he showed little sign of life. Both the doctor and priest arrived at the scene and it transpired later that the doctor managed to bring the unfortunate man around — at least long enough for the priest to hear his confession, give him Absolution and the Last Annointing. Ernie died within the hour; out of deference to his relatives, details of his demise were hushed up, but naturally some of the story leaked out.

It was already common knowledge that the Huckster had trouble sleeping: he was under the delusion that his dead wife nightly stood at his bedside and kept him awake — hence the bolted bedroom door. Apparently sometime during his last three days on earth he tried to make the room more secure by pushing the heavy bed tightly against the door and later suffered some kind of heart attack or weakness. There was evidence that he was conscious for most of the three days he was trapped and that he made repeated and desperate efforts to open the door. So he died alone — alone as far as human company was concerned: a policeman mentioned that 'The rats had been at him', but he refused to say at what stage the rats entered the picture. The onslaught of the rats came as no surprise; everyone knew the Huckster's yard was infested with rats because his yard and house drains were connected by an open sewer to the village drain that runs to the river.

When I heard how the Huckster had met his death I felt relieved that he had had time to make his peace with God and I remembered the prayer of Bill Barden's mother, 'Bill, leave the Huckster to God.'

8. FISHING

Somewhat ungrammatically a friend recently asked me, 'What age did you start fishing at?' What age did I start fishing? Like most of the village children, male and female, I started fishing around four years of age. Of course our quarry was only 'pinkeens'. I never heard the correct name for the little fish, with the sharp spine or needles that seemed to be hinged at the base of the head, and which, possibly at the will of the little fish, stood out at right angles to its body like twin bayonets. I looked up the English term for our pinkeens and it appears that they are sticklebacks.

We had a special place for catching our little fish; it was down the Bog Road about a quarter of a mile from the village at a place called Ward's Bridge. It was, to our minds, by far the best place in Ireland for pinkeen fishing. Possibly our wise parents conditioned us to agree that it was the best; they knew there were plenty of pinkeens in every bog drain in the country, but most of those drains were deep and dangerous for children; in many cases their banks were undercut and hollow and there was always the danger of a bank caving in and endangering life.

Actually Ward's Bridge was only the head-wall of a culvert that permitted the water from the main bog drainage ditch to cross under the road. The solid masonry head-wall was low and broad and could have been designed for the comfort and safety of the young Waltonians, as Mr. L. would say. I only use that word because I suddenly remembered Mr. L., a retired gentleman whom we youngsters always tried to avoid. Mr. L. was 'well read' and never let anyone forget it. He never used a common or simple word if he had a 'jawbreaker' handy. The beautiful, simple word 'fishing' became 'piscatorial pursuits' in his mouth.

I suppose there's more odd beliefs, customs, superstitions etc. connected with fishing than with any other avocation I can think of. The average Irish fisherman will agree that before you can catch a fish you have to earn it. We say 'The worse the weather,

73

the better the fishing'. When it comes to fishing, your true fisherman not only expects to encounter difficulties and experience hardship, he almost welcomes them, because every fisherman worth his salt knows you have to earn your catch. Further on I'll try to point up some of the difficulties and obstacles the youth of my era and locality met and overcame when we were out after fish.

This 'earning your fish' came into being even in the earliest days of our fishing endeavours. At Ward's Bridge I'd say that this delicate balance between effort and reward worked out about fifty-fifty. From a young fisherman's point of view it was a Garden of Eden; but even the original Garden had its serpent. Our fishing ground was called Ward's Bridge although it only bordered Mickeen Ward's little property.

Mickeen was a poor old man who lived alone and as far as I know was a decent sort of man. The Mickeen we children saw was old, cranky and humpbacked. I don't know why he objected to us children fishing from the side of the public road. We were too much afraid of him to do anything 'to get his back up', but from time to time he would put the run on us. Everyone of us, even the teenagers, feared Mickeen Ward. Somehow we associated being humpbacked with disordered creatures; monsters, frightening beings with cloven hoofs, dangerous horns and lashing tails. In our naive world we believed those beings actually existed, that they were creatures who had originally rejected God's control and His order and hence were disorderly, evil and dangerous. The danger — imaginary or otherwise — from Mickeen, could have been an added attraction, or maybe it was part of the price we expected to pay for our fishing. Possibly the element of obscure danger sweetened the overall adventure. We also got a bit of excitement out of apparently outwitting the ogre we believed Mickeen to be. Maybe he in turn enjoyed sending us flying helter-skelter.

Just under the bridge itself the water was about four feet deep. To us it looked fathomless because bog water usually is brown coloured and quite opaque. Our gear for fishing, assembled for us small kids by our parents or older brothers and sisters, consisted of a short stick with about four feet of strong thread. The thread was called 'hussive' and it was extremely strong, reasonably coarse and did not tangle too easily. Usually someone in the crowd of 'pinkeen fishers' carried the tin of worms. The worms were not the big thick soft 'slobs' that North Americans call dew worms. We used 'blackheads'. They are tough and rubbery worms and we found them good for hooking the pinkeens. Actually we did not use hooks, but tied the free end of the thread around the middle of the blackhead and lowered it into the water. The little fish — when they were taking — would cluster around the bait and endeavour to bite the worm, but owing to the size of the bait in relation to the size of the pinkeen's mouth they could not possibly get a grip on the body of the worm. Then a pinkeen would open its mouth to the fullest and attempt to work an end of the worm into it — something like a snake trying to swallow its prey.

The young fisher had to watch carefully for the exact moment when the mouth of the fish would be stretched to its apparent limit. Then the drill was to exert the exact upward pull of the thread so it would not whip the worm out of the little fish's mouth, but with sufficient force and speed to propel the pinkeen from the water. Blackheads (worms) have a rough surface with slightly raised concentric circles and these aid in preventing it from slipping out of the fish's mouth. Each of us kids had our glass jar three-quarters full of the bog water and it was imperative that the captured fish be placed gently in the water immediately on landing it. Like fishermen of all ages, throughout the ages, at the end of the fishing we would proudly carry the catch home to be congratulated.

Looking back I imagine that our parents and elders were not consciously training us to become fishermen and hunters. In my years among Canadian Indians and Eskimos I observed the same pattern of children learning their fishing and hunting skills from their elders, who in turn had received their training from previous generations.

Even after a lifetime I enjoy the memories of those, my first organized fishing trips. Naturally we only went fishing when our parents considered the weather suitable or when they thought it expedient to get rid of us for a few hours. In those times, from May to September all country children and young teenagers would cast off the boots and go in the 'bare ones'. The grassy paths along the banks of the bog drains were kind to the bare feet; in fact the sod that grows like a thick carpet on the boggy (peat) soil has such a sponginess and resiliency that when you ran or jumped on it you'd think you had wings or had discovered the secret of partial weightlessness. When you have lived all your days in the unspoiled, unpolluted countryside you hardly notice — except in retrospect — the wealth and variety of smells and perfumes that is part and parcel of the atmosphere, but it gives that extra something which stays with you. Two odours and perfumes that always evoke for me the joys of pinkeen fishing, are the smells of wild mint and honeysuckle.

On the long and wonderful road leading to becoming the 'complete angler' the next step was taken when I was around seven years old. My parents then felt it was high time that I be allowed to join the other children in wading in the river that flows under the bridge at the foot of the village. The river Gaine flows deeply through boggy land till it reaches the immediate area of the village where the nature of the soil changes to upland. Upland, by its very name, is the land elevated above the adjoining bogland. There is also a distinction between the soil of the bogland and that of the upland; the soils of the latter are mainly derived from sandstone and granites. On the bogland there is no soil development at all.

The present bridge, like most structures of its kind in Ireland, evolved from the pre-historic ford. Hence the bottom and banks of the river in the vicinity of the bridge were composed of small flat stones, gravel and fine sediment. In relation to the boggy stretches of the river, the gravel bottom of the river provided a safe and ideal wading area for the village children and our parents were not worried when they knew we were 'in the river', because invariably some one had an eye on us from the bridge up above or from the open area at the bottom of the village. Naturally we had our minor accidents; some of the flat stones on the bottom of the river — especially near the banks where the flow was slower — were covered with a green growth or scum which presented a very slippery surface to our bare soles. A careless step meant a ducking; but that was part of our training as it were, and in reality we were learning to master our environment. That and other pitfalls and 'danger spots' were like (built in) hazards on a commando training course.

It was in that gravelled, stoney wading area at the bridge that, after I had pinkeen fishing mastered, I tried my hand at the next stage of fishing. It can't truthfully be called fishing because the equipment was an article 'borrowed' from my mother's kitchen, an ordinary piece of cutlery, a kitchen fork with three prongs.

With this primitive spear I went after trout fry, young pike, perch, collicks, stone-suckers and craw-fish.

This stage of fishing had a practical side, because the object of the exercise was to catch small fish, or fry, for my elder brothers to use as bait in their more sophisticated fishing endeavours. No matter how adept any of us young fishermen were with the fork, we found it next to impossible to impale young trout as they were so wary and elusive. I had better luck with the other small types of fish. The favourite quarry was a small fish locally called collick. I have unsuccessfully tried to find the English name for the little fish. The collick is shaped like a trout but is much slower in its movements and reactions. We never saw one that measured more than three and a half inches long and it looks as if that is their ultimate size. They were and still are, prized by fishermen as excellent bait for perch, pike and trout.

The collicks spend their daylight hours under flat stones and when I went after them it meant working upstream and gingerly raising and removing one flat stone after another until I located my quarry. It was important to catch the little fish without wounding it because they were only acceptable as 'live bait'. That's where the perfect fork came into play. In time I became adept at raising and removing the flat stones under which the little fish were hiding and I suppose feeding. If one were awkward in removing the cover the collick was off in a flash and when you next exposed its hiding place it was more wary than originally and it became extremely difficult to spear. The secret of success in the spearing depended on several things: first of all you had to be downstream from the little fish. Then you had to stand within easy striking distance with your feet apart and insure that you were not causing ripples or currents which might alarm your intended prey. Next grasping the spear in your hand — somewhat like you would hold a pen for writing — you would submerge your spear, hand and arm a couple of feet downstream from the fish, move your hand upstream until the spear was about two inches above and centered over the back and just below the pectoral fin. You'd aim for this portion of the fish, but regardless of how smooth and swift your stabbing action was, the fish would dart forward and if your judgement was right you would now have the middle of the little fish tightly jammed between two prongs of the fork. Almost simultaneously you'd slide the index finger down the fork and gently prevent the fish from wriggling free. Then you'd use the fingers of the other hand to form a cage around the fish and fork before you'd raise your catch and gently deposit it in the waiting fresh-filled jar of water. So now you must realize that catching a collick successfully was a 'tall order' for any seven year old.

The fork-spears that the other children used were mostly three-pronged kitchen forks: I was issued (as we say in the Army) a rusty, battered old three-pronged kitchen fork that had seen better days. I was never very bright but I always had an urge to improvise and improve tools and equipment. For instance, about three years later this urge led me to tinker with a clock that was treasured as a family heirloom and such was my lack of mechanical ability and total absence of any appreciation of right and wrong that I found it expedient to 'drown' the remains of the dismantled clock in the deepest part of the river and to this day the family can't account for what happened to their beloved clock. Maybe a broad-minded and charitable psychologist would say that I was amoral. You may ask 'What has clocks got to do with spearing little fish?' The answer 'Plenty, in my case'. Because I made up my seven-year-old mind that I'd acquire a better spear. 'Acquire' in my case meant beg, borrow or steal; I settled for the middle one and borrowed one from home.

My mother had four-pronged forks aplenty, but they were kept in the Parlour and only saw the light of day on very special occasions. The fact that they were 'hall-marked' silver and had been in the family for a long time didn't prevent me from borrowing one of them which after each day's fishing I was at first careful to return to the set. That fork was designed and made to last several lifetimes of normal use and normal use did not include violently spearing small fish on a bed of stones and gravel. Young and all as I was, I realized that I'd be courting discovery and disaster if I returned the battered fork to the mahogany box that held its onetime peers. I'll admit that the handle part of the silver fork stood up well, but unfortunately the prongs, or tines started to resemble battered corkscrews, so I thought it best to find a safe place to keep what I now privately called my fork.

Now that I had a fork that I could (almost) call my own, the next thing to do was to improve it. I did. By trial and error I bent, twisted and manipulated the four prongs until they were the ideal distance apart. This meant that when I took careful aim and plunged the fork down on the back of a little fish there was a fair chance of two alternate prongs sliding down tightly each side like a vice and holding him unwounded. As they say, 'I hammered a job' on my mother's silver fork when I turned it into the best collick spear in the country; but I'm afraid it drastically reduced its culinary value.

The stone-suckers, as far as I can find out from my limited research, are either young eels, elvers or lamper eels. When we were children we believed there was a row of eyes below the stone-sucker's head: now I think they are a series of gills. I suppose stone-suckers derived their name from the way they attach themselves in shallow flowing water to the flat surface of stones by their suction pump-shaped mouth. I'd say the mouth of a stone-sucker resembles the business end of a toilet plunger.

There are two different types of crawfish in our river: the brown-shelled ones with white colouring underneath, and the other kind with pink or salmon coloured undersurface. Sometimes when we were intent on our childish hunt-and-kill operation in the shallows at the bridge, you'd hear a sudden frightened squeal, followed by a rush for dry land. This happened every time one of us dislodged a big crawfish because we had heard stories of childrens' toes being nipped off by their huge pincer-like claws. This dread of the little crustaceans did not deter the more daring from capturing the smaller crawfish because our grown-ups prized small, live crawfish for pike bait.

I was eight before I was promoted from the humble job of catching and collecting bait, to participating in 'real' fishing on the river. In those days before An Bord Iascaigh Mhara (Government Fishing Board) became involved in promoting and improving Ireland's fish stocks, our river, the Gaine, abounded in trout although it also supported a large number of pike, perch and eels. Undoubtedly the other types of fish preyed on the young trout fry and the pike in turn took their toll of larger trout, but I feel that the 'coarse fish' helped to preserve a natural fish balance in the river and probably strengthened the trout stock by eliminating any less than normally agile trout.

Due to my youth, my participation in trout fishing on the river was confined to 'going along' with one or more of my three elder brothers when they fished the river. Although primarily all our fishing was for the larder, my brothers were expert fishermen and had such a yen for it that if they suddenly became rich, fishing would still be their favourite sport and pastime. I was permitted to play only a very minor and humble role in our fishing excursions, in fact I was limited to carrying the extra fishing gear: spare tip for trout rod, landing net, creel and bait. Actually I was serving my apprenticeship under three perfectionists — I thought they were cranks and tyrants when it came to fishing — and without that training or bondage I'd never have become a run-of-the-mill fisherman, let alone the ardent one I became. I've a sneaking suspicion that the brothers must have read Izaak Walton's Contemplative Man because I remember one of them saying — with what I thought to be a touch of bombast — 'Angling in its highest development is both an art and a science'.

Being permitted — at a safe distance — to watch my brothers in action, gave me such a respect for their skill and mastery of angling that I wouldn't cock an eyebrow if I heard an angler — as distinguished from an ordinary fisherman — refer to his pastime as a discipline. I know that the word discipline is almost solely used to describe professions such as medicine and engineering; but I'd like to think that fishing could be called a discipline because training for fishing requires discipline, self-control, character and efficiency. In my own case it early taught me to submit to authority and accept control.

It is generally accepted by fishermen that the culmination of the angler's art lies in capturing fish by using the artificial fly. The angler divides the sport of fishing with the artificial fly into two general types: dry fly-fishing and wet fly-fishing. The dry fly is supposed to float on the surface of the water while the wet fly is fished below the surface by being pulled or trawled through the water. The dry fly is cast upstream and permitted to float downstream towards the angler. The angler's main endeavour is to have his dry fly imitate a live insect or fly. Fishermen claim fly-fishing requires more skill than any other type of fishing; they hold that dry fly-fishing is most demanding of both skill and precision.

The tiny artificial fly is hand made and consists of a variety feathers bound to a minute steel-wire hook. The feathers and the various coloured threads that affix them to the hook are an artistic attempt to imitate the fly or insect upon which the trout feed.

When I was permitted to go along with my elder brothers on their fly-fishing excursions, I used to marvel at the number and variety of dry flies they carried. I knew they spent many a winter's evening tying flies and I even helped them collect bird feathers — although at the time all feathers looked alike to me. They also 'sent away' for trout flies and avidly read and studied books connected with fishing.

When we went up the river after trout, this is how it would go: the brothers would walk carefully — one on each bank of the river — always with the sun at their back because it gave them a better chance of watching a trout 'rise'. Rise is how we describe a trout feeding on surface flies. Sometimes the trout breaks the surface on the water to take a fly; other times the same trout may make a big splash and the odd time a trout will propel part of its body out of the water to try to 'take' a fly that is hovering above the water. If they watched a worthwhile rise my brothers usually would play a guessing game to come closest to the weight of the fish. That guess was often verified when they managed to catch the trout in question.

Immediately they noticed a likely trout break surface they'd give me the signal to stop dead in my tracks and like cats stalking a feeding bird they'd sneak close enough to the rise to determine the type of fly the trout was taking. Regardless of the variety of insects available, a 'rising trout' invariably will settle for only one particular type.

A lot of water has gone under Multy bridge since that afternoon when not yet in my teens I went along with my older brothers Michael and Simon on a fishing trip along the Gaine river. We caught a few average sized trout and then saw one making what they agreed was a 'big rise'. For a long hour they concentrated on trying to tempt that trout with the pick of their huge stock of home-tied flies; but the fish wouldn't even give a second look at their choicest fly. Finally Michael said, 'We'll go home and tie a fly; I know the exact sort he's taking.' So home we went. Michael tied a fly and for good luck Simon made another and within the hour the three of us were back in the trout's feeding area.

By now he was only rising intermittently and one of them remarked 'He's had his fill but we'll mark the spot and be back tomorrow if we can't coax him now.' They watched for awhile and the eldest said, 'Simon, I'll try him first and then you can have a go at him', and he took up his position about fifty feet downstream of the rising trout. Michael owned and treasured a split-bamboo rod that weighed only a few ounces and with it had acquired the knack of being able to land at a distance of fifty feet an artificial fly right on a sixpence. The rest of us held our breath as he made that initial cast. The fly at the end of a few feet of extra fine gut which was attached to the silk blow line described a huge arc, hovered, as it were, over the target area and gently fluttered down. That big trout must have made up his mind not to let that tempting fly get its feet wet, because just before the fly hit the water the trout broke surface and sucked in the fly. At the correct split second Michael 'struck' and after 'playing' the fish for twenty exciting, apprehensive minutes he ordered the landing net. Within seconds the gleaming three and a half pound trout was flapping around on the mossy river bank.

Looking back over the long years I now appreciate the significance of my first important personal major purchase — not a car or a house or even an engagement ring — but a boat. Even in my almost twenty years of service in a vast impersonal organization like the Royal Canadian Air Force I managed to wangle fortuitous postings to geographically backward parts of Canada where the fishing was good — like along the Alaskan Highway, Goose Bay Labrador, Eastern Quebec and the Maritime Provinces. By virtue of my job (Construction Engineering Officer) myself and kindred spirits at our bush stations always managed to scrounge or liberate material and construct a fishing boat. My love affair for boats was of the same intensity which teenagers — and older — have for cars.

The boat bug didn't bite me overnight; and it didn't grow on me — I grew up with it. I well remember some of the vessels in which myself and other children ventured out into the deepest part of the lake; a lake with areas as deep as 200 feet. Most of the owners of boats and cots kept their craft securely locked; other owners didn't bother locking their boats on account of they being so leaky, rotten or falling apart that the owners felt they weren't worth securing. Maybe they consoled themselves with the thought that 'only lunatics would venture out into the deep in them sieves'.

Apart from the problem of us kids obtaining permission to take out a boat, there was always the question of securing oars. Most boat owners lived quite a distance from the lake and to save bringing home the oars they usually depended on their countryman's skill in concealing the oars in the thick undergrowth along the shore line. Some more tricky types were suspected of leaving as a decoy a poorly concealed pair of crudely constructed 'man-killing' oars. Actually, unless there was a storm brewing on the lake most of us would think nothing of venturing out in a borrowed vessel and depend on makeshift oars or paddles for propulsion. Those makeshift paddles could be anything from the floor board of a boat to a shovel or a spade. I remember a story of Paddy Molloy propelling a boat across the lake using only his hard hat — but the lake was glass calm at the time. One important piece of nautical equipment for most of those gift horse craft (Irish saying: Never look a gift horse in the mouth) was a bailing tin or bucket. Incidentally, a man who was handy with a shovel could bail out as much water as if he were using a gallon bucket. Some boats were so leaky that it was not unusual to see one member of the crew leisurely rowing and two others bailing like mad. Surprisingly, it did not give us a disregard or disdain for water safety; rather it made us skilful in handling boats and also imparted a healthy respect for the water — a respect that went deep because so few of my generation ever learned to swim. Ability to manage a boat plus an awareness of the dangers involved in boating and fishing paid off in an unusual local record: within the last one hundred years thank God, there has not been one single drowing fatality on the lakes and rivers in our twin parishes.

I mentioned already that in rural Ireland families fished primarily for food. For several reasons perch was the most sought-after fish. They were plentiful in our coast-to-coast network of canals, rivers and lakes and catching them did not require exceptional fishing skill or expensive gear and equipment.

Perch is so plentiful both in Europe and North America that it is unnecessary to try and describe it except to remind you that it is a small, spiny-finned fresh water fish. The first thing I learned about — the hard way — is what the book calls the anterior dorsal fin. This fin appears to me to be a membrane stretched on a half dozen sharp, strong spines. Those spines permanently protrude about half an inch from the fin and they are as sharp as a darning needle. In addition to the deadly spines the perch is so well covered with tough close-fitting scales that it is almost impossible for a novice to scale one. When you realize how difficult it is to remove those scales you will agree it says well for the edibility of the perch.

In our locality there have always been two schools of perch fishers: the ones who fished from dry land and those who fished from a craft on the rivers or lakes. I belonged to the larger group who preferred the open water. My type of fisher felt superior to the dry-land fishers and this feeling was not based on fishing comfort, or number of fish caught. We believed that the others were missing the best part of the fishing, the thrill and pleasure of being out on the water in a craft (am tempted to say that they missed the boat). I purposely used 'craft' because some of the contraptions in which we risked our young lives could not, even loosely, be called boats. Some of them did not, in the true sense of the word, even float; unless you could say that an iceberg floats.

The most common methods of catching perch were trolling and still-fishing. The former was not popular even though more action was involved, namely the work of rowing the boat and trolling two or more long lines in its wake. There was the problem of preventing the lines from tangling when the rower made a sharp turn and also the inevitable mix-up when you'd hook a couple of fish simultaneously. In my youth there were few outboard engines used on the lake; hence rowing was the order of the day.

There were two types of craft on the lake: the rowboat and the cot. The wooden rowboats were all practically of the same design and construction and measured eighteen feet long, four feet wide and three feet deep. With a sound rowboat and a good pair of oars, an experienced and virile boatman could weather any storm on the Irish lakes and rivers. The other lake craft was the cot, which was a flat-bottomed boat originally designed to transport material such as turf, wood, hay, building materials etc. on our inland waterways. These cots were of wooden construction with extra thick planking for the bottom or flooring. Their overall measurements were about the same as our rowboats. As the cots were primarily used for carrying loads, they did not warrant paint; instead they were given a thick coat of boiling tar or pitch to waterproof and protect the wearing surface.

Looking now at a few of the remaining cots in this area you realize that when it came to building rowboats, they definitely were not innovators. Of course the same holds true for the now world-famous seagoing currach, a light and remarkably seaworthy, all-purpose boat used extensively along the west coast of Ireland. It has been established that the currach's basic design and construction has remained unchanged for the past two thousand years. The English-speaking world, at least, is familiar with the history, construction and seaworthiness of a certain currach which recently sailed across the stormy Atlantic. Tim Severin, in his medieval-type currach succeeded against enormous odds, violent storms, deadly ice packs and encounters with whales and other sea creatures, and he has recounted his story in 'The Brendan Voyage'. The Brendan's hull was nothing more than forty-nine ox hides stitched together to form a single skin, stretched over a wooden frame.

The same reluctance to change either design or construction holds true for the cot. This is evident when you compare the cots still used on Derravaragh with two ancient dug-out boats discovered a few years ago, deeply buried in mud at the north end of the same lake. One of these resurrected boats was dated as belonging to the fourth century. Our cots were so designed that they could sail in shallow water; also their flat bottoms made it easier to pull the craft ashore or launch when the water's edge was a layer of soft mud. This flat-bottomed construction coupled with absence of any kind of rudder, meant that few oarsmen, even on a calm day, could row a cot in a straight line. With a strong side wind blowing it is virtually impossible to maintain a straight course. However, cots were more popular for perch fishing especially when one eighteen foot cot could accommodate a party of eight or ten fishermen. Boat owners were loathe to lend their workhorse-type craft for perch fishing, especially on account of the anchor. Our standard anchor was — and still is — a large stone weighing around 200 pounds and for an anchor chain the huge stone had a suitable length of rope. This rope, like much of our crude fishing gear, was often a hay rope which the average one of us could "twist' in twenty minutes. This is how we would go about 'twisting', meaning making a hay rope. You and a partner went to the nearest farmer's cock of hay, pulled out handful after handful until you had a pile of good sound well-saved hay. You'd tease up the bundle and using your thumb and forefinger as a device for measuring the diameter of the finished rope you'd pull a wisp of hay the desired bulk or thickness through the circled thumb and finger, and twist the wisp until you'd have the beginning of a rope. Then your partner would keep twisting and with your other hand you would feed the loose hay continuously through the circle until you'd have the desired length of rope. By the way, everyone felt certain that the hay rope stretching down in the water attracted perch and had many other advantages over ordinary hempen rope. For instance, the hay rope had no monetary value so it was unnecessary to raise the anchor stone and retrieve the rope; also if the fishing hole turned out to be a good one, we would attach a piece of light timber as a float or marker so that there would be a ready-in-place anchor for our, or a neighbour's, future visit to the fishing hole.

When I recall the fishing gear in general use when I was a boy, I compare it with the fishing equipment and modern facilities my children have, and almost demand. With an effort I resist the old 'when I was your age. . . .' sermonizing, because at the back of my mind I feel that if the bottom fell out of things my children and other children would extemporize and 'make do' as I did at their age. When I was in their shoes, as we say, the only item of our fishing gear generally bought in a shop was the hook that held the worms we had to bend our backs to dig for. Even digging the worms, especially blackheads, was part of the 'earn your bread by the sweat of your brow' ethos. The only good worms for catching perch are blackheads and in summer they stay three feet down in hard soil tightly curled up in a knot (we believed to keep themselves moist). Like aborigines living off the land we made our own fishing gear and I've already mentioned the primitive cot, the anchor stone, and hay rope. Our fishing rods were saplings cut out of a ditch on our way to the lake. Most of our fishing lines were homemade, in fact by the time we were in our teens most of us had learned to make, or plait hair fishing lines. Incidentally, tail hair from stallions or geldings was preferred because we understood it lasted longer than hair from a urine-splattered mare's tail.

'Still-fishing' for perch involved sitting at your appointed place in the cot and 'plumbing'. This consisted of attaching a small pebble to the hook end of your fishing line, paying out slack, and when you judged the stone was on the bottom and the line taut, securing a float — actually a cork out of a porter bottle with a slit in the cork which grips the line — then gradually slipping the cork downwards on the line until it remained four inches below the surface. Then you drew in the line, removed the stone, baited your hook with a worm, a minnow or a collick and settled back to 'watch your cork'. Needless to say, the plumbing was to ensure your worm was 'fishing' about four inches clear of the bottom, the ideal level for perch. A handy fisherman can fish four rods simultaneously — two long and two short ones. The long rods are about ten feet and the short ones no longer than a walking stick. We called the short ones 'sniggers', from an Irish word meaning jerk. When fishing, the sniggers were held in the hand and moved or jerked up and down to give an appearance of life to the bait dangling at the end of the line.

We never used a creel or bag to carry home our catch but threaded a sapling through the gills of the perch — naturally with the bigger perch showing to advantage. Talk about being on top of the world! That's how I used to feel as I walked home after a successful morning's fishing, secretly hoping I'd run into some of my pals and grig (make jealous) them with my fat hank of perch.

Charley Reilly — a keen fisherman himself — owned one of the handiest cots on the lake and if he were on good terms with your entire family and your inner circle of pals and you approached him 'cap in hand' he might take you perch fishing. If, like himself, you were a grown-up and he approved of your boathandling capability he might even lend you his cot and oars. Regardless of being flahoola (princely, generous) with his cot and oars, Charley was not the most popular fellow around, because he was inclined to be brusque. Well, brusque is a bit of an understatement. Everyone around said that Charley Reilly was 'as thick as a ditch'. And as well as being less than courteous in manner, when it came to doing any ordinary kind of work he wasn't exactly the handiest person in the world. I heard a neighbour say 'Charley is naturally awkward, but you can't blame him, sure awkwardness runs in the family like the wooden leg.'

Actually Charley Reilly was a God-fearing, law-abiding man but unfortunately, as everyone agreed he did take himself too seriously. Maybe you would keep that in mind as I try to give you a brief account of an incident that most of us at the time thought to be funny — even hilarious. One evening Charley 'half-grudgingly' took out four local lads for an evening's fishing. One of them afterwards said 'Shows how much I love perch fishing when I'd willingly go for an entire evening with Charley Reilly, 'specially when I knew I'd have to put up with his kemares (antics), being nagged into doing every little thing his way. He'd tell you how to put a worm on the hook; him that sticks his own hook into his own fingers more often than into the maggot. A man so awkward that just blessing himself he's known to have put his thumb in his own eye.'

When Charley and his guests had rowed out to the deepest part of the Roach Hole, one of the boys — actually they were all fully-grown men — offered to let out the anchorstone. 'I've been letting out anchorstones before you were out of petticoats' says Charley. He was stating a fact; in those far-off days before diapers — disposable or otherwise — were invented, babies, both male and female from the time they first crawled until they were fully toilet-trained toddled around without restraining undergarments of any kind.

That dirty dig about the petticoats didn't go down too well with the boys, but they knew that if they didn't 'back water' with Charley he'd row them to the nearest shore and tell them to leg it home. He now had a captive audience and couldn't resist a further bit of show-off with 'You young fellows may have plenty of muscle — if you knew how to use it. Move back there, give a man elbow room and I'll show you how it's done.' There already was plenty of room for Charley, because regardless of how many fishers he had on board, he always monopolized the entire stem area of the cot. By the way, we always call the bow of the boat or cot the 'stem'; we refer to the tail or end of the craft as the 'stern'. The stem seat was the coveted one for perch fishing because that was where the anchor rope was affixed and even when the lake was rough there was little or no movement of the craft at this point. On the other hand the stern of the cot swung freely in a wide arc because no one ever used two anchors.

This is how a fisherman lets out the anchorstone from the stem of a cot. First he makes sure the anchor rope is several feet longer than the depth of water where he intends to anchor. Then he attaches the free end of the rope to the (usual) ring set into the stem post of the cot or boat. He next ensures that the rope is securely attached to the anchorstone. He then carefully coils the rope on the floor of the craft, leaving himself free standing-room to lift up the heavy rock which he rests momentarily on the gunwale before gently lowering it into the water. He then pays out slack rope until the stone rests on the bottom. Naturally he only uses enough free rope to permit the craft to swing freely.

I hope you kept in mind those normal steps an average man would follow to successfully and safely 'let out' the huge, awkward anchor stone. But as I already intimated, Charley Reilly was not exactly your average man. He now stood up in the cot, spat on the palms of his hands, rubbed them together and bellowed 'Stand back all of you' (actually they were all sitting motionless), 'and I'll show yous how it's done.' He grabbed the huge stone, got it up as far as his bent knees. Then with 'main strength and ignorance' managed to hoist it chest-high and like an Olympic weight-thrower, heaved. Out went the anchor stone plop into twenty feet of water. One second Charley, red-faced from exertion and short-lived triumph was standing upright in the bow of the cot — the next split second he was gone. Like the tail of a comet disappearing into space he followed the anchor stone into the depths of the lake. One of the boys described it: 'Like a cormorant diving into the lake after a fish, Charley Reilly dove after that enormous anchor stone because he had no choice; the poor awkward fellow had his leg tangled in a loop of the anchor rope.' Another eyewitness elatedly broke in with 'Sure it was no trouble at all rescuing Charley — in fact it was a pleasure shared by every soul in the cot. We wouldn't have pulled him and the anchor stone up so soon except that we couldn't wait to see the look on his face.' For the rest of Charley Reilly's long, robust life, *never* was he allowed to live down that anchor stone episode.

When I cast my mind back to our preparations for early morning perch fishing excursions, three events stand out and one of them is special. The special one is evoked every time I get a whiff of the mouth-watering smell of roast beef when it has reached a certain temperature — that would be the stage about three hours after it has finally been taken out of the oven. Needless to say refrigeration, for me, would completely cancel both the delicious smell and the scrumptious taste. Early in my teens the time arrived when I was considered grown-up enough to be taken along for morning perch fishing. By then Tommy, my elder brother, had started to treat me on a man-to-man basis, and I felt I'd finally arrived when full of importance he announced, 'In the morning you and I have to call in at the Friary and waken up the cook at four o'clock. He promised to come with us after perch.'

Jack Cunningham was the Friary cook — nowadays he would be given the more impressive title Chef. Jack did the cooking for about one third of the lifetime of St. Louis College. St. Louis, as the Friary brochure says, 'Was, from it's inception in 1899 until it's closure in 1956 a Franciscan Secondary School. It was in the main responsible for an extraordinary revival of Franciscan activity in Ireland and on the Missions of the Irish Provinces overseas during the first half of the twentieth century.' Counting friars, teachers, students, staff and labourers, Jack with one assistant had to cook for around three hundred. As my brother and I approached the grounds of the Friary he warned me to be especially careful about making a noise; in fact he made it clear that it would be my last 'early morning go' if I even sneezed. Seeing I was in my bare feet there was little chance of me awakening anyone. Just the same while we were in 'the grounds' I carefully walked on my tippy toes. There was an exhilarating feeling of adventure, secrecy and even danger in this pre-dawn operation of going to the 'command centre' of the Friary grounds and complex of buildings to waken up the cook.

Tommy and I like commandos went around to the back of the Friary and when we were about ten feet from a certain window he ordered me to stand still while he approached the one he called the cook's window. He left me standing there in the shadow of the kitchen wall and like a hunting cat he moved closer, gently drummed on a pane with his fingers and although I was 'blessed with a pair of ears that could hear the grass growing' I never heard that window being lifted. I learned afterwards that Jack had greased the sash beforehand. I heard murmurings — not a glimmer of light showed — then Tommy materialized at my side and whispered 'He'll meet us at the back gate in ten minutes'.

We went to the back gate, sat down on our 'hunkers' and it was no surprise — my nose, like a retriever's, had already picked up the scent — when my brother handed me two thick cuts of bread and me already knowing all the time what was between the cuts, because hadn't the mouth-watering smell of

prime roast beef, like a lilac bush in bloom, hung over my
brother since he left the cook's window! Between the
well-buttered cuts of bread there was a thick slab of juicy roast
beef. If I live to a thousand never will I taste anything so
succulent as that beef. Tommy sampled his sandwich and as
confidently as if he was an authority on cuisine, declared, 'In
the Friary they always put down a roast as big as an ox: the
bigger the roast, the better the taste'. Judging from my
oft-recurring taste memory, my slab of beef must have been
carved from a king-sized roast!

Then there was the time I really upset the applecart — except
it wasn't a cart at all — it was a piece of furniture loaded to the
gunnels with glass ornaments and other bric-a-brac. That
afternoon I heard my brother and Ned Fay the Telegram Boy
work out an elaborate plan for 'a real early call' to go perch
fishing the following morning. In addition to delivering
telegrams, Ned did odd jobs for a local publican, 'lived in' and
had his own room upstairs in the pub. Ned said 'Tommy, Mrs.
— will be mad if you waken the house trying to get me up
because you know I'm a notorious heavy sleeper; the last time
you threw that handful of pebbles up at my window to waken
me she threatened to give me the sack and a bag to put it in.'
Both boys agreed that before Ned retired for the night he would
tie a length of thick fishing line to his wrist and pay enough
slack out the window to hang down for Tommy to reach it when
the time was ripe. They agreed the downpipe that passed close
to Ned's window would conceal the hanging line.

The village pump — it's still there and working — is right
across the street from where the old thatched pub stood. That
same evening — it must have been after ten — I was sent to the
pump for a can of water and seeing there was no light in any of
the upstairs windows I said to myself, 'Ned's sound asleep by
now, I'll take a rise out of him; I'll give that cord that's around his
wrist a tug or two; I'll have my can of water already filled and
seeing I'm in my bare feet I can run home like a red shank.' Even
in the dark I'd no trouble finding the thick hair line as I took a
good grip and pulled. The weight at the end of the line was
heavy and seemed to be resisting my pull, so I pulled a bit
harder, felt it give and the exciting thought came to me 'I'm
actually pulling Ned out of bed' so I gave a mighty heave — the
line came slack in my hands — and crash. I felt sure that

somehow I had pulled the foundations out from under the house, the ground under my feet shook so much. Before the echo died and without a soul ever clapping an eye on me or connecting me with the catastrophe I was down the street and safe home. Poor Ned Fay! He'd a hell of a time trying to pacify Mrs. —— for the broken piece of furniture she called her 'whatnot' and the smashed ornaments. I'm sure you guessed it. Ned, a methodical person, before retiring for the night had lowered the line to the desired height and left enough slack to comfortably reach his wrist when he later went to bed. Being tidy he didn't like leaving a loose line on the floor so he tied the end of it, with a half hitch, to Mrs. ——'s prized whatnot, then blew out the candle and went for a short walk.

In spring and summer there are two daylight periods when perch take best; in the evening for an hour before and an hour after the sun sets, and again for slightly longer periods before and after sunrise. They take best in the hour before sunrise. Our grown-ups had a monopoly when it came to sunrise perch fishing. This was because it was looked on as 'hardship' to leave your warm bed around four o'clock, fish all morning, stay on your feet all day and do a normal day's work. I don't have to spell out how a sleep-hungry schoolboy sunrise-perch-fisher would fare under the stern, unrelenting eye of a Schoolmaster with his ever-ready, palm-hungry cane. As far as any person 'in their health' going back to bed in the daytime, it just wasn't done. Even yet you are apt to catch a whispered remark like 'Oh! they say Sean is overly fond of the bed; he goes to the trouble of getting up early, building up a slow smoky fire, opening all the windows and sneaking back under the quilt.'

Every one of us youngsters hungered to be taken 'early fishing' even though we knew that the early rising connected with it somewhat nullified the glory of carrying home dozens of big perch after a couple of hours of glamorous fishing. The snag was that the early riser — especially if a member of a large family — would be accused of upsetting the entire household at an unearthly hour. The upset was, and is, connected with the peace, serenity and quiet of the countryside. Maybe that's the difference between urban and rural life; down here in the country most of us are conscious of the other fellow's existence and rights — and certainly a good night's sleep is a right.

In the quiet countryside, if one or more occupants of a house have to sit up all night on account of something like illness in the family, attending a sick neighbour or helping a cow calve, it's as much 'as your life is worth' to disturb sleeping members of your household. Although our alarm clock was dependable it was only used for telling time because of my mother being such a light sleeper. Then I suppose all mothers, especially those with large families, have to be light sleepers and ours never let us down when it came to getting any of us up early. Never once did she hint let along ask for the early morning tea we always took up to her and it would warm the cockles of your heart to see the look on her face when you handed her that big steaming mug of strong tea. It is only in retrospect I appreciate the real part of that 'call me early' exercise — I'm sure there is no need to spell it out for you.

PART TWO:
SOME PERSONALITIES

9. BILL BARDEN

When the Barden family was the topic of conversation, and that was often, Bill's name came up more frequently than the rest combined. For instance, if the subject was 'poaching' someone would surely say, 'When it came to poaching, Bill Barden was the daddy of them all'. In season or out of season, if an invalid wanted a drop of hare soup or a breast of pheasant or even a nice trout you only had to give a hint to Bill Barden and it was as good as done. If he'd a mind to, Bill could have made a good living poaching rabbits, but I am afraid that rabbits did not present enough of a challenge to his hunting skills.

If the talk got around, as invariably it did, to fighting-men, meaning men battling each other with hands or fists, it was a toss-up whether the first name to be mentioned would be John L. Sullivan, Dan Donnelly or Bill Barden. If you are in one of the dozen or so pubs in this locality and 'for divilment' you want to start a 'bit of diversion' just gradually bring the talk around to Mohammed Ali, Joe Louis, Jack Dempsey and world heavyweight boxers in general, and before you have the froth blown off your second pint of Guinness, everyone at the bar will be elbowing each other to get a word in edgewise about John L. Sullivan, Dan Donnelly and Bill Barden.

John L.! They speak about him reverently as if it were only yesterday instead of 1889 when, as the 'book' says 'This remarkable man who has not inaptly been described as the last of the gladiators, defeated Jake Kilrain the world's heavyweight bare-knuckle champion in seventy-five rounds'. In Irish pubs and places where they gather for a drink and a bit of relaxed conversation, men brag of John L.'s exploits and speak as intimately of him as if he were a blood relation or had been born in Kerry instead of Boston, Mass., U.S.A. Talk of hero worship! How glowingly they speak of John L. Sullivan's herculean strength and physique and revel in accounts of his courage and pugnacity. Then someone else will butt in and say, 'Sullivan! He couldn't carry drinks of water to Dan Donnelly'.

Dan Donnelly was the most outstanding figure of Irish boxing in its early days. Even today, his name is enshrined in song and story; many a heated argument have I heard on how long John L. would have lasted in the same ring with Dan Donnelly. Of course it is a foolish argument; impossible to prove who was the better fighter seeing that Donnelly died thirty-eight years before Sullivan was born.

Dan Donnelly, born in Dublin in 1788, is generally regarded as the first Irish boxing champion and the only professional pugilist on whom the honour of knighthood was conferred.

By the time Dan had reached manhood, his country was wallowing in the aftermath of the 1798 Rebellion. In that year the downtrodden, ill-fed, poorly-armed Irish, spurred both by desperation and patriotism arose in revolt. The 'rising' was smashed and the people, broken in spirit felt they had no leader left to do battle with what they called 'the oppressor'. This was the Ireland in which Daniel Donnelly grew up.*

Of the many interesting tales told about Dan Donnelly, the one that interests me most was that Dan Donnelly's arms were so long that without stooping he could fasten the top buttons of his gaiters. You are hardly old enough to remember that gaiters were a cloth or leather covering for the instep and ankle; in Donnelly's day the top of the gaiters reached almost to the wearer's knees. I assumed that the story of the abnormally long arms was an invention and then someone casually said, 'But I saw Dan Donnelly's right arm in a glass case in a pub in Kilcullen, Co. Kildare near the Curragh where Dan trained and triumphed.'

Mention of the arm gave me something tangible, so I drove to the little village of Kilcullen, only a few miles from our most famous race course, the Curragh, which has been a Royal race course from time immemorial. In addition, for the past two hundred years, it has been the site of the biggest and most important military station and army training centre in the British Isles.

When I arrived at the 'Hideout' which is the name of the principal pub in Kilcullen, the proprietor Mr. Jim Byrne, took me into his spacious lounge whose walls are embellished with

Encyclopaedia of Ireland, Allen Figgis, Dublin, 1968. p. 436.

curios, souvenirs and ornaments from foreign countries. The assorted collection attested to the proximity and long tenure of the one-time British Army camp, because most of the relics were obviously brought back by military men from places where the Union Jack proudly flew when the Empire was in its heyday. Place of honour in the lounge is given to a glass case which exhibits Sir Dan Donnelly's right arm.

When Dan Donnelly died, the medical doctors vied with each other for the opportunity to study the body of what they believed was a superhuman. Sometime after Dan's funeral, his grave was robbed, his body dismembered and parts of it passed from one surgeon to another. His enormous arms became a curiosity. Dan's famous right arm has, in a manner of speaking, been in the public eye continuously ever since.

Mr. Byrne kindly gave me some well-proven research literature on Dan Donnelly and also filled me in on some local aspects of Dan's unwritten history. Dan's most famous fight took place in Donnolley's Hollow, close to Kilcullen. The date of the event coincided with the Battle of Waterloo, but to the Irish, the outcome of the battle between 'their man' and George Cooper the English champion was of greater importance, because to their mind Dan Donnelly had now 'assumed the mantle of their champion; here at last was an Irishman to fight their cause against a representative of the dreaded and hated oppressor'. Donnelly won the fight in the eleventh round. An on-the-spot reporter wrote,

Finally Donnelly put an end to the hostilities by knocking Cooper senseless to the ground by two terrific punches, the second of which caught Cooper on the mouth, knocked out all the front teeth and broke his jaw bone.

Regardless of Donnelly being a national hero and there being 'bad blood between England and Ireland', there is no record of any Irish — or English — outcry when Dan was knighted by George IV. In fact, Donnelly has the distinction of being 'the last man so honoured during the Regency, and the only pugilist ever to be knighted'. Sir Dan returned to Dublin, and ballad-singers have described the wild scenes of enthusiasm that greeted him as he was chaired through the streets of Dublin, and attended Donnybrook Fair. Though alert and cunning in the ring, these traits deserted Donnelly outside it. He was an easy prey for all sorts of tricksters and it is said that 'the only blow which ever knocked him out was Poteen punch'.

At the age of thirty-two, Dan died penniless on 18 February 1820. His funeral cortege was huge. Thousands of his admirers lined the route. Carriages and carts, loaded with flowers, were followed by the hearse which was hauled by grief-stricken supporters. His gloves were carried on a silken cushion, and he was laid to rest in the Bully's Acre, Kilmainham. His untimely end was referred to in the following lines by Lord Byron when speaking of Donnelly's reputation:

> He won it in a field where arms are none
> Save those the Mother gave to us. He was
> A shining star which had not fully shone;
> Yet promised in its glory to surpass our
> Champion star ascendant; but alas! the
> Sceptered shade that values earthly might
> And power and Pith and Bottom as the grass —
> Gave with his fleshless fist a buffet slight
> Say, bottle-holding Leech, why ends so soon the fight?

If Dan Donnelly's body was considered unique, I'm sure the same could be said of Bill Barden's physique. Our local poet Tommy Gorman never made a poem about him, but I recall his description of how Bill was put together. Tommy said, 'We have a word that described Bill's build — it's "butty", from the Irish 'buta'. Bill only stood five feet five inches in the bare ones, but in his prime he weighed fifteen stone (210 pounds). You know how God designed the trunk of an oak tree. He made it round and thick and gnarled for strength and ruggedness. Well He built Bill Barden on the same lines. Bill's torso was so broad and deep that his chest gave the appearance of roundness; it looked the same thickness viewed from front, back and sides. His arms and legs were stubby and immensely powerful. Bill's neck! Well, he never buttoned the collar of his shirt because he complained that they never made them big enough — Bill had a neck on him like a bull.'

Like most of the Barden family, Bill was a most dependable worker in his own line of endeavour, which was labouring. I already mentioned his poaching skills, but it was as a rough-and-tumble fighter that he was renowned. Until he was around middle-age, he carried out a one-man vendetta against the Peelers, as the Royal Irish Constabulary police force were

called — when none of them were around. I suppose you know
they were christened Peelers after their creator, the Englishman
Sir John Peel. Bill told me he never held a grudge against any
individual member of the force but never explained what had
started 'the bad blood' as he called it.

I think Bill's crimes were mostly 'drunk and disorderly',
possibly with 'resisting arrest' thrown in for good measure. If he
had been in trouble with the law for what we call serious crimes,
he would never have been so welcome in all our homes and so
fully trusted by everyone in the neighbourhood. I suppose the
general public, including the Police and even the Judiciary, were
and are inclined to treat fighting, even fighting while 'under the
influence' as a weakness instead of a crime; as a matter of fact
when the police sergeant's wife was away, Bill was their
favourite 'to mind the childer' as he put it.

If Bill liked you and you were in his good books he might
admit that he had 'done time'; if he were in a confiding mood he
might even give you a good look at his wrists. Quite often, I
had noticed that in keeping with his general build, his wrists
were massive, but on closer inspection I realized they were
either deformed or had years before been badly mutilated.
Once when he was in the mood he pulled up his cuffs, stretched
his hands towards me and said, 'Look at them rusts. Two
policemen had to put all their muscle into the job of closing the
handcuffs on me and me at the time submitting because I had a
bit too much porter in me. Them handcuffs must have been two
sizes too small for me because they had to force them deep into
my flesh before they could get them to lock. Then when they
thought they had me one of the Peelers called me a bastard.
That sobered me up. I bet you I'm the only man in the whole
world that ever broke a pair of handcuffs with a sudden twist
and a God Almighty heave.'

As far as I know, Bill was the only ticket-of-leave man around.
Ticket-of-leave was a written licence granted by the English
Government whereby a penal convict was given liberty for good
behaviour before the expiration of his sentence. It came into
domestic use about 1840 when the 'Colonies' refused to receive
more convicts.

The fracas cost Bill more than the injured wrists. When Bill
was showing me his 'rusts' he must have thought that I was too
young, or that I did not show enough sympathy, because it was

a dozen years afterwards before he asked me, 'Did you hear of the Treadmill?' I had a fair idea about that apparatus, but sensing a story, I diplomatically answered, 'Very little'.

The 'very little' that I knew at the time was to the effect that a treadmill was originally a mill operated by manpower and later adopted as a means of punishment. It consisted of a large wooden wheel about twenty feet wide, with steps on its peripheral surface — somewhat like a mill wheel. Workers or criminals were obliged to stand on a step at a time in the position of walking upstairs; weight set the wheel in motion and they maintained themselves upright by means of a horizontal bar fixed above them, on which rested their hands. They could not support their bodies by hanging on to the bar because then their legs would dangle to be walloped by each succeeding step as it swept downwards; so they had to keep climbing and climbing until they collapsed or were allowed off.

Bill said, 'I wish to God that I could say that I know very little about the wheel', and rolling up his pant legs asked, 'What do you think of them shins?' The front of poor Bill's shins had ridges and corrugations on them like the ribbed surface of the old-time domestic wooden washboard. He said, 'It's a full forty years since I got them tracks on me shins; tracks I'll carry to me grave; tracks made by the cursed tread-mill. Even yet I waken up at night in a cold lather of sweat from dreaming I'm back on the wheel and often I've to get up and go for a walk because I'm afeared of going back to sleep again and back on the tread-mill nightmare.'

Bill had, as he said 'To my everlasting sorrow first-hand knowledge of the contraption' and offered to explain its operation to me. He asked me to go with him and have a look at Mullvaney's mill which was about a quarter of a mile outside the village. The mill wheel which was then in working order was of the overhead type and turned by water from the mill-race. The wheel, which as I sit here I can see from our kitchen window, must be about thirty feet in diameter. Using the ponderous, slow-moving mill wheel as an object lesson, Bill made the working of the tread-mill brutally clear to me.

As a result of Bill's lecture, I will try my hand at describing the working of the treadmill. Imagine yourself alone on a perpetually moving escalator. It is a 'down' escalator and you are obliged to go upwards. You are already half-way up and so

confined and boxed in that you only see two steps — the one
you are standing on and the one above it. The horrifying,
nightmarish reality is that you have nowhere in the universe to
stand except the step that is under your feet at that particular
moment; but that step is slowly sinking under your weight and
your only refuge is to step up and on to the next one that
inexorably is descending to take the place of the step that is
already sinking out of your reach and sight. When you scramble
on to the next step it takes your weight only long enough to
allow you to step on to the next step and so on and so on to
exhaustion and collapse. There is no power in the world that
will keep that wheel from turning: the punishing wheel is not
only in the driver's seat — it is the driver.

Drunk or sober Bill was not much of a talker; in fact he gave
the impression that in a man, talkativeness could be a sign of
weakness. 'Bill' I asked, 'What was so wonderful about the old
times that everyone pines for them?' He was loading his old,
partially-blackened clay pipe, one with a very short stem which
he called by its Gaelic name, 'dudeen', and when he had the
pipe drawing he answered, 'My brothers and sisters and my
parents and their parents before them had more dinner times
than dinners, and we well knew what hardship was; not one of
my breed ever ate idle bread. I don't suppose I owned a total of
ten pairs of boots before I was twenty and many's the Saturday
me brothers and me father and myself all went without a shirt
on our backs, that was because me mother was washing the
shirts so they'd be clane for going to Mass the next day. Oh yes!,
we went through plenty of hunger, hardship and hard times,
but to me they still were the good auld days.' 'How the hell
could any sane person call them good?' Bill stopped talking and
I thought I may have been too abrupt or even rude, but consoled
myself with the thought that on one occasion he had carefully
explained to me, 'Friends don't have to pick and choose the
words they use talking to each other; they should know the
mayning behind the words.'

Bill asked, 'Did you ever watch a family of birds in a nest?
They're secure. Sometimes they go hungry and sometimes the
weather is atrocious, but they put up with it because they're
together. Our own family was a big family but us children were
like skaldeens (scallacán — young birds in a nest before the
"down" covering their bodies becomes feathers), we were

secure; we stuck together through thick and thin. What held us together? I'm not ashamed to put a name on what held us together; it was love. I didn't understand it at all until both me mother and father passed to their eternal reward, but they had lashin's and lavin's of love for every single one of us, and I'm telling you we were a hard, wild bunch of childre (*sic*).

'The day came that they carried out me mother's coffin and one by one we moved out of the house that "was a nest to us all"; then we knew that the auld times — for us — were gone never to return.'

Bill looked kind of wistful and added, 'Maybe that's what everyone means when he raves about the auld times — times like when we were still in the nest and suckled on love'.

10. TOMMY GORMAN

It is safe to say that conformity is not a typical Irish trait. My village has always had the 'oddball' — the one who refuses to conform even to our general and admittedly erratic pattern of social behaviour. We call such a person 'a character' and pronounce it char-ak-ter. In fact this area always had more characters than a stray cur has fleas and when it came to *colourful* characters everyone agreed that Tommy Gorman — village baker, classical scholar, poet and philosopher — was the daddy of them all; or to use a local *and* apposite phrase, 'he took the biscuit'. Tommy was immensely popular and highly respected and as far as baking was concerned, it was handed to him that in the length and breadth of Ireland he had no equal. I don't know how many generations of Gormans were bakers, but I do know that our village of Multyfarnham has a long history of baking. The *Annals of Westmeath* state that

In 1644 Multyfarnham was the granary of the Catholic forces for the counties of Longford, Westmeath and Cavan. Great quantities of wheat were levied in these counties to make bread for the forces scattered through the districts named. Large ovens were made and brought to Multyfarnham, Athlone and Birr, and the best bakers in the kingdom were employed to bake.*

One of the large stone buildings bordering the yard of our Old House is still called The Granary.

In Tommy Gorman's time — that was around the time I was born — most householders baked their own bread — homemade bread made on the hearthstone; but baker's bread was considered such a delicacy that when they could afford the twopence for a big white loaf, most families 'went for' Gorman's bread.

---

*James Woods, *Annals of Westmeath, Ancient & Modern,* Dublin 1907. Reprinted by James Woods Memorial Committee, Ballymore, Co. Westmeath, 1977, p. 113.

·All his life Tommy Gorman talked to himself, but none of us thought that was anything out of the ordinary, after all wasn't he a poet! and everything he said was worth quoting. I for one used to enjoy listening to his soliloquies. When he was unhappy you could hear — addressing himself — 'Why didn't you go long ago. Why didn't you take the red bundle and go to America?' The red bundle was reference to the only bit of luggage the average Irish emigrant took on the one-way passage in the Famine-era ships. Those hapless travellers travelled light, all their earthly belongings wrapped up in that pathetic portable red bundle.

Tommy sold only a portion of his baking 'over the counter' in his shop, and took the remainder of it out in the country to his customers. Initially he made his bread deliveries with a smart well-groomed pony and bread van, but by the time he was in his fifties his bread business was on the down grade and he was reduced to using an ass and cart. If there had been visiting tourists in those days, we'd have been inclined to show off Tommy Gorman travelling the country roads making deliveries with his ass and cart. It was not uncommon to see a rapt audience — non-existant as far as Tommy was concerned — silently following within earshot and listening to him delivering lectures and homilies to another audience — an imaginary one. He said 'Strolling the roads, leading my ass, or he leading me, is the time my mind works best; that's when I compose my best poems, the ones about local happenings — especially happenings with humorous overtones.'

Tommy and his donkey were never in a hurry; in fact every mile or so the donkey would stop in his tracks to nibble some of the roadside grass; then Tommy after a decent interval would tug at the reins with a 'Come on Neddy' and Neddy with his half-swallowed mouthful of grass would plod on behind his master.

Did I mention that Tommy was absentminded? Well he was; especially when, as he said 'I'm in the throes of composing.' Around here they still chuckle when someone recalls that lovely June day that Tommy Gorman was out delivering his bread. There was Tommy shuffling along the road and as usual talking to himself and in this instance reciting for his own amusement his favourite poem; the one entitled 'Johnny Tormey's Barrow'. I remember one of the lines went: 'With bits of tin and leather and nails six inches long'. He was walking a few feet ahead of the ass with the reins loosely held under his oxter to leave both hands free so that for instance, he could load the short pipe 'he never went without'. Part of his absentmindedness was the number of times he let that pipe go out. Now try and picture our poet: head down and so engrossed in creating he hasn't noticed that at Neddy's last stop to eat roadside grass, he hadn't turned around when he gave the customary jerk to the reins with 'Come on'. He doesn't realize that the straps of the winkers were loose and his final tug pulled the winkers off the ass's head. That stop for grass was a couple of miles back. The donkey and the load of bread are still there but walking slowly along the middle of the road comes our poet still 'courting the Muse', with the ass's empty winkers trailing behind and every time it catches in a loose stone, or is hooked by a briar Tommy tugs the reins with a 'Come on Neddy'.

I may have already mentioned my Mass-serving days. Now when I go to Father Mac's eleven o'clock Mass and kneel down — still on the men's side of the Chapel — instead of praying properly, my mind flits back over the years and I see three other altar boys and myself 'inside the rails', feeling terribly important, decked out in our black soutains and snow-white surplices. Then invariably the lighter, hilarious moments connected with my acolyte activities assail me.

I suppose everyone some time or another has had that ridiculous, overpowering temptation to burst out laughing at the wrong time and the wrong place. Unfortunately, with me that irresistible impulse to laugh at an inopportune moment is not confined to childhood days; there have been times in my so-called adult life when it was all I could do to keep a straight face. One such occasion was a very important and impressive function towards the close of my professional military career. It was a ceremonial Mess Dinner and yours truly was there — a Senior Staff Officer in full regalia, medals and all — seated within breathing distance of the Air Vice-Marshal.

At the conclusion of the meal, the A.V-M stood up, as he said 'To say a few brief words — off the cuff you know'. For a man who hadn't prepared his speech he was a wonder — but they say, 'It takes brains to get to the top of any profession'. After awhile I got a sneaking suspicion the A.V.-M was speaking longer than the occasion demanded. Then it dawned on me that somehow he had missed his peroration. With a mixture of incredulity, horror and amusement I realized that like a faulty record player he was giving the entire 'impromptu' speech all over again — word-perfect. As I sat there sweating in my tightly-fitting 'Mess kit' trying hard to keep a neutral expression, I had the bizarre feeling that if some hardy — or foolhardy — soul didn't jeopardize or hopefully further his own career by gently breaking the news to the Big Brass he'd surely sail into his third rendering.

Nowadays when I'm supposed to be 'attending' Mass I recollect dozens of funny, incongruous happenings in this same Chapel; but my church-going memories of Tommy Gorman stand out.

Even in the present permissive era, late arrivals at Mass are frowned on. In Tommy Gorman's day our Parish Priest, Father Murphy didn't frown — he glared — and if you could picture what Father Murphy looked like, you too would feel what it is like to get hit with a real glare: even on a hot day, a scowl from our P.P. would send cold shivers down your spine. You know that saying, 'A Black Irishman'? That's one of our breed with fair skin and black — almost blue — hair. Father Murphy had swarthy skin, jet black hair and eyes of the same colour; big eyes set far back in his head and surmounted by heavy eyebrows for all the world like a pair of black awnings. When he glared it was like a searchlight shooting out a jet black beam — a beam that could transfix a gossiping pair at the back of the chapel, or spear a luckless fellow exchanging meaningful glances with a girl across the aisle — the women's side of the chapel.

Tommy Gorman was always late for Mass, but his unpunctuality was expected and accepted. Even Father Murphy put up with it although they say that when he first came as P.P. he made an effort to do something with Tommy Gorman; even begged him to 'Get to Mass on time, try always to remove your hat, and *never* keep that dudeen (short black pipe) stuck in your jaw when you come to my Mass.'

On Sunday Tommy wore shoes and leggings, freshly blackened. We never said polished; in fact there was only one kind of polish on the market and it was sold in small dry, hard slabs wrapped like a chocolate bar. I remember its name was 'Martin Day Blackening'. The leggings were designed to be worn as an adjunct to boots having fairly long uppers, but

Tommy being an individual, wore the leggings over, or above a
pair of low-cut shoes and the thick hand-knitted grey socks he
wore always managed to work out in the gap between the
bottom of the leggings and the top of the shoes. Another more
impressive piece of apparel was the dickey. The dickey was a
heavily starched, detachable, combined shirt-front and collar.
The collar part of the contraption that Tommy wore was about
three inches high (or deep) and must have been extremely
uncomfortable for our hero, because he had a short neck. The
dickey was popular with the housewives — it saved much shirt
laundering because it completely obscured a shirt. As a matter
of interest it was mooted around that 'certain men whose
women were poor laundresses' sported a dickey without a shirt
underneath.

To get back to Tommy, winter and summer when he was
'dressed up' he wore a light overcoat he called his 'mac' — full
name Mackintosh. Invariably his headgear was a bowler and
quite often on Sundays he was well inside the church before he
remembered to remove the hat. That reminds me of the
exquisite occasion when he went the whole length of the Chapel
still wearing the hat. That Sunday as Tommy made his entrance
through the door at the back of the church a titter started at the
back and swelled as he slowly shuffled towards the front and
the occupants of each seat (we don't use the expression 'pew'
except in relation to Protestant Churches) waited for Tommy to
pass them. The temptation was strong and universal for each
seat full of worshippers to turn around and get a sight of
Tommy even though they knew he would eventually shuffle
into their line of vision because he always occupied his Sunday
seat which was only one row away from the Altar rail. I can still
hear the sigh of relief from the audience when Tommy knelt
down, placed his elbows on the armrest formed by the back of
the seat in front, tried to rest his head in his hands and felt the
hat with the points of his fingers. Without giving it a second
thought he casually doffed the bowler and placed it carefully on
the seat beside him.

Every Sunday from my server's vantage point I knew that
Father Murphy never really settled down to say Mass until
Tommy Gorman had finally arrived and the congregation were
satisfied that Tommy was down on his knees — and praying.
Then I'd get the feeling that Father Murphy breathed a sigh of

relief and silently prayed 'God I thank You for permitting
Tommy Gorman to make *his* entry: maybe now I can start Your
Mass in earnest.'   .

I'll finish with another true incident; that was the Sunday
Tommy walked up the packed church and apparently no one
noticed that in his hurried dressing for Mass he had managed to
put on his overcoat without removing the coathanger. My
explanation for the hundreds of keen-eyed church-goers
missing this unusual addition to Tommy Gorman's wardrobe
was that as he went by they only gave him the usual 'sideways
glance'. As you know the sideways sweeping glance permits
one, without lifting the head from the reverential praying
posture, to take stock of everything in a 180 degree arc — but
ONLY up to the level of the glancer's eyebrows.

Even when Tommy knelt down to pray it's strange how few
noticed the skeleton of the body of the hanger bulging under his
tightly-fitting coat; especially when down on his knees, he
brought his elbows forward on the arm rest, then the hanger
was plainly outlined. When he lowered his head in the normal
attitude of prayer, the hook of the hanger protruded vertically
and grotesquely at the back of his neck. I realize that the
average-built person in the same predicament would have been
aware of the hook the second he'd have held his head erect; but
Tommy had a pronounced hump — we call it a cruit — and
normally he carried his head well forward. So there was our
master baker intently attending to his religious duty and most of
the congregation attending to the hook.

Came time for the sermon and everyone settled back in their
seat. Tommy also sat back but still carried his head a bit forward.
Father Murphy was well into the sermon when Tommy must
have looked up at the ceiling for some reason, because there in
sight of the entire Chapel, he half-turned around and accused
one of the 'good boys', seated behind him, of tickling him. It
happened again and 'me bould' Tommy turned around and
publicly told off the unfortunate lads; then he once more
focused his attention on the sermon. It happened again but
before there could be a real scene the man on Tommy's right
whispered 'Mr. Gorman there's a hook sticking out of the back
of your neck.'

Tommy put up his hand, gingerly felt the hook, followed its
outline with his fingers and satisfied as to its nature, turned to

the person who had tipped him off and in a whisper that carried to all corners of the Chapel said 'Mr. Brown you are only half correct; it *is* a coathanger right enough; but its out of my coat it's sticking, *not* out of my neck.' Then for the remainder of Mass, Tommy 'went through all the motions' as natural and unconcerned as if a well-placed coathanger was a *must* for every well-turned-out Master Baker.

Gorman's shop and bakery were just across the street from our house; in fact when he lit the two oil lamps in the bakery we could, and did, watch Tommy and his current apprentice go through every step of baking, from measuring the flour into the trough (Tommy called it trow), to drawing out the perfectly baked loaves from the primitive coke-fed oven. We marvelled at his skill with the long oar-like piece of wood he called 'the peel' which he used to put the loaves into the oven; later to move them around, and finally to withdraw the finished product.

Everyone in our house looked forward to Sunday because then we could count on Tommy Gorman coming over for two solid hours — hours of amusement and enlightenment. Every Sunday without fail, right after eleven o'clock Mass, Tommy would cross the street to our house to spend a couple of hours 'around the fire'. He gloried in an appreciative audience and big and all as our kitchen was, while Tommy 'had the floor' it was always packed. Young and old, we hung on every word that came out of his mouth. His knowledge was encyclopedic; it was handed to him that he was better read than even the clergy and in those days it was accepted that every priest was so highly educated that he could speak fluently and intelligently for two solid hours *and* without previous notice, on any given subject.

I'd nudge my mother to get Tommy to talk about the Nugents and the swanky garden parties they used to give at their baronial mansion, Donore. The Nugents were considered the most important family around, especially as they originally owned most of the land in the area — this included the ground on which our village stood. Then Tommy with eyes sparkling would regale us with stories of 'The Baronet introducing *me* to the assembled Lords, Dukes and Earls *and* their Ladies as a top-notch classical scholar, and I can tell you that old Sir Percy himself backed a sure winner every time he pitted Tommy Gorman against the best brains of that erudite assembly.'

Tommy never ran out of ammunition to hold an audience spellbound, but the time came when he'd throw an enquiring eye at the clock on the dresser and mutter 'My time is up, I'll have to go home and balance the books'. There was I, hungry for crumbs of knowledge from Tommy's storehouse of learning and he rushing away to do the books. Later on as I looked across the street and watched him pouring over his accounts I felt a deep personal antagonism, almost jealousy for those damn accounts because they stood between me and what, at the time, I suspected were brilliant lectures by a man who 'had more knowledge and deeper wisdom in his little finger than most professors of the day had in their heads'.

When he was only in his early sixties Tommy Gorman made his last entry in his earthly account book and God chose that same hour to close Tommy's Book of Life. I have no doubt whatsoever that Tommy's spiritual account showed a favourable balance because he was a God-fearing man. A shocking and — to me — sobering tally of Tommy Gorman's lifelong weekly struggle with 'the books' showed up when it transpired that the 'nest egg' he had amassed was barely sufficient to give him a decent burial. His oft-repeated 'Naked we came into this world and naked we'll leave it' surely presaged his precise book balancing.

11. JOHN BRENNAN

In 1960, my wife, six children and myself left Canada and came to live in the little Irish village where I was born. We bought an old house on the main street and were barely settled in when we won our first regular visitor, John Brennan.

Every Saturday evening, regular as clockwork come rain or shine, up the main street of the village you'd see John Brennan stepping along smartly with his large shopping basket in the hook of his arm. Watching the man's spry movements you'd find it difficult to believe that he was, as he put it, 'pushing the hundred mark'.

When I first introduced John Brennan to the 'Canadian family' as my foreign-born wife and children were called locally, John with a twinkle in his eye asked, 'Why don't you present me as an *old* friend?' I answered 'John you are ninety five years young; its your friendship that's *old*.' From then on he used to drop in for a chat every Saturday evening when he'd be up in the village for his weekly groceries, his two ounces of plug tobacco and at least a couple of pints of porter. John had been a close friend of my parents and their parents before them and without delay he took my wife and six kids into his heart. He said, 'I had their father in my heart ever since I used to croon to him and rock him to sleep in the family cradle.' My wife took to John immediately and before long developed genuine affection and respect for this venerable family friend. Imagine an intimate friend of the family stretching over four generations!

I remember how gratified and proud I was to see John Brennan 'céileing' in my house as naturally as he did in the 'old house' where my parents and grandparents had spent their lives. I was delighted to see how eagerly and enthusiastially this Canadian-reared family of mine looked forward to John's Saturday evening visits. Here he was now, regaling my children and their mother with fascinating tales of the 'old days'; but I had mixed feelings when John with tongue in cheek and a twinkle of mischief in his 'good eye' (he always had an eye that

113

was a little behind the other one for close work) told the kids tales out of school about 'that father of yours'. John related how 'himself' (yours truly) before he even learned to make the Sign of the Cross managed to come out with 'Go hell John" (go to hell John). Another time John cast up at me 'I mind the day and you still in petticoats you roared at your mother in the crowded chapel, 'I want to go up in the gallery and shit on the sheet (sit on the seat).'

He confided seriously to my wife Eileen that all his life he was in love with my mother, 'Even though she wouldn't give me her shoes to clane (clean).' When Eileen broke faith and leaked it to me, I wasn't the least bit surprised, in fact I was proud of it because my immediate family always had a sneaking suspicion that John Brennan carried a torch for Bridget Hand as he called her. (Even today, lifetime friends of married women usually call them by their maiden name.) Looking back now, I realize that John always treated my mother with an old-world courtesy now as rare as hen's teeth.

Recently there has been a spate of writing about the Great Famine of 1845–48. The first accurate census of Ireland was taken in 1841. It revealed that there were over eight million people in the country. The greater proportion of those people were living off the land at bare subsistence level. Their meagre standard of living was aggravated by high land rents, rapid growth of population and a most unsatisfactory social structure. Another unfortunate aspect was their undue dependence on one main food crop — the potato. The failure of the potato crop, caused by the potato blight in the years 1845–47 brought disaster on Ireland; just imagine! In the ten years after 1841 death and emigration reduced the population by one and a half million. I asked John Brennan about the Famine. He said, 'You talk about the Famine! Ireland never gave an easy living to her own people, my father and mother both lived through the Hard Times and kept the spark of life lit in their children — I myself was born only a few years after the worst of it was over. My parents and grandparents never called it the Famine — that fancy name was invented years after — but they never tired of talking about the Hard Times. But the Hard Times didn't start in 1845 or end in 1848, the dates the men that wrote our history give to the Famine. For a terrible long time before, and for a fairly long time after it, no man, woman or child in Ireland ate idle bread. I often recall my people complaining that humans had to work harder than asses to keep body and soul together. Avic! (my son) you still hear old people say "They were real min (men) in them days". Sure they *were* real men, nevertheless the Hard Times weeded them out like when you're thinning turnips you pull out and throw away the donny [sickly] ones.' John continued, 'You yourself mind walking along the shore of the lake in the dapping season (fly fishing) when the greendrake that the gentry call the Mayfly is up? You see the purty (beautiful) greendrakes come up to the top of the water, climb out of their skin bag (cocoon), dry out their gauzy shiny wings and fly away over the waves to join the millions of their kind. But walk along the shore and look down where the water laps the edge of the land and there in the froth and foam you'll see thousands of greendrakes — spent, broken, dying and dead. Speaking of the Hard Times! My father said that the corpses and the sick and dying on the sides of the road in the ditches and the hovels always reminded him of the greendrakes on Derravaragh shore.'

The Irish, like most other races at some period of their history, have been decimated. Now after a lapse of some one hundred and thirty years I wonder how the 'thinning out' of our people affected the descendants of the six million survivors of the Famine. The decendents of those survivors now number in the region of twenty four million — four million living in Ireland, and twenty million living abroad. I can't vouch for the historic memories carried by the Irish abroad, but I do know that the Famine will never be forgotten by the people living on this island, 'Not', as they say, 'while grass grows, and water flows'.

John Brennan was living proof that 'only the hardiest of the hardy survived'. His own words spoken when he was ninety eight years old, were, 'I was never sick a day in my life because I come from hardy stock.' He was right about the hardy old stock — all his brothers and close relatives on his father's side of the family lived well into their nineties. Because John firmly believed that proper eating and drinking coupled with a diet of hard work was the key to long life he repeatedly reminded us about the type and amount of food he ate. His diet, to us, sounded monotonous and when I hinted that we liked variety he ominously retorted, 'Time will tell'. And he continued, 'Since I found myself getting on in years I trained myself to eat less quantity but not to change the kind of food I was long used to.' His meals for an average day were: breakfast of rashers and eggs — and of course plenty of strong tea and homemade bread; dinner — boiled bacon and cabbage. The cabbage was cooked in the greasy bacon water, potatoes boiled in their skins and eaten with plenty of homemade butter. 'Buttermilk!' he said, 'Strong sour buttermilk, nothing tastes better right after a dinner of bacon and cabbage.' For supper he had boiled eggs and homemade bread and tea. The last thing at night was a good meal of stirabout (porridge) 'from our own oats ground in Mullvaney's mill'. John, like most of his generation, claimed that plenty of stirabout would cure any stomach destroyed from drinking too much whiskey or from bad eating habits. He'd ask, 'Did you ever see how quickly a hot oatmeal poultice would clean up a bealing (swelling) finger or any other inflamed part of the human body?'

In addition to coming from hardy stock and enjoying a healthy life-style it is probable that John's determination to outlive his own generation significantly helped to lengthen his life span. To the casual eye he could pass for a man in his mid-sixties and as for the quality of his mind, 'My brain is as sharp as ever it was' he would brag. There were times when I had a sneaking suspicion that as he grew older — and as a bonus — John awarded himself extra years; years he felt certain he'd eventually earn.

John said he hadn't eaten baker's bread a dozen times in his life and the times when he did were when he happened to be visiting and didn't want to hurt the good neighbour's feelings by turning it down. He remarked, 'I first noticed years ago how people failed just a little at a time, once they gave up eating oaten bread.' I asked 'What is so special about oaten bread?' He explained, 'Look at what a good feed of oats does with a pony or a hunting horse!; immediately they start to behave for all the world like a man that takes a good stiff glass of poteen (home distilled whiskey). There's nothing in the world like bread made from your home-grown oats. What did the unfortunate emigrants take in their bundles for the long sea voyage to America, in the leaky, wooden sailing ships when I was a gossoon. Oaten bread, baked hard as a slate on a griddle on the hearthstone.' By the way, speaking of food with substance, John called it 'food that sticks to a man's ribs.'

After three memorable years in Multy we decided to return to Canada for an indefinite period. So in 1963 as we were getting ready to go to Cobh, County Cork to 'catch the boat', John Brennan came to say goodbye. His final words were, 'I'm ninety five years of age but when you all come home I'll be waiting here to welcome ye' and to Eileen he said, as he hugged her, 'Good-bye me darlin', don't worry about me, I'll be saying a prayer for your safe return.'

Three years elapsed before I set foot again in Ireland and this time Deirdre and Patsy, two of my daughters, returned with me for a month's vacation. So after our arrival in Multy, the three of us walked down the Avenue, took the path across the Bridge Meadow at the corner of the Friary graveyard and crossed the big field at the back of the Friary buildings and came to Brennan's stile. It was a wooden stile and required a fair amount of agility to climb across. Deirdre said, 'It's only three years ago since John Brennan helped me across this "bockety stile" as he called it.' The stile is part of a fence between the Friary land and Brennan's. The same fence separates the upland from the bog — Brennan's little place is all bog and at a much lower elevation than the adjoining upland.

John's people were small farmers on Donore estate and sometime before his birth they were 'moved' to this smaller farm in the bog portion of Abbeylands — ancient and present site of our historic Franciscan Abbey. By dint of hard work and frugal living, the Brennans — it took three generations of them — managed to drain, clear, break and cultivate their twenty-five swampy, boggy acres. Brennan's was typical of what we locally call a small farmer's snug place. We use the word 'place' to identify the whole complex of farmhouse, farmyard, farm buildings, garden, fields and livestock. It also includes fences, gates, drains, roadways and other farm-type utilities; it even covers farm equipment. The first time a stranger to our ways hears us say 'small farmer' he may imagine we are referring to some undersized individual endeavouring to perform man-sized tasks on a farm. On the other hand if it's a 'big farmer' he hears, he may get the image of a giant of a man engaged in farming. In reality the above adjectives only refer to the acreage respective farmers possess; a small farmer is one owning any acreage from ten to fifty and needless to say the fortunate owner of a farm exceeding fifty acres would be called a big farmer even if he were no bigger than the once famous Tom Thumb.

In Ireland the word 'snug' has many connotations. Used in the context of 'snug farmer' it could mean any, or all of: comfortable, thriving, prosperous. Snug has another meaning here, because snug is an area in that well-frequented and well known oasis for thirsty travellers — The Irish Pub. Most of our country pubs have a snug, which is a small room set apart for the exclusive use of privileged customers or clients. It's a place that ensures privacy for deals or bargaining and is frequented by those who prefer drink to company — in other words, by solitary 'heavy drinkers'. Invariably the snug has an open fire and is cosily furnished along the lines of a farmer's comfortable parlour. I know a line of poetry that could describe the atmosphere of the snug: 'Secure, close and warm as an infant snuggles up to the mother's breast.'

The two daughters and myself stood there at the stile looking down (physically) on Brennan's, and the whole place as they'd say was a going concern. There was movement without bustle. I suppose you could say that there was orderly disorder about the place; cattle grazing in the fields around the house, pigs giving the odd squeal, hens picking around in the yard and the geese and ducks paddling in the muddy drain that sloped down to the bog road and hopefully drained the most-times muddy yard. Speaking of mud, everyone here calls it muck. It could be a coincidence, but our Gaelic word for pig is muc — pronounced muck. Which reminds me of an old saying here, 'Where the muck is, the luck is'. Using that yardstick, Brennan's farmyard must have been as lucky as the proverbial four leaf clover. The geese guarded by the menacing and belligerent gander appeared to spend as much time in the fields around the house eating grass as they did paddling and feeding in the deep bog drains at the lower end of the farm.

A couple of hundred yards away we saw Jim — the only son — pottering around the yard. John's wife was dead for many years so he looked after the son about whom John complained 'never brought in a wife'. The looking after included treating Jim like a growing boy when in reality he had been drawing the Old Age Pension for years.

At the time of our visit Deirdre was eighteen and Patsy was sixteen. To use a cricket expression, John had just made the century and was terribly proud of having accomplished what he

had 'early in life set out to do — to be able to walk without a
sthick (stick) the day I get to be a hundred years old.' I was
wrong about John adding a year here and there as he went
along. A few weeks before we went to call on him he had
received an official letter from the President of Ireland
congratulating him on reaching the venerable age of one
hundred years. The letter also contained the standard
government gift for centenarians—ten pounds. 'That magnificent
sum', John was quoted as saying, 'amounted to two shillings for
each year of John Brennan's long laborious life.'

When Deirdre, Patsy and myself got to Brennan's yard, Jim
came to greet us and said they had heard we were back and that
his father was dying to welcome us. Deirdre afterwards
remarked 'The father looks younger than the son'. Jim led us
into the unlighted kitchen and then I remembered that although
his eyesight had failed somewhat over the years, John had not
had electricity installed. His excuse — 'it's against nature to turn
the night into day, doesn't the sun shine long enough even on
the shortest day of the year?' When asked, 'What about reading
after dark?' John replied, 'As a gossoon I read and learned my
Catechism at the fire by the light of the rush candles we
ourselves made. I even remember the hullabaloo people made
when tallow candles first came out.' Now as I crossd the kitchen
to where John was standing with his back to the fire I did not
have to say who I was or enquire about the state of his health;
the second I put my foot across the threshold and stepped into
the kitchen John recognized my voice and almost shouted, 'Be
God, if it's not the little fellow I used to jockey on my knee when
he was in petticoats'. He even gave me a 'sly dig' about the
Yankee shirt I was wearing. His remark amazed me because the
kitchen was poorly lighted and being used to well illuminated
buildings, I couldn't see my hand in front of my face. With a
boisterous hug John almost squeezed the breath out of my body.
When I told him I had two of my daughters with me John's
eyesight apparently failed him; and in a 'put on' weak voice he
whispered, 'My sight is poorly, will both of you garahallas (girls)
stand over here close to me till I get a good look at ye.' In a flash
'me bould' John threw his arms around each of the girls in turn
and gave each of them a hug that would prove as John said
'There may be snow on the thatched roof but there is still fire on
the hearth'.

Then to show my venerable friend that I remembered his
lifelong boast, I enquired, 'John, where's your walking stick?'
'Sthick is it you're talking about?' and turning to the girls he
bragged 'If someone will lilt a bit of a jig or an Irish reel I'll dance
a few stheps for me darlings'.

A couple of hours passed and even then I almost had to tear
away the girls because — like their mother before them — they
were completely under John Brennan's spell. Nothing would do
this centenarian opportunist but he'd buss the girls before we left
even though he knew for sure we would soon return to pay him
another visit. As the girls and myself climbed back over
Brennan's stile, they assured me they enjoyed the visit and
'loved being treated as women by a mature man'. While we
walked home I told the girls how John always had an eye for the
ladies and after all he had been a widower for the past quarter
century. He often said he'd marry again but he never met a
woman that 'could replace my wife in my heart'. I explained,
'The manly bit of bussing he just gave both of you is only part of
what we call courting. Patsy, you're familiar with the expression
'bundling'. In John Brennan's time bundling was an accepted
courting custom both here and in England. Technically, it
consisted of lying without undressing, in the same bed with
one's sweetheart, and to prevent hanky panky, the courting bed
was not supposed to be in a room with a locked or closed door
but in part of the house where the rest of the family went about
their normal business. Needless to say bundling was supposed
to be confined to formally engaged couples; in Ireland it was
reserved for couples going seriously — when the suitor meant
business. Country homes with a courting daughter usually
reserved a snug, dimly-lit corner of the kitchen for the lovers'
nightly romps. When the day's work was over and some of the
nightly ceiliers had arrived, the daughter and her suitor would
casually retire to the 'courting corner' and hang up a blanket or
shawl as a makeshift screen and proceed to do a bit of discreet
courting outside the clothes.

We were back in Canada when we got word that John Brennan
passed away peacefully at a little over 102 years and that local
people with sad finality — and when it was too late to do
anything about it — said that it was pneumonia that took him;
and the result of sheer neglect. To me, John Brennan
represented many of the finest characteristics of our Celtic

culture and as we go along I will surely speak of him again and again, because his way of life, his home and his little farm could be a prototype of the seventeenth and eighteenth century Irish homestead.

Present day visitors to our shores — especially if they have ancestral roots in Ireland — feel an atavistic tug at their heart strings every time they encounter, almost anywhere in our still unspoiled countryside, some of the few remaining genuine Irish farmhouses complete with their white-washed walls and thatched roofs. Brennan's was one of those farmhouses. Their dwelling was a couple of hundred paces from the main road. The house and the adjoining farmyard, farm buildings and haggard snuggled in the most sheltered part of their twenty-five acre farm.

If you throw an eye over our Irish landscape you'll notice that all the older-type buildings invariably were sited to get the maximum shelter from the elements and were designed and built to conserve heat. You may also observe that farmhouses and the houses of people with less worldly goods were all one-storey buildings. I believe the height, or lack of it was influenced — maybe dictated — by the limited local choice of building materials which were clay and stone for the walls, and timber and straw for the roofs. Houses constructed of those materials were called mud-wall, thatched houses.

The foundations, intersections of the walls and chimney of Brennan's house were of stone, but the walls themselves were composed of a mixture of different clays to which water was added; then the builders formed the walls somewhat like we now use concrete. The kitchen had a clay, or earthern floor and the roof was the then standard wooden-framed, straw thatched roof. The house measured about fifty by twenty-five feet and contained two bedrooms, a parlour and the kitchen. The kitchen took up half the area of the house; but its size is understandable when you examine the functions of the kitchen in an Irish farmhouse of that period. From a modern point of view the most unusual thing about the layout of the house was that it had but one doorway and very few windows. This small number and size of openings in the wall was part of the householder's effort to conserve heat and to avoid the much-dreaded draught. As you ramble around our country you may notice that the average person never hesitates to take shelter under a hedge or in the lee of a wall; but that same person would 'avoid like the plague' sitting in a draughty vehicle or building.

The doorway was unusally wide, about four feet, with the door itself separated into two halves which were generally called the upper and the lower half, but when we specifically say 'half door' it refers to the lower portion only. The windows were few, only four, and each so small that it provided an opening only large enough for a person to scramble through — if the glass were first removed. In addition, the little windows were of a fixed type and not designed for opening and closing.

I often heard John Brennan brag, 'When my father built this house he knew what he was about; he turned its back to the cold biting north wind blowing down from the lake, and the gable end of the kitchen without a porthole or window in it turns a square shoulder to the bitter, frosy east wind itself; our doorway catches the warm sun as good as if Rosse the astronomer himself had marked out the plan of the house.' John assumed that his listeners knew all about the Earl of Rosse, a world-famous astronomer who lived at Birr Castle, County Meath, barely fifty miles from here. In 1845 the Earl built and used a telescope which, until 1915, remained the largest in the world.

Perhaps I should say a few words about thatched roofs, seeing that the odd house is now being built with the roof thatched in the traditional style. Thatching a roof is not a job for a do-it-yourself type: it calls for a skilled thatcher. There are several kinds of straw suitable for thatching; we have oaten, wheaten and barley straw. The latter is the most widely used because it retains its colour and lasts longer. Regardless of the type of straw used, the important item is the method of threshing the straw. Straw thrashed by the primitive flail or even by modern harvesting machines is unsuitable for thatching, because machines bend, break and crush individual straws and if those broken straws were used for thatching, they would quickly lose their water-repellent quality. We consider that barley that has been 'scutched' is the ideal thatching material. Scutching is one of the primitive methods employed to remove the seed from stalks of grain and consists of beating the stalks of grain 'a wisp at a time' on the smooth curved suface of a keg or barrel to shed the seed.

Brennan's had the usual number of buildings, we call them outside buildings: a shed for farm machinery which in those pre-tractor days consisted of a horse-drawn plough, harrow, rollers, and a hand winnowing machine (for winnowing corn and grain), a mowing machine, haygathering rake, wheelbarrow and a pulper. The pulper was a machine with rotating knives for slicing turnips, mangolds and potatoes for raw cattle feed. There was also a stable for loose cattle which held about ten bullocks. One end of the stable had an area set apart as a byre to house a few milch cows and some of their calves. Another little building was the henhouse with boxes for the hens to lay their eggs and a dark corner set apart for hatching hens and chickens. Close to the henhouse there was a separate shed for ducks and geese.

The pig sty was always the shed furthest from the house because no matter how well pigs are bedded down and fed, invariably they are noisy and apt to smell. The Brennans usually kept four or five pigs. One of these pigs would receive special attention — food, bedding and cleaning — in order to be 'fattened up' so that in the fullness of time it would be 'slaughtered for the house'. Most householders with a bit of land, even the cottagers with their single acre of garden kept a pig for slaughtering, and in most country houses it was a common sight to see large flitches of bacon — each the full length of a pig — hanging from the kitchen rafters.

A slaughtering was and still is an occasion — a small gathering of select neighbours who 'could always be depended on' — and it still carries discernible traces of long ago when killing, curing and storing the year's supply of meat for the family was a religious rite. As of yore, the entire 'killing party' repaired to the kitchen for refreshments at the completion of the killing, the scalding (to remove hairs), the paunching, the dressing down, the dismembering and the final act when the entire carcass was split lengthwise and each half laid out flat on a stone-cold flagged floor.

Salting the flitches commenced the following day. I well remember taking part in 'a salting' when we did our own slaughtering. Usually four people used the traditional 'crubeens' for rubbing the salt well into the fresh pork. Crubeen is a commonly used name around here; it's the Irish word for pig's foot (crūibín). When the salting 'took; and after a local 'expert' pronounced the sides of bacon 'ready for hanging' the flitches would be taken to the house and hung on the sturdy iron hooks permanently affixed to the kitchen rafters.

The longer the flitches of bacon were left hanging the better cured and 'smoked' they became, and I assure you that in most of the houses there was never any shortage of smoke up among the rafters. Not all the smoke generated by the burning turf on the open hearth managed to find its way up the chimney; a reasonable (or breathable) amount of turf smoke missed the cavernous maw of the chimney-place and meandered up through the rafters. This peat-scented smoke imparted a delicious 'something' to the hanging flitches of bacon. As long as a flitch would last, the housewife would cut bacon for the next meal direct from the hanging flitch. Speaking of home-cured bacon, John Brennan said, 'If I were laid out for my own wake and got a whiff of frying rashers from our own home-cured flitches I'd sit straight up with my teeth watering.'

Brennan's haggard was close to the farmyard in a 'sheltery' area well fenced off from the farm animals. Space in the haggard was reserved for the stacks of corn, barley, oats and wheat. A high and dry corner of the haggard was kept for ricks of hay and turf. These ricks were expertly built and thatched to make them rain and wind proof. The big rick of turf was sited as close as possible to the kitchen to facilitate carrying in fuel for the turf-hungry kitchen fire. Of all the produce of the farm and the bog so snugly stored in Brennan's haggard that stack of turf was the most precious commodity. A year's supply of turf was almost a matter of life and death because the farm had no trees suitable for firewood and the purchase of coal was beyond their modest means.

In the Irish Midlands we are fortunate in the number and ready availability of bogs. Clonave bog is only a couple of miles from the village and is even closer than that to Brennan's house. Wish I had time and space to tell you in detail how much a part the cutting, rearing and bringing home of the turf played in all our lives. Every household around here has a long established right — without paying any fee — to cut as much turf as they wish. This right is based on what is called Turbary, which is an ancient English law that 'gives the right of digging turf on another man's land'. Like the rest of the villagers, we still have the right to cut our own turf on Clonave bog.

Given normal drying weather it took about three weeks actual work for a family to harvest (a word never used in this context)

their year's supply of turf. Of course the whole operation —
depending on the weather — was usually spread over the entire
summer. Nearly every family cut and reared their own turf on
the bog, and although not exactly a communal effort it did give
neighbouring families an opportunity to mix and observe each
other's style of work.

Somewhere else I wrote about the cutting, rearing and
backing down of the year's supply of turf to the banks of either
of the two Inny Rivers that are connected with Lough
Derravaragh. Previous to the construction of access bridges on
both those large rivers, Clonave was virtually an island, hence
all the turf for our side of the lake had to be brought home by
cot.

Bringing home the turf by cot, up the Inny River, across the
lake and up the Gaine River to where it runs parallel to the Bog
Road was considered the most difficult part of the entire turf
operation. From the turf bank on Clonave bog the dry turf was
'backed down' to the Inny River. The backing down was done
by asses pulling carts with crates attached, that held about a half
ton of dry turf. Asses were generally used for the backing down
because although their hoofs are small in relation to those of
ponies or horses, asses manage to work on soft, soggy ground
where the larger animals would bog down or flounder. Each
family piled their turf in a separate loosely-built rick at the edge
of the Inny River, then when weather permitted, they would
row their own or a borrowed cot to the rick, load it with turf,
push or be pushed out into deeper water and row back to the
unloading area at the Gaine River.

Owing to the hard work involved in rowing an empty cot to
the loading area it was considered practical to load as much turf
as possible for the return trip. This meant building layers of turf
that came up three or four feet higher than the gunnel of the cot.
Our expression 'loading to the gunnel' means that the weight of
the load submerged the cot until its gunnel was almost at water
level. A friend described his loaded cot: 'I loaded that cot 'till a
mouse could drink off the gunnel.' A well loaded cot left no
room for a passenger; in fact the final sods were usually built so
close around the rower that he — or she — resembled an
Eskimo in his kayak.

I said 'he or she' because in our district the rowing of boats or
cots was not solely restricted to men. Incidentlaly, in those days
neither sex exhibited any tendency to embarrass or to 'show off'

the other; there was a recognized sharing of work and workload, and no woman was expected to do a man's work and vice versa. In fact, if a woman — in the line of her family's normal work — undertook to do the type of work usually done by males, everyone — male and female — applauded.

Now, rowing a cot, even on a calm day, is a challenge to any man; and I should know, because by the time I was in my late teens I had slaved and suffered so many hours pulling cots that I could have given lessons to the unfortunates that once rowed the Roman galleys. Speaking of cots, maybe I should first try and say a few words about them. Cots are flat-bottomed boats designed to transport bulk material. A unique and aggravating feature of those cots is the difficulty of rowing one in a straight line. When you try to row even a partially empty cot it acts like an air-borne bubble on the surface of a calm pond — it moves in any or all directions, heavily loaded, the same cot displays the manoeuverability of a towed iceberg. To sum it up; we ROW boats but PULL cots.

Most of us on the Multy side of the lake fancied ourselves with a pair of oars but we 'couldn't carry drinks of water to the Clonavers'. We alibied, 'They all, men, women and children, have to be good on the water. Aren't they surrounded by it. Even to go to Mass or bury their dead they have to row across the lake.' Be that as it may, we knew there were women in Clonave better with a pair of oars than any of us males. Usually someone added, 'I bet John Brennan's garahallas would put any of them to the pin of his collar.'

In those days we all looked forward to the annual regatta on the lake where the traditional cot race was the favourite event. 'It is popular.' they said, 'because racing a cot is a man's job.' Making a good showing in the cot race demanded strength, endurance and 'a way with cots'. The crew of a racing cot was made up of a coxswain and two rowers, each rower using a single oar. When I was thirteen, on account of being small for my age, I was steersman (coxswain) for the Nallys at a regatta.

First a few words about the Nally brothers — Andy and Jimmy. On the hurling field, the bog, or the lake the Nallys had no equals. Both were big men — powerful men. I recollect someone saying, 'Shoulders! Just watch Jimmy Nally coming through a doorway. He has to come in sideways or his shoulders 'ld get stuck in both jambs'.

By the time the regatta was under way, 'the waves had their

coats off' and Andy said, 'The rougher it gets the better we'll be'. There was a lot of truth in that because both he and his brother owned and rowed the only large cot on the lake; in fact it was known far and wide as the Big Cot and it was six times bigger than the average. Although the Big Cot was larger than some canal barges that take a pair of horses to tow, the Nallys propelled that big boat with oars — oars so big and awkward that it took two men to lift and put one oar in place on the thole pin or rowlock. People around here still speak with awe when they retell of the Nallys, 'In a storm, taking seven hard, gruelling hours pulling AGAINST the win' to travel two miles and when that gale was at its worst, Jimmy saying "We may not be moving a foot forward but be Jasus we're not being bet back an inch either"'.

The length of the course for the cot race was two miles, from a point on Donore shore northward around a single anchored keg and back in a straight line to the starting point. A violent west wind was blowing which meant that the competing craft — racing boats, row boats and cots — were at all times subjected to a strong side wind. If you have any idea at all about rowing you will recollect that with a strong side wind, the oarsman on the lee side has all the work to do, yet there were times in the race that I had to 'put the rudder on' the rower on the easy or windward side.

From the starting gun our craft was well out in front and we were on the return leg of the course, so — barring some misfortune like breaking an oar — we were bound to win at a canter. Breaking an oar would be our greatest hazard because by this time it was blowing a gale and to keep on the course Jimmy was pulling his oar so powerfully that he was putting an alarming bow into the strong, well-seasoned ash oar. I forgot to mention that invariably the rowing seats of cots were rough from the primitive carpentry and exposure to the elements; also that in those days none of us — the males anyway — wore underwear; hence a male rower's posterior was subjected to more than a fair share of wear and tear — in polite company it was referred to as chaffing. Anyway as our cot ploughed towards the finish line well ahead of the field I thought I'd give Jimmy a word of encouragement. So over the roar of the waves and the cheers of the crowd, I yelled, 'Jimmy can you stick it?' Through clenched teeth he ground out, 'I've plinty of skhin left on my arse'.

Some of my happiest childhood memories revolved around being sent with a brother or sister to Mrs. Brennan for twopence worth of new milk or for a big can of buttermilk. Farmers never charged for buttermilk, yet no one dared call it free because 'free' smacked of charity; and charity evoked memories — bitter memories — of the Famine which scourged and decimated our people. There never was any milk shortage in our village because it is surrounded by well-stocked excellent grazing land and local farmers sold us all the milk we wanted. We never use the term dairy milk, we call it newmilk, possibly to distinguish it from buttermilk. In those days a lot of buttermilk was drunk as a beverage. It was also used with stirabout and for making homemade bread. Nowadays, people appear to be losing their taste for buttermilk as a drink, but the odd household still bakes homemade or soda bread and sour buttermilk is an important ingredient in that type of bread-making.

Although Women's Lib was unheard of in those unenlightened days, everyone including her husband referred to her kitchen as 'Mrs. Brennan's kitchen'. Not that the good woman was the type who 'ruled the roost'; it was just accepted that in the Irish kitchen the Lady of the House ruled supreme.

Mrs. Brennan had the name of being the 'best maker around of butter and buttermilk'. I vividly remember the pleasure of the trip — we considered it an adventure — when we were sent there for milk; especially if the weather was right for 'going in the bare ones'. I still recapture the sensuous feeling of that boggy path, springy and warm caressing my little bare feet. It was only a short walk across the fields and when we arrived the first thing we'd see was Mrs. Brennan in her snow-white pinafore at the half door, greeting us children with 'Ye are as welcome as the flowers in May'. Then with arms open wide, as if she were marshalling a flock of downy ducklings she would solicitously usher us into her big whitewashed kitchen and seat us around the fire.

As I was the youngest she always gave me what we considered the seat of honour in the deepest corner of that — to us — fascinating fireplace. The seat I was so proud of was a three legged one, called a 'creepy'. I wouldn't be surprised if the creepy stool was specially designed to overcome the uneveness of the flagged floors of that era. The creepy was also extensively used as a milking stool. Its seat was circular, about ten inches in diameter and roughly two and a half inches thick. I have nothing but my own guesswork to go by, but it is reasonable that on uneven ground it is easier to find a comparatively level base for three legs rather than for four or more.

I know everyone has some special childhood memory, but my most treasured one is 'myself like a king on a throne' riding that old three-legged stool in Brennan's snug, smokey chimney nook and savouring the foamy mug of fresh cows milk and huge slice of delectable homemade soda bread swimming in butter that was her specialty. We children revelled in Brennan's hospitality; a type and standard of hospitality rooted in ancient pagan Celtic culture where hospitality was considered a cardinal virtue; a hospitality that bore the traditional Irish hallmark, not only since Christianity came but long, long before. At that stage of my life their open fireplace intrigued me. Our kitchen at home had a monstrous iron grate and though it's normal for everyone to believe their possessions superior to the other fellow's, in my heart I knew Brennan's fireplace was far ahead of ours. I was not alone in my criticism of our iron grate; didn't I overhear my grandmother grousing about our grate and muttering about newfangled ideas!

A friend recently remarked, 'Pretty soon a kitchen like the Brennans had long ago, may only be seen in old paintings, faded photos or maybe in a museum.' I find it hard to appreciate that something so vital as that kitchen could disappear from the face of the earth. Outside our own home, I spent more time in Brennan's kitchen than in any other house right from the time I could toddle to the day when on the threshold of manhood I went down the Bog Road to say farewell; and she bid me 'God speed' while John added 'So our haro (hero) is off for foreign parts — but with the help of God he'll soon be back'.

If I try to describe Brennan's kitchen where shall I start? I already mentioned the half door, so in memory I'll open that half door and try to picture the kitchen. You step inside and when your eyes become accustomed to the dimly-lit kitchen you see that the inside walls are spotless. That's because hardly a month goes by that the whole interior doesn't get a fresh coat of whitewash. The floor is a 'clay floor' and so far, I have not unearthed the trade secret of how such a floor was laid. Its builder could have used materials other than clay for the floor surface, because stone flags, field tile and timber were plentiful, but most people liked — and chose — the traditional clay floor because for generations those clay floors withstood the wear and tear to which Irish farmhouse floors were subjected. The earthen floor looked like a solid, unbroken sheet of dark grey mahogany and if your eyesight was sharp enough, you could see that the surface was so compressed and polished from ceaseless walking and repeated sweeping with the 'besom' that its wearing surface resembled polished bog oak.

The central or focal point of the kitchen was — of course — the hearthstone, but I may hold my fire, as it were and describe it later. Mrs. Brennan's pride and joy was the kitchen dresser with open shelves displaying her prize delph. The dresser itself was very old and must have been fabricated by a master craftsman. The material he used was bog oak which had lain buried deep in the nearby bog for millenia. Her full set of Willow Pattern had not a crack or flaw; she said it was 'because they are more for ornament than use'. She did not know their exact age, but believed they had been in the family since the seventeenth century. She beamed every time one of us asked her to tell the story of the characters on the delph — everyone uses the word delph, where English North Americans say dishes. As the good lady recounted the tale, the story took on a distinct Celtic flavour. Chang was an Irish bard and Li-Chi was daughter of the High King of Ireland. The lovers, disguised as Chinese, eloped to an island on the Shannon and were about to be captured and separated when a benevolent fairy magically changed them into a pair of beautiful pigeons. The tale always ended on a happy note with Mrs. Brennan pointing to the love-birds flying away together to Tír na nÓg the land of Eternal Youth — the Celtic heaven, where there is no sadness, suffering or long farewells.

In the middle of the kitchen there was a massively constructed, well scrubbed wooden table big enough to seat a dozen. The table was the most frequently used piece of furniture in the house and a list of its various uses would include almost every function of the entire household and farm. All the family meals were prepared and eaten at that table and every single scrap of food that went into the eternally simmering huge pig's pot suspended from the crane over the fire was also made ready on it. There was no spring well near the house and of course no piped water on the premises, so all the water for the house had to be carried in pails, hence the dishwashing was done and most of the family laundry was washed, starched and ironed at that same table.

When a bunch of the neighbours would drop in for their nightly céilie, the overflow from around the fire sat at the table, playing cards or just talking. Then there were the special occasions when the freshly scrubbed table draped with Mrs. Brennan's prized snow-white stiffly starched Irish linen tablecloth was used as an altar. That was when the Parish Priest — as was the custom — came to the house to say Mass.

There were other times — rare times, thank God — when there was a death in the house and the spacious kitchen would be filled to overflowing by neighbours attending the wake. In our countryside culture it has always been considered fitting to wake our dead in the kitchen. They say it is the natural place because, first, it provides ample room for the gathering of neighbours and 'clownies' to congregate and pay their respects both to the family and the departed; the other reason is that we consider the kitchen to be the pulsing heart of the household and the hub around which the lifetime activities of the now dead person revolved. That word clownies is from the Irish *clann* meaning tribe, and we use it to include relatives by blood and marriage down to, and including fourth cousins twice removed. Speaking of wakes, I have yet to meet a sober Irishman who witnessed the type of wake attributed abroad to Ireland. Undoubtedly the Irish wake with accompanying high jinks is connected with the stage Irishman.

I suppose everyone knows that we never wake a corpse in the coffin (casket). Regardless of how poor a family may be they always manage to wake their dead in traditional style. The usual setting is a bed — or a large table made up like a bed — complete with snow-white linen sheets and pillow slips. The top sheet is always folded down, just far enough to disclose a rosary beads entwined in the stiffly folded hands joined in prayer. Sometimes there is a departure from the traditional white shirt, or shroud; that is when a member of the Third Order of St. Francis is being waked. They then wear a brown shroud that has been blessed for the occasion. A large percentage of Catholics belong to the Third Order and although not an article of faith, it's a widely-held belief that if the dying member has received the Last Rites in good faith, and is, even partially, clothed in the 'blessed' shroud, then he is spared an indeterminate stopover in Purgatory.

In a remote corner of the kitchen there was a sturdy bench usually loaded with vessels filled with newmilk, cream and buttermilk. There were also several shallow pans called keelers, holding milk at the various stages from fresh to ready-to-churn. Those shallow pans facilitated skimming off the cream which was then kept at temperatures which caused the cream to sour — we call it ripen. It's this ripening of the cream that gives the resultant butter the unique taste or tang peculiar to country butter. To anyone like myself reared on country butter, dairy butter is almost tasteless; as they say, 'More like lard than rale (real) butter'.

The barrel-churn stood in the dairy corner of the kitchen. Today this piece of dairy equipment would be labelled primitive. The churn itself was just a plain sturdy oak barrel built by the local cooper. The working part of the churn was called a dash and consisted of a straight wooden handle projecting downwards through a hole in the tightly-fitting lid. The lower end of the handle was attached solidly to the dasher, which was the heavy piece of wood — sometimes circular — with holes in it. In our area the favourite dasher was shaped like a crucifix — we felt it was a kind of insurance because of the extraordinary amount of lore, superstition and religion connected with churning. I suppose those strange beliefs and practices originated because, while butter making is as old as civilization itself, knowledge of the chemical process is relatively recent.

Sometimes our trips to Brennans coincided with the churning and the churn would be out in a clear part of the kitchen where the churner would have plenty of elbow room — and he'd need it! The churn would be about one third full of sour cream to which Mrs. Brennan would add what she called 'The right amount of water hated (heated) to the exact temperature'. Now I realize that her successful churning was a combination of cleanliness, age-old ritual and luck. She called it luck, but in reality it was a 'mixumgatherum' (*sic*) of practices both pagan and Christian.

Even today you hear the word pisreóg connected with milch cows and churning. Pisreóg is an Irish word which means witchcraft, sorcery, a charm, a spell, wizards, diviners. For instance, everyone who has experience of using the dash-churn will remember the times when 'you and six more strong men could take your turns working that damn dash up and down for hour after hour and still the butter refused to break'. The long delay or non-appearance of butter was always put down to a certain neighbour who was suspected of 'working pisreógs and taking the butter for herself'. You might also hear, 'No wonder hur (she) with one cow turns out more butter than if she had a small herd.' I really can't explain why it was always a she they blamed! I suppose it was a guard against some sinister visitor 'taking the butter' that gave rise to the universal practice of never leaving another's house during a churning without first 'taking a hand at the dash'.

Recently I was sounding out one of my own generation about pisreógs and had difficulty concealing my surprise when he said, 'Some people around here still practice the black art'. He asked, 'Did you ever hear tell of Connor Sheridan the silenced priest who lived in that townland over there? Well, a neighbour of ours Mat, with two fine cows milking, still had to buy butter. If that unfortunate man churned from here to eternity he'd never get the butter to break, so in desperation he told his troubles to Connor Sheridan who advised him to take a clean, clear glass naggin bottle and the first thing in the morning milk one of his cows into the bottle and bring it to Connor's house. Mat followed instructions and when he arrived Connor made him welcome, brought him into the kitchen, told him to put the bottle of milk on the table and invited him to a cup of tea with him as he sat at the fire. He next poured the tea into Mat's cup and then filled his own. Then he said "Put some of the milk out of your bottle into my tea and do the same with your own cup and then put the three-quarter filled bottle back on the table over there." Connor inquired, "Who do you think is taking your butter?", and the other answered, "There are several people I suspect but I can't prove anything". The silenced priest kept silent for awhile, then he said, "Look over at your bottle on the table and tell me if you recognize the person whose face you clearly see in that bottle".

'Mat looked, shivered and said, 'It's a trusted friend of the family alright, but I never thought it of her.' Connor said, 'Now your troubles with butter are at an end.' They were.

As soon as the butter broke Mrs. Brennan would use a strainer to collect the mass of tiny grains of butter floating in what was now buttermilk. Next she would salt the butter evenly and beat out excess water. To beat out the water, she would dexterously use two wooden 'clappers' which were somewhat like the kitchen utensil we call a spatula. Seeing that we children were there to take home a big can of fresh buttermilk, she would go to great pains to make what she called an extra special pat of butter. This would weigh about a pound and she'd mould it into some geometric shape and imprint her own design on it. Singularly, Mrs. Brennan's curlicues always consisted of a series of interlocking circles, arcs and spirals. It was many years afterwards that I saw the self-same pattern — imprinted 8,000 years earlier — on large boulders recently uncovered in a series of Bronze Age tumuli in County Meath. Then she would pop the pat of butter into our big can of freshly churned buttermilk with 'A little gift for your darlin' mother'.

In the kitchen there were several kinds of seats: a homemade sugán chair; wooden benches without backs, called forms, some designed to seat one person, others to accomodate up to half a dozen. In the cosiest corner of the kitchen, tight against the back wall and convenient to the fireplace, stood the settlebed — a seat in the daytime and a bed at night. Brennan's settle (the commonly-used name for it) was bigger than the modern double bed. Our house did not have a settle; even then they were fast becoming a rarity and they intrigued me.

Settlebeds had no legs; they simply were built like a box with a ponderous, tightly-fitting lid. Every morning the settle was made up: the quilt, blankets and sheet were taken out and aired in front of the open fireplace; the well-filled feather tick that lay on the top of the straw palliasse was turned over and 'shook up' (kneaded, pummelled etc.); then the remainder of the bedding was put in place, including the bolster, the pillows, and finally the heavy lid was closed. This lid then provided a large surface for people to sit or recline on during the day. In *'The Deserted Village'*, Oliver Goldsmith beautifully describes the settlebed's dual role:

> 'The chest contrived a double debt to pay,
> A bed by night, a chest of drawers by day.'

I was sixteen years old before I got the chance to sleep in a settle. Sleep is not the precise term, because there were two separate factors that tended to make it impossible for me to sleep. First, I had not quite recovered from an earlier traumatic experience. Twelve years previously, my grandfather was being 'waked'; he was being 'laid out' upstairs and the (so far) empty coffin was temporarily stored in the room of the kitchen. It was the first coffin I had been in contact with and it both attracted and repelled me. Jack Cowan, a first cousin of my mother was a 'time server' in the British Army and was home on furlough at the time. Maybe I was making a nuisance of myself; that's the only reason I can think of to explain what happened next, this scarlet-coated soldier grabbed me, opened the lid of the coffin, put me in and shut the lid. When I read how such traumatic infant experiences are supposed to affect one in later years, it makes me wonder because I have no unusual fear of enclosed space — even worked as a miner. But I never got into a settle without first thoroughly checking to ensure the ponderous lid wouldn't close while I was virtually a prisoner inside that contraption.

The second barrier was of a more bloody nature. In a feeble attempt to be facetious I could say that in those not so far off days before D.D.T. no one slept alone — because the fleas, lice and bedbugs were no respecters of either royalty or commoner. In the (then) British Isles the best known flea killing compound on the market was Keatings Powder. The owners of the settlebeds which I temporarily occupied were either too poor to buy Keatings, or their domestic fleas had developed immunity to the powder. I remember that in one of the settlebeds in question, it occurred to me that if all the fleas in that box jumped simultaneously I would go down in history as the world's first passenger in an air-borne bed.

12. THE HANGING

The fact that I have lived for ages in other English-speaking countries has sharpened my ear for specific accents and also made me more aware of how different people express themselves differently. Although the general standard of education is appreciably higher in Ireland than it was in my youth, I notice that the quality and standard of everyday communication has not altered. In addition, most country people are still bilingual *in one* language. I'd better explain. Many of us conversing with each other use an older and broader-sounding kind of pronunciation. You may hear sthick (stick), sthone (stone), towld (told), mowld (mold), hur (her), buther (butter) and so forth. We also include innumerable archaic words and phrases reminiscent of Shakespearean works like: 'I'm afeard' or 'I can't abide him' or 'I mind the Boer War'. Our normal vocabulary, even here in the Midlands where the Gaelic (Irish) language went out of general use almost two centuries ago, contains thousands of Irish words and phrases.

Our English sentences reflect Gaelic construction and grammar. To pick a few examples, here's one describing poor hospitality: 'He never asked me if I had a mouth on me'. Another is about a chance meeting of acquaintances where the salutation is posed as a question, while the response includes a query; 'Is it yourself that's in it Mike Murphy?' 'Sure Pat O'Brien, who else but myself could it be?' As much as possible we avoid using the personal pronoun 'I' and the possessive pronoun 'my' and *never* consciously use the 'one' in expressions such as 'one does', 'one's wife' etc. Amongst ourselves, with total disregard for good grammar or precise English, we avoid the possessive 'my' and instead, use expressions such as 'meet the wife', 'the misses', 'herself' or 'lady of the house'.

Actually strangers seldom hear us use what our parents called 'that rough, uncouth talk' because any of us 'at the dhrop of a haich' — or is it aich? — will slide from one pronunciation to the other. Invariably the 'other' (that is, modern sophisticated

136

speech) is *always* used when conversing with superiors, doctors, opposition lawyers, visiting ministers of religion to mention but a few. At school we used different English on the playground than in the classroom. Past pupils recall unforgettable occasions in my old school when the teacher himself, losing patience and almost sanity let slip the odd expression that betrayed both his country and county origin – he came from Cahirciveen in County Kerry. Each generation of parents endeavoured and still do, to have their darlings use impeccable English, but I'm pleased to report that our current crop of Irish youth still speaks both languages fluently, albeit generously sprinkled with Americanisms.

My parents were sticklers for good English. I recall an evening when I was a little lad and my elder brother Tommy came back from running an errand to the shop up the street and said 'When I was in Moughty's, Jim — came in and went to a terrible lot of trouble testing and fiddling around with the coils of ropes that are always piled in the corner near the till. I nearly forgot my own message watching Jim putting loops and slip knots on the different thicknesses of rope. He looked puzzled over something and then he stared at me, held a length of half inch rope in his hands and — you know the way he talks — said, "Would you think this strong enough to hang a man?".' The whole family with mouths open were listening to Tommy and my mother said 'Well what did you say? How did you answer him? I know full well everyone makes fun of him just because he never descends to using rough, coarse English like the rest of you. It would serve you all better if you made an effort to speak like Jim — instead of jeering behind his back.' Tommy answered 'I knew he was codding me so I thought to myself, I'll take a rise out of him and make out to take him serious; so I said to him, "What size of man have you in mind to hang with the rope?" "About eleven stone," he said. So I examined a length of the half inch rope, even tried stretching it, shook my head and with a straight face pointed to the three-quarter inch rope and said, "That's about right".'

We all enjoyed Tommy's telling of it because he was a bit of a mimic and while he was recounting it the rest of us could close our eyes and see Jim and him in earnest conversation. It didn't occur to any of us that Jim, a middle-aged, athletic man happened to weigh about eleven stone (154 pounds). When my mother cross-examined Tommy and eventually was satisfied that he had not been cheeky or insolent she said, 'Well its no harm in the world to indulge in a bit of harmless humour'.

A few hours afterwards a neighbour found poor Jim lying exhausted under a big ash tree with one end of a rope around his neck in a hangman's noose and the other end tightly secured to a big thick branch about fifteen feet from the ground. Jim must have studied cowboy pictures of people being hanged because he had picked a perfect branch that grew at right angles from the tree. He even had a long ladder resting against the branch and well clear of the rope. Judging from the way the sod under the bough was cut up and trampled, it was obvious that after each abortive jump Jim must have reclimbed the ladder to the bough, cast himself off, plummeted to the ground, recovered and repeated the drill.

Jim had every detail perfect for executing the perfect hanging except that the rope was seven feet longer than the distance from branch to ground.

A neighbour afterwards remarked, 'I can't fathom how Jim botched the hanging and he always such a conn-i-shure.' Then she added, 'But then nobody's perfect.' Jim died thirty years later in the county asylum.

13. THE NUGENTS

The Nugents' connection with our village goes back a long, long way — even by our critical local standards; standards so exclusive and restrictive that families, Irish families who moved to the village three generations ago, are still regarded as outsiders even though they originally lived twenty miles away.

The Nugent family is descended from Nogent de Retrow of the illustrious house of Bellsme, in Normandy. In the reign of Henry II (1172) Sir Gilbert de Nogent with his brothers Richard, Christopher and John, came as part of the Invasion of Ireland, with Sir Hugh De Lacey. As a reward for assisting in the Conquest of Ireland, together with subsequent intermarriages with the De Lacey family, the Nugents acquired vast estates in the Irish Midlands.

The Multyfarnham branch of the Nugents owned a large demesne in this locality and built their 'Big House', a Georgian mansion, on the shore of Lake Derravaragh about a mile from the village. In fact the land on which the village was built was part of the Donore estate although the village itself already existed ages before the Nugents were ever heard of.

Members of the Nugent family served with distinction in the armies of Ireland, England, France and Austria. Through centuries of religious persecution that illustrious family clung to the public profession of their Catholic religion. But they must have walked a political tightrope seeing they were never dispossessed of their titles or estates. It is noteworthy that over the centuries the Nugent family provided political protection to the Friars of Multyfarnham and next to the Delemares were the chief benefactors of the Abbey. In fact historically the Nugent family is credited with the title 'Defenders of the Friars in the Penal Days'.

Visitors to our Franciscan Abbey usually find it of interest to examine and study the many monuments and plaques that bear witness to the antiquity, fame and pious works of this family. The oldest of these memorials is a flagstone set into the inside wall of the Abbey Church. It bears a coat-of-arms with the inscription:

SUMPTIBUS	'at the expense of
NUGENT DE FILII:	James Nugent, sone
NUGENT DE DUNOWER	of Richard Nugent
QUI OBIIT 18 FEB.	of Dunower who died
ANNO DOMINA 1615	18 Feb. 1615 A.D.

It's less than fifty years since this part of the world boasted of two distinct strata of society — the upper crust and the lower layer as it were, or should I say the cream of society and the skim milk? Anyway, living in our present society I find it difficult to appreciate how the ones at the top — the Nugents — and The Others peacefully coexisted. But by all accounts the Nugents were not the least bit paternalistic and there is no evidence that they looked down on the rest of us. Loosely speaking, I would say the exercised, and we accepted, the outmoded 'divine right of kings'. Like the rest of the gentry the Nugents felt a pride of ownership in regard to their tenants and 'in company' were known to brag about the exploits and quirks of their people. Maybe there was a certain proprietary pride involved and it is understandable that in the telling, the narrators never came out second best in a confrontation or competition with the common people.

The following actual, though innocuous episode may illustrate my point of one-upmanship. Sir Walter Nugent was a stickler for punctuality and one day Doolin, his overseer, reported to him that one of his workers, Pat Fay was becoming lax in reporting for work in the mornings and lately was slow about returning to the job after the dinner hour was up. Fay was a cut above the average labourer on the estate. At any kind of skilled or semi-skilled work he was almost as good as a tradesman. But then Pat Fay and his whole family had a 'taste for work'. Taste in this context has no connection with 'perceiving flavour through the mouth'. A tasty worker is our top encomium. With the scythe, Pat was the equal of two good workers. When mowing, his swath would be finished and he'd be taking his ease at the other headland by the time other mowers were half way there. It was said that Pat Fay or any of his 'blood' could whet a scythe that would split a hair; he also had the knack of mowing and did it as easily as a cat walks.

So Doolin touching his cap to Sir Walter said , 'Sir, I have discovered that Fay goes home for lunch and is inclined to go early and come back late'. Then to give the impression that *he* would put up with no nonsense, suggested the Sir should fire Fay as a warning to the rest. It was customary to address the lower class by their surnames; 'Doolin', said Sir Walter, 'leave the matter in my hands because he is too valuable a man to sack.'

So the Baronet stalked Fay without the latter smelling a rat and within days the Sir caught him sneaking in the back way twenty minutes after the one o'clock deadline. The Sir confronted him and roared 'Fay you are late.' 'Yes Sir I am, but this morning my missus run out of food for the lunch I always take to work with me so we agreed she'd bring my lunch to the Back Gate and I'd eat it there; I suppose me and her must have dawdled too long while I was eating it, I'm a slow eater'. 'Twas said that Fay could put a better skin on a lie than the devil himself. Sir Walter looked sternly at Fay for a few moments, turned around and walked away from Pat and over his shoulder remarked, 'Your wife looks after all your comforts. I see she even shaved you at the Back Gate.'

There were hundreds of right-of-way paths on Donore estate, especially paths leading to the lake. To give credit where credit is due, the Nugents, their gamekeeper, their herders (locally called herds) and their gatelodge-keepers placed no restrictions on local people traversing their wide acres, using the short cuts, going down the front avenue, bathing, boating or fishing in the lake. But the Nugents and their gamekeeper waged unremitting war on poachers. As a matter of record a Nugent got up from his deathbed to be driven to the Garda barracks to complain 'My pheasants are being poached when they fly out of the demesne to neighbouring farms'.

I'm a bit vague about the Nugents' rights or claims to the lake itself but they owned the land surrounding the entire Multy end of that body of water, roughly six miles of shoreline. A friend of mine, 'a man of the cloth', told me a story that could clarify this poacher problem. He said. 'I was out shooting ducks and snipe in Ballnaclune Bog along the Roach Hole.' The Roach Hole is that area where the River Gaine flows into the lake and where the River Inney, that eventually joins the Shannon, has its beginning. My friend continued: 'Out of the corner of my eye I saw the young Sir coming towards me and cutting off my line of retreat. My setters were out in the open or I'd have made a beeline for the Clonave road which is only half a mile away. On the other hand seeing I was in my thigh-high waders I could have walked out into the lake and hid in the bullrushes and reeds that grow so thickly in that end of the lake. There was a third course open to me and I took it. I just walked to the edge of the lake and stepped into the water. I never let on that I saw the young Baronet closing in on me; just stood there with my back to the land trying to give the impression that I was wrapped in thought or happened to be standing stock-still admiring the scenery.

' "Hey you!" I turned around slowly as if reluctant to tear my eyes from the landscape. Then in what I hoped was a conversational but slightly surprised tone said "Good day Sir, were you addressing me?" The boyish Baronet, his face red from the half-trot, anger and self-importance, stood on high ground and towered over me. There we were eyeball to eyeball, me in the water and he on dry land. "What right have you to trespass and poach on my land?" I held my fowling piece casually under one oxter; took my time lighting a fag; watched the young Baronet grow more angry by the minute and putting on what I felt was my best Abbey Theatre manner and in the tone of an elderly governess towards a recalcitrant infant answered "Your land! But my dear fellow can't you observe that I'm not on land at all, let alone *your* land, in reality I'm out here in the lake and up to my ankles in water." '

When I was in infants' class in Multy National School, Sir Walter Nugent was the last of his direct line to own Donore. I remember that it was about that time the Old Sir, as he was called, got married. He was not a young man at the time — they say he was around sixty. The village celebrated the Baronet's wedding in fine style. There were bonfires, barrels of free porter, food galore and dancing in the main street. Our Parish Priest, Father Murphy, gave a memorable speech that included '. . . and may you, Sir Walter, live to see your children's children.' That remark *was* memorable and Father Murphy was often criticized — behind his back of course — for trying to flatter the aged Baronet. As time went on the scoffers were confounded because doughty, virile Sir Walter lived to see and enjoy three grandchildren.

Sir Walter's choice of a bride met with universal local approval. She was around twenty, a six-footer and beautiful — regal is the word. In addition the new Lady Nugent proved to be a superb horsewoman. When, over the long years, local people spoke approvingly of Lady Nugent's sterling qualities, someone would remark 'Isn't she an O'Malley from the west of Ireland, a blood relation of Gráinne Uaile!' The 'someone' was referring to the celebrated sixteenth century Grace O'Malley, Sea Queen of the West.

Someone, someday, will make a movie about our sixteenth century beautiful red-haired buccaneer whose feats as a ruler of her area of sea around Ireland's west coast earned her the title 'Gráinne of the Heroes'. Grace O'Malley's adventures — maritime and marital — become legendary and read like fiction except that her daring exploits are recorded in State Papers. They are also preserved and kept alive in the spoken tradition of islanders around Clew Bay, County Mayo.

Gráinne's body lies in an ancient abbey (1224) on Clare Island where she had her home and headquarters. There the islanders relish retelling the historically true story of Gráinne's trip to London when Queen Elizabeth invited our Sea Queen to appear at the Royal Court. The flamboyant red-haired pirate managed to steal the Royal show and refused to play second fiddle to Elizabeth. Eventually the English Queen offered to make her a Countess but Gráinne haughtily replied that she was a queen — at least equal to Elizabeth.

Joe Weddock, head gardener at Donore, was about the only local who claimed even a nodding acquaintance with the Nugents. The first time I heard Joe brag of being head gardener at Donore, I had a bizarre picture of him cultivating heads — human heads. Then again, it could have been heads of cabbage or lettuce. Actually, though born in Multy, Joe was never accepted as a local because his parents came from another county. He was combination footman, coachman, gardener and part-time groom and described himself as an 'all round functotem'. I suppose he was wearing his 'footman hat' the day he was involved in giving Lady Nugent a leg-up on her sixteen hands high hunter. Naturally, she was correctly dressed for riding; in those days riding breeches for ladies definitely was 'de trop'. I'll try to describe the leg-up ceremony. The female rider stands at the near side (that's the left hand side) of her mount.

The groom assumes the correct stance. This means that he bends low, cups his hands together thus making a cradle into which the lady rider-to-be places her booted and spurred foot. Then at the appropriate moment, the lady gives the pre-arranged and mutually understandable signal and concentrating all her weight on the foot cupped in the groom's hand she co-operates with him as he gives an upward heave. If both groom and rider's timing and co-ordination are 'on' the rider is deposited safely and securely in the saddle. In passing, I must mention that on occasions, grooms have been known to become over-enthusiastic with their upward heaves and lifted the would-be riders up and over the steed's back.

The Lady was ready to mount. With hands cupped, Joe bent forward to receive the Lady's foot, but the Lady disdained his proffered assistance and unaided, leaped nimbly up into the saddle. Flushed with exertion and triumph and understandably craving approval, acclaim and even a modest bit of applause she queried, 'Weddock, did you admire my agility?' Breathlessly Weddock replied 'I'm afraid me Lady that I didn't get enough time to admire the whole of it; it flashed past the corner of me eye for all the world like the glimpse you'd get of a fox's bush when he slips into his hole'.

Sir Walter Nugent died in 1955 and was the last of his line to own Donore. His son, Sir Peter Nugent, heir to the baronetcy, lives about twenty miles from Donore.

14. THE PARISH PRIEST

For hundreds of years — and today — the Parish Priest has been, and is, the most important and influential person in rural Ireland. Parish Priests, in fact the entire Irish priesthood and all they represent, were a target of that foreign power that for centuries strove so diligently to subjugate this country.

The Penal Laws that Edmund Burke, statesman and essayist in the late eighteenth century, described as a 'wise and elaborate contrivance to oppress Irish Catholics', were crude — and in the long run — ineffectual, especially when compared to the 'modern machine' the apostles of the permissive society employ to spread their gospel of liberation and permissiveness: a gospel which in my youth bore another name — license.

Like their predecessors, these prophets of 'modernity' also use that shop-worn label, 'priest-ridden natives' as a propaganda and psychological weapon. I have had the good luck to spend a fairly long life in Ireland and other parts of the English-speaking world and am satisfied that here in Ireland, our priests do their appointed job to the best of their individual ability and diligently try to lead and guide us in matters connected with faith and morals; but in other matters — including politics — they act or react as the average lay citizen does. In fact, any priest in Ireland who would try to use the altar as a political platform or podium, would find himself preaching to an empty church — if his bishop had not already 'had a word with him on the side'.

The charge of 'political meddling' levelled by English politicians against our clergy and the attitudes of the Irish laity to their priests could be based on the behaviour of both the invaders and the invaded in the bloody period between the middle of the twelfth and the beginning of the nineteenth centuries. In the *Irish Ecclesiastical Record* dated October 1866 I read:

And when the penal laws took the place of the trooper's sword and torture, when that system was adopted, which Edmund Burke has designated "a machine of wise and elaborate contrivance, and as well fitted for the oppression, impoverishment, and degradation of a people, and the debasement in them of human nature, as ever proceeded from the perverted ingenuity of man" the priest was the one who, above all, was aimed at. Others suffered for his sake and he for theirs, and both for what was dearer to them than life. The priest was true to the people, and the people were true to the priest. Even when death stared them in the face, they were ready to receive and protect him.

Thus the Irish priest earned the title 'Sagart Aroon'. Sagart Aroon in English, is usually translated 'Dear Priest', but Aroon in Gaelic has a more intimate, endearing, loving connotation — somewhat like 'beloved pastor.'

Our Sagart Aroon is the Very Reverend Michael MacManus, but except on the odd formal occasion, we call him Father Mac — even to his face. In fact, that intimate abbreviation suits him so admirably that sometimes it requires mental effort to recall his full name. Our twin parishes of Multyfarnham and Leney are fortunate to have had Father Mac as our parish priest (commonly abbreviated to P.P.) since 1953.

I was about to say, 'When Father Mac is being discussed' but thought it better first to explain what we mean when we say 'being discussed'. No one will argue when I come out flatly and say that we are a nation of talkers. Ever since the universal advent of radio and television we talk and talk interminably. I suppose that is why some of my countrymen are credited with being good story-tellers.

If you listen to a crowd of us Irish engaged in conversation, you will be struck — assailed is a more apt expression — by the intensity of the participants. Participants is not precisely the word I was groping for; a person could participate — I suppose — in a talk-fest, just by listening and keeping his mouth shut; but when a group of us get together, the 'conversation', like a football or a hurley ball in a furiously fought game, is kicked around, often driven sky-high and never stays within bounds in a game that is without rules or discipline.

I notice that in novels, on stage or screen, each person — in correct order or sequence — says his piece. In Ireland, no one person ever gets a chance to 'hold forth' and monopolize the conversation. If a particularly forceful talker 'has the floor' someone else invariably is trying to get a word in edgewise and that 'someone' sooner or later will edge into the game. This obsession to be heard, may account for the fact that a protagonist often finds it expedient to 'come out' with something more interesting, or better again, more startling, in order to capture and retain his share of the audience. In fact, it is not unknown for people to disclose (hitherto) confidential, or even dangerous information, as a stake to stay in the game and get a chance to say their piece.

To get back to 'being discussed'. This usually means that the individual under discussion is being viewed under a collective microscope. We would not, for instance, say we were discussing the Queen, or Princess Grace of Monaco, or some other world-famous figure and the reason is that we don't know them intimately. But we do use that term for someone we know 'the breed, seed and generation' of because in the rural area there are few well-kept secrets. In reality, in rural Ireland there are hardly any secrets at all, because it's considered appropriate and quite normal for people to take an 'undying interest in the neighbours', and this includes leaving no stone unturned in order to know the other fellow's private business, intimately.

The highest encomium I can give Father Mac is that when he is 'under discussion' the concensus is that he is 'the heart of the roll'; and when his sacred calling and priestly functions are being discussed and dissected, special emphasis is placed on his record of never missing a 'sick call' in his twenty-five years of ministering to our twin parishes' spiritual needs.

How shall I explain to 'non-believers' what a 'sick call' is? The ideal Catholic — if there ever was such a one — at all times is ready to meet his Maker. This means that he is free from mortal sin, or to put it another way, 'in a state of grace'.

I could say that we Irish are high on the list of races that 'puts things off', and undoubtedly this includes putting off 'making our peace with God', which is our way of saying, 'receiving the Sacrament of Penance or going to Confession'. The latter entails confessing mortal (as a minimum) sins to a priest; having the necessary sorrow or regret for committing them; having the 'firm resolution of sinning no more', and obtaining absolution from the priest. Universally we believe that if one dies with an unrepented sin on his soul he will go to hell for all eternity.

Even if one is in the prime of life and 'healthy as a trout', it's considered a serious matter to be anything less than in a state of grace. Just had a peculiar thought: most men fear death, but I wonder are Christians doubly fearful of dying? I won't try to answer but from personal experience would say that a 'believer' feels that he is playing something akin to Russian Roulette if he has not 'a clean slate' at all times. Nevertheless, most of us gamble on the old death bed repentance and at the back of our minds feel reasonably sure we can fall back on the 'sick call'.

The sick call is the S.O.S. sent out when a Catholic is considered to be mortally ill, or at death's door. The priest 'getting the sick call' invariably makes haste to get to the person who is *in extremis* in order to administer the 'last rites'. The last rites mean that if the person is still conscious, the attending priest hears his confession, gives him absolution and annoints him. This is followed by the priest giving him Holy Communion, which in this case is fittingly called Holy Viaticum — meaning food for a journey — the lonely journey into eternity. If the patient is unconscious, I believe there is a provision for 'conditional absolution', but it's so long since we learned our Catechism (by heart) at school, that I'm a bit rusty on details.

Here in Ireland where, for instance, road-traffic deaths are becoming commonplace it is very seldom that anyone 'dies without the priest'. If a priest is not available and the patient appears in imminent danger of dying, a lay person usually tries to get the dying person to repeat after him the well-known prayer, 'An Act of Contrition'. Then if the patient is still unable to communicate, the ministering person will whisper that little prayer into his ear.

Speaking of gambling with one's immortal soul! Here in Multy we are doubly fortunate on that score; a gambler would say that the odds of anyone dying without the priest are considerably shortened, because we have the Friars and there are several of them; also they have two phones and always have a car available to answer sick calls; and as a parishioner said, 'Don't they always work hand in glove with Father Mac!' I can also add, 'What priest has a more perfect record than Father Mac himself who never missed a sick call'.

I was living in Canada when Father MacManus was appointed parish priest of my home (twin) parishes, and on my annual trips back to Ireland I became acquainted with him. It would be a loose expression to say 'I became familiar with

Father Mac because I have a feeling that very few people could honestly claim real 'closeness' to him. But then, one of the attributes of a successful parish priest could be the ability of not 'making fish of one and flesh of another'. Our rural community is composed of nebulous layers of social strata which we call class distinction, but I doubt if anyone — especially an outsider — could discern a distinct or tangible demarcation between many of the classes. But it's there, and as one of his lady parishioners elegantly said, 'Father MacManus' ability to transcend the boundaries of class and creed, is nothing short of miraculous'.

When we came back here in 1960 with our six children, Father Mac proved a tower of strength when we developed schooling problems. Subconsciously, I must have had a mental picture of our P.P. when I used that metaphor, because in more than one of the many 'write-ups' covering his football career, Michael MacManus has been aptly described as a 'towering figure' and Father Mac's physical shadow has not grown smaller with the passing years.

In 1960, anyone in the vicinity of the village who got up early enough was bound to see Father Mac exercising his two racing greyhounds. These graceful animals were near and dear to his pastoral heart. In fact the only time I saw the good priest 'feeling drim and drew' (down in the dumps) was when I paid him a visit that coincided with the 'putting down' of one of his champion greyhounds that was incurably ill.

Early one morning I met him walking briskly with his two dogs on a leash, and without mincing words he made it clear that if I wished to converse, I would have to walk with him 'jig for jolt', because any man knowledgeable about dogs will explain to you that to train a racing greyhound, there is no substitute for road work. Road work means that a dog has to have a walk of at least ten miles a day — every day. The walking must be continuous and no rests for 'goster' (Irish: idle talk), and definitely no halt at any of the pubs that seem to proliferate in our fair country.

It would do your heart good to see that huge, strapping priest — no longer young in years — striding along the quiet country roads and he looking so healthy you could, as they say, 'Bleed his cheeks with a straw'. When I used to see him religiously exercising the dogs, I would remark to my wife, 'The road work may be good for the dogs, but it surely is good for Father Mac now. Anyone seeing him for the first time would have no trouble believing the stories of his football prowess in the twenties.' I'll come back to Father Mac's football fame when I'm finished with greyhounds.

Now to try and explain what greyhound racing is, and the important part it plays in our Irish life-style. Ireland has an age-old legacy of dog racing. In fact, for a couple of hundred years, 'coursing' here has been as popular a pastime as horse racing. Coursing is the name given to the so-called 'sport' of a brace of greyhounds chasing a wild hare. Originally the chase — called open coursing — took place in the open country, where the wild hare in its natural habitat took a fifty-fifty chance of being mangled by the speedy greyhounds' fangs. Incidentally, greyhounds have been clocked at 45 m.p.h. In the open — especially on ground familiar to the pursued hare — it usually manages to escape its much speedier pursuer by 'turning'. With one dog, the hare travelling at full speed chooses the split second when the dog's fangs are clamping on it to execute a series of sharp, erratic 'turns' which temporarily, at least, throws the dog 'out on the turn' and frustrates it. With a brace of dogs pursuing it, the hare's 'turning' is further restricted, because in evading one dog, the hapless animal could turn right into the second dog's snapping jaws. In coursing, it's not unusual for a hare to feint a turn, or a double turn, and cause the greyhounds to collide with each other and in the ensuing confusion, escape.

Another kind of coursing is held in 'park enclosures' using hares that are already trained to run up an open field towards an escape through which the pursuing dogs cannot follow. 'Park coursing' has largely superceded the 'open coursing'.

When the first mechanical hares were put into operation here, it was natural that the Irish greyhound, so expert at chasing live hares, should take to track racing 'like a duck to water'. Now there are over twenty licenced greyhound-racing tracks operating in Ireland, while the breeding of greyhounds for track racing has become one of our major industries with the world's largest greyhound sales being held annually in Dublin. It is acknowledged that Irish greyhounds are supreme in dog racing.

In 1960, I happened to read in *Newsweek* about a recent report 'carried back' to the Papacy by one of its agents who, apparently, had made a 'flying tour' of Ireland. The gist of the agent's report was: 'I had noted certain irregularities among the Irish clergy.' Reading the full account, I remarked 'Mind you! there *is* an historical precedent for this report — but that was a hell of a long time ago — 1166 or thereabouts, when another Roman 'visitor' reported back to the Papacy that the Irish clerics 'were living it up' or whatever the then current expression was.' Now the 1960 watchdog 'sniffed out' that priests were observed 'putting up' for weekends at the better-class hotels: the odd one was even detected in the bars (pubs). Many were observed attending race meetings with a goodly percentage openly 'taking a flutter' on the horses. Many others were noted publicly attending some of the government-licenced greyhound tracks. The worst was to come. It was common knowledge that numbers of priests owned registered track-racing greyhounds.

Rome took strong and immediate action. Church authorities issued an edict, which amongst other provisos, sternly forbade Irish priests to own racing greyhounds. Once the Church ban became operative — as was to be expected — the number of cleric-owned registered dogs dropped to zero. But peculiarly enough, the overall number of racing greyhounds did not appreciably diminish.

To get back briefly to the historical precedent. The 1166 'report' provided Henry 11, the English King, with the 'longed-for excuse to occupy Ireland in the cause of ecclesiastical reform'. So in October 1171 Henry, with 'a considerable army' started the occupation of Ireland — a bloody occupation of this entire island that persisted until 1921, ending with the signing of the Anglo-Irish Treaty. Then the British Army of Occupation moved out. But they only vacated twenty-six of our thirty-two counties. Two thirds of the inhabitants of those Six Counties call themselves British and steadfastly maintain that the north-east corner of Ireland is part of Britain.

For over 150 years, Gaelic football has been the most popular field game in Ireland. The Gaelic Athletic Association — commonly called the G.A.A. — has a playing membership of one hundred thousand, while the game itself boasts spectator participation of one third of our population. Recently, Father Michael MacManus was honoured by selection for the Meath G.A.A. Hall of Fame Award.

Gaelic football is something like soccer, except that any of the players, fifteen men to a side, when playing, are permitted to handle the ball. A player may catch the ball, but is required to kick or handpass it to another player almost immediately. By far, the most spectacular characteristic of the game is the high catching of the ball. Young Michael MacManus — Mick Mac to his idolatrous football fans — excelled at the 'high catch'; in fact, he was credited with saying, in a moment of euphoria, 'In my prime, going for a high ball, no man ever bested me.' If he did actually say it, it was no idle boast or exaggeration. In my teens I watched him play a match that was an unforgettable occasion for me, and he surely must have been in his prime at the time, because the tall, athletic, powerful young man dominated the entire game. The goalie from either team would 'loft the ball' right out to mid-field; several players would cluster in the area where the ball was about to descend, and as the ball dropped, the mass of athletes, like ballet dancers, would surge skyward, but invariably and inevitably young MacManus would outjump the pack, secure the hard-fought-for ball and unerringly pass it to one of his forwards deep in enemy territory.

Recently, when Father Mac's Hall of Fame Award was written up in the press, the specific items that I found most illuminating were: he was ordained in the Irish College in Paris in 1927; in the following year playing for County Meath in the Leinster Championship against County Kildare 'he turned in one of the finest-ever individual displays'; and this following quotation from the Westmeath Examiner (27 November 1976) gives a fair picture how conservative, straight-laced, 'rank conscious' etc. the Church in Ireland was, less than fifty years ago. It goes:

Strangely the name of MacManus never appeared in reports of those games, as in those days priests playing field games, especially at intercounty level, was something of a rarity and although he was listed under different noms de plume, everyone knew that the brilliant midfielder was indeed Father Mac. However, the Church Authorities eventually 'caught up' with him and after serving up another superb display in the defeat of Dublin in the 1930 Championship he was forced to bow out of the playing scene.

That ruling on priests playing football — amateur football at that — contrasts drastically with today's accepted public image of our clergy, where no one is 'scandalized' when some 'priests in good standing' in the Dublin Diocese — for example — are engaged in extra parochial activities: writing plays for the Abbey, books, poetry; painting; appearing in cabaret shows, guest singing in pubs and on dance hall stages, and so forth.

In 1977, I was part of a crowd of his parishioners that packed the Old School of Multy to celebrate Father Mac's Golden Jubilee — his fifty years of priesthood. The parish spokesman presenting the two major gifts from appreciative parishioners, could have — but did not — mention that the timepiece he was presenting could *not* in Father Mac's case, be connected with the well-known 'gold watch syndrome', because our pastor was still 'in harness' and undoubtedly had more mileage in him than even the second gift — a brand new car. The thought crossed my mind: how appropriate! Both watch and car are some of his 'tools of the trade' — the parish pastor's trade — as it were. And, doesn't the word 'pastor' conjure up a picture of the Biblical shepherd, one who has care of flocks and herds?

15. THE POSTMISTRESS

Here we are in the middle of June 1979; yesterday we voted in both the local and the European Parliament elections. A stranger would never suspect we are suffering from the world-wide fuel crisis or that the country has been paralyzed for the past four months by a postal strike. Down here in the country and in most of the Midland towns, life is being lived to the full. Personally, I'm amazed and relieved to find that the postal strike plus a work-to-rule campaign by the telephone employees have not appreciably, or even noticeably, upset our way of life. I've been a mail-watcher all my life. Now I find that after four months of postal strike — and that includes wire service — I am almost used to it and actually have more time for myself.

We are not cut off completely from our brood in Canada. We can't phone them, but *in emergencies* they manage to contact us. This brings me to something else. At school — in my day — we were constantly reminded, 'As the twig is bent so will grow the tree'.

In the field of child-rearing my own bit of twig bending hasn't been anything to write home about. I always did my level best to maintain correspondence with my mother and kept it up faithfully with an elder sister after my mother died. But my example did not rub off on my own children. In fact my eldest son Mike hasn't written us a line in years — not even a Christmas card. He suffers no pangs of conscience on that score. Once, looking squarely into his deep-set grey/green eyes I asked 'Mike, why didn't you write?' He looked distressed and bewildered as if I had asked him to do something completely foreign to his nature and totally beyond his capability. He was shocked because it appeared to him that after all our years of closeness and mutual love I failed to fully understand him. He answered 'Dad! *you* know I never write'. Unlike me, his mother understood. Later when I was grousing and giving out about filial obligations she gently reminded me 'Don't forget the times Mike spent up to fifty dollars on a single long-distance phone call to us.'

We had such a call this past Christmas. The phone rang and as naturally as if he and I had never been separated both by time and distance Mike quietly said 'Hello Dad'. Then followed a mutually fulfilling exchange of thoughts and feelings. Half an hour later I called his mother to the phone and left them to *their* privacy. After what seemed to be a terribly long time she joined me and I silently noted that she had unshed tears in her eyes — are there tears of happiness? She said, 'Mike asked me to tell you that he loves us both.'

I fully understand why Mike delivered that all important and poignant message secondhand. He had no hesitation in telling his mother he loved her, but it did not come easy to him to say the same thing to me. You see, my father and *his* father before him, held some unusual views on what they considered to be manly behaviour. He hammered into us injunctions such as, 'A man's strength is his beauty' and he included strength of character in that homily. He gave us to believe that sentiment — at least a public show of it — is unmanly. His credo was, 'Men don't cry — outwardly.'

We have an Irish saying 'Blood is thicker than water'. Mike's uncle — my brother Simon — hardly ever wrote to *his* parents. My mother used to say to me, 'It would wring blood from a stone if you read some of the heart-scalding letters I wrote to your brother Simon and no answer.'

During the First World War, Simon joined up when he was sixteen. He chose the Connaught Rangers, a famous fighting regiment, and spent his seventeenth birthday in the front line trenches. When it came to writing home he was tarred with the same brush as my Mike. In the army he rarely even used the handy pro-forma type of letter cards dreamt up in the interest of censorship. They were the postcards that permitted only limited information and were so designed that the sender had only to cross out unwanted words. The sender's home address was the only handwriting required.

Regardless of Simon neglecting to write, the rest of us felt sure he was mother's favourite. She was not the kind of person who passed the buck by praying for quick and easy results and sitting back with 'Let God do it'. No! she was a woman of action. As she put it, 'I took up my pen and wrote a stiff letter to Simon's Commanding Officer.' The Commanding Officer was in turn a man of action. The Company happened to be back at

base for a well deserved rest when the C.O. got my mother's
letter. He ordered a general parade and when it was assembled,
roared, 'Lance Corporal Nevin stand forth.' Our young warrior
— with visions of a medal — stepped out smartly, took his stand
in front of the C.O. and saluted. The Big Brass bellowed 'Why
the hell don't you write to your mother?' Even this
confrontation failed to produce more letters home.

Forty years after the war, brother Simon visited us in Canada
and when we all sat around and he and I talked of Ireland and
our family life there, he — like a true son of Erin — painted such
a glowing picture of life in Ireland that if there had been a plane
handy we'd all have climbed aboard. Then I capped it all by
digging out an old family album and showing Simon a faded
photo of my mother in a wasp-waisted crinoline dress with
three of her children at her side — Simon was one of the three;
his blue eyes clouded over, filled with tears and in a choked
voice he muttered 'Me poor old mother'.

Even in these modern times when most of us question long
established beliefs, we still steadfastly swear by the seal of
Confession. But a couple of generations ago few people had the
same confidence in the security or secrecy of the local postal
service. In those days there were many loopholes in the safe and
sound delivery of letters — not to mention the danger of them
being opened and read in transit. To save a long walk, a rural
postman would think nothing of holding back a letter until he'd
meet the addressee at Mass — or worse again — he'd hand the
letter to a third party with, 'If you meet someone in this fellow's
area will you ask him to deliver this letter — it doesn't look too
important anyway.' Then again, the gum in general use at the
time coupled with our damp climate meant that envelopes were
poorly sealed. I suspect that's how sealing wax and signet rings
came into being.

I remember my parents holding serious discussions as to
whether a particular letter should be trusted to the village
mailbox or posted at a location where letters did not pass
through our local post office. There were other times when they
deliberated if in the interest of security the envelopes of certain
letters should be gummed or sealed. When the latter was
indicated I savoured the smell of the burning wax and loved
watching my father use his signet ring to stamp it. Our villagers
strongly suspected that certain letters were read *en route*; but

like the weather they felt they couldn't do anything about it.
Nevertheless I never heard of any legal prosecution for opening
mail illegally.

As far as our family was concerned we were all on the best of
terms with the local postmistress, Katie. Actually my mother and
Katie were close lifelong friends and the latter took a special
proprietory interest in me on account of being my Godmother
— here we say 'she stood for me'. Katie was a frail almost
delicate spinster devoted to her postmistress job. She lived
alone except for her niece Veronica whom she reared, and her
main outside interest was her church work. As long as her
health held out she never missed the six o'clock morning Mass
at the Friary.

I mentioned already that an Irish village resembles a large
family. Members of families don't always get on with each
other, but they *do* take an interest in each other's business; an
interest that sometimes goes beyond the bounds of idle
curiosity. I'm not implying that any of them would go so far as
to open and read other people's mail, but the general opinion
was that some of the local mail that passed through Katie's post
office was being tampered with. I still have a soft spot in my
heart for my Godmother who passed away peacefully fifty years
ago and I'd give anything to settle the vexed question; did she,
or did she not, steam open and read private correspondence?

There was no absolute proof that she did — but I'm sure you
know how hard it is to hoodwink the neighbours in an Irish
village. The nearest I ever came to verifying the rumour was a
story 'carried' by another God-fearing lady. The 'carrier' went
by the name Anastasia and worked as a part-time maid for
Katie. It was common knowledge that Anastasia herself had
more than her fair share of curiosity and openly resented the
strict house rule that never *under any circumstances* could she go
into Katie's bedroom.

The odd time that Katie was 'laid up', her niece 'attended' to
both the post office and the sick room. I vaguely remember
when I was around eleven, visiting my Godmother when she
was 'slightly indisposed'. I recall the bedroom being cosy and
warm. She had a nice coal fire going in the small fireplace and I
was fascinated at the variety and richness of the holy objects in
the room: religious pictures of all kinds, holy water font,
crucifix, a statue of Saint Anthony and red votive light burning

at the feet of a statue of the Mother of God — a statue big
enough for a small chapel. Katie made me a cup of tea while I
was there and boiled the water in a lovely little shiny tin kettle,
so different from the black utensil in our kitchen. She boiled it
over a small methylated spirit stove that reminded me of one in
Dr. Daly's dispensary.

Anastasia's tale told in 'strictest confidence' was to the effect
that when the postmistress was ill it was Veronica's job to sort
the mail and hand it over to the postman to deliver, but that
invariably, the niece kept back a certain number of letters which
she then carried in a cardboard box to Katie's bedroom.
Anastasia claimed that on one occasion she caught a glimpse of
Katie's table 'with all the paraphernalia for steaming open
letters on it'. This included the spirit stove, the kettle, a stick of
sealing wax and a bottle of gum. For additional evidence she
elaborated on the smell of burning sealing wax. Then she made
a big thing out of the niece 'ducking into the aunt's bedroom
with a bottle of sticking gum under her apron'.

I remember the last time Anastasia visited our house. She left
in a hurry. Of course my mother knew most of the gossip — as
she called it — about Katie and other peoples' letters, but she
never believed it and what's more didn't *want* to believe it.
When my mother overheard Anastasia repeating the gossip, she
threw at her 'Bearing false witness against your neighbour' and
in a cold accusing voice followed it with 'You have just
committed the grievous sin of detraction'. But Anastasia held
her ground as she was further grilled:

'Did you ever actually see her open other peoples' mail, read
it and reseal the envelope?'

'Good Lord! no, but I often smelled the hot sealing wax.'

'How did you find out all the other details I overheard a
minute ago?'

'Oh, I surmised the rest.'

'You surmised it did you! Well surmise youself out of my
house and *never* darken my door again as long as you live.'

Around that time there was an incident that sorely perplexed
the few people involved. Two individuals the same day and on
the same postman's route, each received a letter; but the
postmark on each envelope did not tally with the sender's
address at the top of the letter inside it. The contents of the
separate letters made no sense to the persons who received

them and to complicate it further, at first neither party knew of the other's dilemma. I'm afraid — even after all those years — I can't safely give you any more information as there is still 'bad blood' over the mix-up.

Many a time even when Katie was still in the land of the living — and the odd time since — I silently listened to the subject being threshed out without winnowing any provable evidence. Katie took her secret — and possibly many of her neighbours' secrets — with her to the grave.

16. GRANNY'S DEATH

I know it's ridiculous to generalize about the characteristics of an entire people and for instance, make a sweeping statement such as, the Irish are a fighting race, but if an outsider were to judge our attitude to death — and to life — by observing how we behave at funerals he might conclude that we are a morbid, death-loving people.

My wife, returning from a local funeral remarked, 'Met our friend Bill in the graveyard. I have a feeling he actually enjoys going to funerals.' He does. Maybe it goes back to the not-so-far-off days when our people lived in abject poverty and all that kept them going was the firm belief in a better life the other side of the grave. Bill, like most of us here, feels a strong social obligation to attend all funerals of his family, and to him family includes all those related by blood ties or by marriage.

When people discuss the Church's switch-over from Latin, I always recall Bill's reaction at a funeral when just as they put the last sod on the grave, he was overheard to remark, 'This wasn't like a real funeral at all; it didn't sound right to me and if Father Mac himself wasn't doing the funeral service I'd swear I was attending a Protestant burial!'

Speaking of death, I know that no one wants to think of dying let alone speak of it, but the more I mix with people here in Ireland the more I realize that they accept death and dying as naturally as they accept other less grim realities. For instance, my generation — and undoubtedly previous ones — had it drilled into them that the capital letter M formed by the lines or marks on the palm of your hand spell out in Latin the words Memento Mori — remember death! Without bible-thumping or harping on religion I would venture to say that most of us in Ireland have a firm belief in the 'hereafter'; witness the striking figures from a recent survey that found ninety-six per cent of Southern Ireland's population goes to weekly Mass. Incidentally that incredible percentage may reflect our social awareness more than it does our sanctity; because in our tightly

knit society every one is painfully sensitive of our public image
— meaning 'what will the neighbours say!'

Down the ages the ritual, rites, rubrics, ceremonies etc.
connected with the outward observances and practices of the
Catholic Church have been the subject and vehicle of artists,
painters, sculptors, poets, composers, writers and playwrights
and in more recent times portrayal of church ceremonies has
provided colourful, touching and often poignant background,
plots and settings for movies. I sincerely hope that someone,
someday, will make a movie — a sensitive, factual movie —
built around that *so final* one of the Church's Seven Sacraments,
the Sacrament of Extreme Unction. It has other names: The Last
Anointing, The Sacrament of the Dying. It's modern (palliative)
title is Sacrament of the Sick.

What a subject for a movie! It has all the pathos and meaning
of life itself. The circumstances connected with the Last
Anointing contain the material, the essence of reality, of life and
death, including, to believers, eternal life — life beyond the
grave.

Normally Extreme Unction is administered after the mortally
ill person has confessed his sins and received absolution. The
priest performing the rite uses chrism, which my Catechism
says is olive oil blessed by a bishop on Holy Thursday. The
priest dips his fingers into the chrism and with it anoints the
organs of the five senses, pronouncing at each anointing 'By this
Holy Unction and by His most tender mercy may the Lord
forgive thee whatsoever sins thou hast committed by sight' (and
he touches the eyes), 'by hearing' (and he touches the ears), and
so on. When the priest gives Holy Communion to the dying
person it bears the significant name, Holy Viaticum, meaning
food for a journey — a one-way journey!

I had about reached the age of reason when I became part of a
drama enacted at our house while the family was busily making
preparations to have my grandmother anointed. Normally an
anointing is sudden and unexpected; other times the 'Last
Anointing' is administered once to people with 'a mortal
sickness' or what's now called 'terminal illness'. When there is
adequate time before the priest answers the sick call to
administer The Last Rites, the women of the house do their
utmost to make the place spotless. The sick room receives
special attention and a small table is always placed close to the

'sick bed', is covered with a snow-white linen tablecloth and usually has a crucifix, a holy water font and two blessed candles already lit. Preparations are always of the highest order because we believe and accept the Real Presence — meaning that it is Jesus Christ Himself under the appearance of a wafer of bread, that the priest carries in the small silver box called the pix.

Our family has no photo or likeness of my grandmother. Personally I don't need them because I remember her as well as if it were only yesterday she was with us. She was tall and carried herself straight as a ramrod. A lady with a pale face and smooth skin, hair not completely grey and always well-brushed, and unusually white teeth. She gave credit for her unblemished skin to washing her face nightly in a mixture of warm buttermilk and oatmeal. She was justifiably proud of her teeth and was known to say, 'When I go I'll bring my own teeth with me thanks to cleaning them the old way — with soot out of the chimney mixed with salt and baking soda.' She was true to her word. They say she was a strong character who stood squarely up to life. She was never heard complaining — not even about her sixty years of marriage to my grandfather Hand, who they say took over forty years to drink and gamble away a business and a fortune that included grandmother's dowry of ten thousand pounds — a sizeable fortune in those days (*c.* 1847).

Grandmother never had to take to her bed. As far as I know she was not stricken with any particular disease or sickness but she was well into her eighties when she started failing and it was accepted by our doctor, the family and herself that she was dying a perfectly natural death from old age and was, as they say, gradually and gracefully slipping away. She spent her daylight hours, as she remarked, 'Thank God, in the bosom of my family', seated like a reigning queen in her big, comfortable armchair beside the kitchen fire. I use the word 'reigning' because she had all her mental faculties and to the end retained her accepted and respected position of being head of the house with the final say in all family discussions.

She was sitting bolt-upright in her chair and we were all there: counting my parents, my grandmother and my brothers and sisters there was a full dozen of us in the kitchen. We had just said the family rosary and because it was November, the month of the Holy Souls, the long rosary was longer than usual; especially the decade that grandmother Maria always 'gave out'.

We thought her contribution longest of all because she said her prayers in Irish; she claimed 'They were sure to be heard because God has a soft spot for the Irish'. I do not doubt that her lifelong prayers paid off when they were most needed; especially her unfailing communication with her Creator which was the Thirty Day's Prayer — the one for a happy death.

The kitchen was anything but quiet, the usual conversation, or free-for-all, was in progress with everyone talking at once. As well as I can recollect, grandmother was taking part in the general talk. I remember her saying to my mother 'Bridget, give me a long drink of that nice cool water Molly has just brought in from the pump.' She slowly drank the water, handed back the cup to my mother, carefully looked at the circle around the fire and in a clear, calm voice said 'Your weary watch will soon be over'. She then settled herself in her chair, took her beads from the folds of her lap, closed her eyes and from the movement of her lips was silently praying. A little later she said, 'It's getting dark, Tom (my father) please light the lamp.' Before anyone could thoughtlessly say 'But the lamp is lit', my father said to her 'Maria I'll light it.' Slowly Granny's head relaxed backward on the headrest of her chair. My father stood up, moved closer and gently closed her eyelids, while we all knelt down and said the accepted prayer.

Death with dignity! If I ever settle down to praying in earnest it will be for grace to meet death as naturally and serenely as my grandmother did.

PART THREE:
THE SUPERNATURAL

17. JERRY FLYNN

It is mid-April and we have the latest spring within living memory, a lot of rain, plenty of harsh winds, little sunshine and no growth. In normal years, everyone aims to have most of the potatoes 'in' by St. Patrick's Day (the seventeenth of March), at the latest. This year my gardening became more of a chore than a pastime, so we arranged for Thomas Anthony Nugent to 'do' the garden.

Tom is as 'tasty' a worker as there is around and already has made a brave start on our garden. Since he took over the garden Eileen and myself had got into the habit of sleeping in till nine a.m., by which time Tom always has an honest area expertly tilled. Then there was a gap and 'no Tom', but there was an understandable excuse for his absence because he had just celebrated his seventieth birthday by going on 'a tare' (binge). Eileen made enquiries around the village and I checked the pubs, but no word of 'our man', so she talked me into driving out to his house in Fulmorth to make sure that Tom was still in the land of the living. Although Fulmorth is only a couple of miles away, I had never been down the full length of the bohereen that goes past Tom's place. So we drove from the village and the end of our first mile took us to Multyfarnham Railway Station that was made famous, or infamous, by the Big Mail Robbery in 1976.

A few hundred yards past the Station stand the big impressive buildings of Wilson's Hospital. You meet Fulmorth bohereen before you reach the entrance gates at Wilson's, but I thought we would stop outside the main gate and I'd refresh my mind by rereading the plaque commemorating local participation in the Rebellion of 'Ninety, Eight'. The plaque set into one of the piers of what was once a typical demesne wall, was erected to the memory of the insurgent United Irishmen of Westmeath who assembled here in 1798 to assist General Humbert's Franco-Irish army. The marble plaque has an inscription in Irish followed by an English translation that reads:

They Rose in Dark and Evil Days
1798

Next we drove down the narrow, winding, well-maintained bohereen; past a dilapidated farmhouse and stopped at a wider part of the little road where it passes Finnegans. It would do your heart good to see the way they maintain their place. Then we met Marcella Finnegan who confided to Eileen that 'Your husband and myself were in the same Confirmation class'. She was ready and willing to direct us to Thomas Anthony's and I told her 'I'm trying to do a bit of writing and I'm dying to find out more about Jerry Flynn'. I didn't think it advisable to let on that I subscribed to the almost universal local belief that Jerry Flynn was 'a changeling'. My reluctance about even hinting that there could be a shred of truth in that fairy story was because the Finnegans have a reputation for being 'level-headed people' and I considered they would be the last in the world to believe in pisreógs, which is the Irish word we use for magic, spells, witchcraft etc. Besides, Marcella is, by Irish standards, highly-educated and well-read.

Imagine my surprise and relief when I found that she not only subscribes to the legend of Jerry Flynn but implicitly believes that Jerry was a changeling. She said, 'Step out of your car and I'll show you where Jerry Flynn's house stood.' Then walking a few yards with us she pointed to a briar and bush-covered area at the foot of Knockmorris Hill. 'But isn't that a fort?' I asked. 'Yes, it's a fairy fort and Flynn's house stood right in the middle of it; five generations that I know of, of Flynns lived in it.' When she said 'fairy fort' I queried 'Fairy! why fairy fort?' Almost pityingly and with a straight face she answered, 'Why not fairies? When I was a child we watched for hours the crowds of little fairies dressed in their red and green outfits, playing and dancing Irish reels in those big fields up there. Up there, where with your naked eye you can count that bunch of hares chasing each other.' Immediately it struck me, if she could count those little animals at that distance I'm not surprised that over a half century ago you were able to watch and follow the intricate steps of the fairy dancers. Just the same, I thought she was pulling my leg and cagily I asked. 'Has anyone ever seen the fairies within the past fifty years?' With conviction, regret, wistfulness and a vestige of disapproval she replied, 'How could anyone see them anymore; didn't the Prayers after Mass put a stop to all that!' That was a reference to the once lengthy church prayer that went: '. . . rest for all the wicked spirits that wander through the world seeking the ruination of souls.'

After we had said our good-byes to Miss Finnegan, Eileen and I got into the car, headed for Tom Nugent's and as we drove past the place where the Flynns once lived I resigned myself to just glancing at the fairy fort, because — as usual — I intended to visit it sometime in the future. After passing the fort we dallied to watch and admire the antics of the bunch of wild hares as they flashed in circles across the big, bare green fields that clothe the slopes of Knockmorris. Knockmorris, meaning Morris' Hill, rises steeply from a small bog which has an area of about twenty acres. The bog has a large pool or *lochán* (meaning little lake), which originally lapped the outer bank of the fairy fort; but that was ages ago, before succeeding drainage schemes lowered the old water level. Irish hares normally mate in the month of March and I suppose this gave rise to the saying 'mad as a March hare'; but because of the late Spring the mating antics of the wild hares had been postponed a month, it was now mid-April, and right before our eyes on a square mile of spring green stage the wild hares were performing their own primeval ballet.

Thomas Anthony's house is but a couple of yards past Flynn's place. Thomas Anthony himself said, 'I'm in fair fettle, but not quite up to gardening till next week.' He thanked us for calling in and gently though regretfully (I thought), refused offers of anything — including me driving back to Multy for a 'naggin' of whisky. It was no surprise at all to Tom when I told him I was on the trail of Jerry Flynn. He and I had previously talked about Jerry's strange powers so now he directed me to call in to see Mrs. Brady who lived half a mile further along the bohereen, because the Bradys had been near neighbours of the Flynns.

We continued along the bohereen and stopped in front of Mrs. Brady's. She immediately invited us in and offered us a cup of tea. For Ireland's sake I was proud of Mrs. Brady and her kitchen; it was comfortably furnished, spotlessly clean and snug with a 'lived in' appearance. I told her of my quest and she was so ready to co-operate that I suspected that our mutual friend Tom had already tipped her off. She spoke quite intelligently about Jerry Flynn for well over an hour but I found a vagueness

— but not a studied vagueness — when I tried to tie her down
on fairies and their ways. She did however give us quite a bit of
interesting background on the Flynns including stories and tales
that both Eileen and I found intriguing. Before she bid us adieu
with her 'May God be with ye' she told me how I could contact
surviving members of the Flynn family. Incidently, even a
trained reporter would find it hard going to run down a lead in
Ireland; he'd find himself up against something intangible,
tenuous and terribly frustrating. It's not reticence or
unwillingness on people's part; it could be shyness and a fear of
ridicule, but I suspect it's a refusal to bare their private, inner
feelings, and although they are my own people and they accept
me fully, yet in some vague way they always hint that there is a
much better informed source — a source that sticks to the gospel
truth. Sad to say, I have yet to corner this gospel-truth type!

As a result of plenty of legwork, including visits to Sean
Weir's pub and being 'sent from Billy to Jack' I collected an
intriguing jumble of tales, legends and lore about Jerry Flynn.
After a lot of cross-checking and running the bare facts to earth,
I'll try and give you a brief account of the story of Jerry Flynn —
as it is widely accepted here by a surprising number of normal,
intelligent people.

The Flynns, just ordinary labouring people, lived down the
bohereen a few hundred yards from where Mrs. Brady was
born. Up to fifty years ago there were three dozen houses strung
along the side of Fulmorth bohereen; today there is about one
fifth that number.

Around 1850 Mrs. Flynn gave birth to a baby and as was not
unusual in those days the midwife had a hard time delivering
the child, so the next day the Parish Priest was sent for 'to attend
the new mother'. When the priest arrived at the house he was
shown into the bedroom and as he went over to the mother in
the bed he's supposed to have said in a strangled voice, 'There's
something in this room that actively resents me;
something that's trying to drive me out of this room.' Then
pale and sweating the priest asked, 'What's that under the quilt
behind you?' The mother flung back the quilt and there was the
baby with a head that for all the world resembled one of those
giant puffballs you meet in the fields. The head was bigger than
any infant's you ever saw and its skin had a queer
semi-transparent unnatural grey-green hue; though it had the
face of a child, it had the features of an old, old man.

When the startled priest clapped his eyes on the child he stepped back with 'I can't attend you until someone removes it from this room.' Mrs. Flynn's husband carried the child out to the kitchen and put it in a cleeve beside the hearthstone. Cleeve is a basket or container for carrying turf and is handwoven from osiers and sallies. Then the hapless father spent two full days making a box that turned out to be a combined cradle, crib and pen; planked the *thing* down in it where it stayed day night for the rest of its life.

Word got around that there was something strange about Mrs. Flynn's new arrival. Old women knowledgeable of ways and ancient practices — practices the clergy were down on — warned the mother that the *thing* in the box at the fire was not the child she gave painful birth to; that the fairies had taken the human child and put one of their own kind in its place. The women advised there was only one certain cure and that was for the mother at the dark of the moon to take the changeling to the edge of the lochán and leave it (between the water and the foam) and if she did so, the next morning she could go to the edge of the lochán and her own child would be waiting for her. But the poor unfortunate mother must have been under a spell, because their advice fell on deaf ears and this in spite of the fact that everyone within the roar of an ass from the lochán was finding it hard to get a wink of sleep on account of the night-long heart-wrenching sound of an infant crying and sobbing its heart out on the cold shore of the lochán. That expression, between the water and the foam, came up again and again. It was used by several people but none of them could — or would — explain its significance. I know that in a storm on a lake the wind blows foam off the top of the waves and forms a foamy ridge on the strand a couple of feet from the water's edge.

Even in the confines of his crib — big and all as it was — Jerry never learnt to walk. The best he could manage was to drag himself from one side of the box to the other. Before he was past the infant stage, queer stories about his 'gifts' began to circulate. He surely had the gift of second sight. Although communications were poor in those days, never a day passed that people from over a hundred miles away didn't arrive at Flynns to get help from Jerry to find or recover items and farm animals lost, stolen or strayed. People still around today — intelligent, educated people — swear that Jerry, who had never been outside his parent's house in his life, was always able to give the exact location of the missing articles and supply details of their disappearance. It appears that Jerry loved to show off his strange powers. Maybe it would be better if I gave it in the exact words of a near neighbour of Flynns. Here it is: 'Never a visitor or stranger darkened their door but long beforehand me bould Jerry 'id have the family prepared. And hours ahead of the arrival, Jerry'd announce the time, the reason for the visit and supply such a clear description of the stranger that when you'd clap your eyes on that stranger for the first time you'd swear you'd already met him before.'

People still marvel at Jerry's gift for music. My friend Tom Nugent said, 'No matter what musical instrument — even a kind he never met before — you'd put into Jerry's pen, the minute he got his hands on it he'd knock music out of it. And the music! Not songs, reels or jigs but a strange kind of music with all the sounds of nature. Playing, he could bring out the exact sound of any animal, bird or insect; if you closed your eyes and listened while he played you could hear the wind blowing through a field of ripe oats and another time hear it bend and break trees.'

They tell how another one-time céilier at Flynn's never tired of telling about the crowds that congregated there every night, some to play cards and the rest to sit at the fire chatting, telling stories and 'drawing out' Jerry: and when Jerry's mother wasn't looking, some of the 'good' boys loved teasing and playing tricks on the 'yoke in the box'.

Jerry, caged in his box, could not possibly see the cards on the table over in the middle of the kitchen and he couldn't even get a peek at the hands of cards held by the players; but that didn't stop him if he were in the mood from taking a hand in the game because he knew every hand each player held. Jerry was not beyond shouting to a friend in the card game, 'Give a short prod with your ace of hearts, the joker is held by someone on the long side of you'. Better again, no matter how good a hand of cards you held if you once got on the wrong side of Jerry, you'd never win a trick if you didn't make up with him first: not if you played 'till Doomsday.

Then came the Sunday when the Flynns, walking home from Mass in Leney, saw smoke and flames in the distance, rushed up the bohereen and found their house such a blazing inferno that neither they nor the gathered neighbours could risk going in to save poor Jerry. Within minutes a crowd was standing helpless with the poor parents in a state of shock waiting for the fire to die down so that someone could find Jerry's ashes. The house had the usual thatched roof: an old roof, with successive coats of straw built up to a thickness of two feet. The entire roof — joists, rafters, crossties, rooftree and thick mass of dry thatch — were like tinder; worse still, the underside of the roof would be encrusted with layers of soot from a century of smoky turf fires. One second the entire blazing roof was in place; the next instant it fell in with a swoosh that expelled a shower of sparks like fancy fireworks.

The onlookers were silent but you could see people's lips moving and you knew they were silently saying their prayers and suddenly someone half way up Knockmorris gave a shout and came running towards the crowd roaring, 'Be God! but Jerry and his cot is up there in a sheltered part of the hedge safe and sound.' Four strong men carried Jerry down, cot and all, and at once everyone excitedly asked Jerry to tell what happened. His father, right there in front of the crowd of neighbours, said, 'Jerry me son, how did you and the box manage to get out of the house? You and I know that your box is a foot bigger every way than the widest part of our doorway; how did you get it out seeing there isn't a scratch or scrape on it?' With a straight face and for the first and last time that Jerry ever mentioned the matter he answered, 'I don't know, maybe the hate (heat) shrunk my box.'

As was to be expected, Jerry never grew very much; even in his prime he was no bigger than a boy of seven. He was around middle-age when he died and had the best attended wake in the district. Everybody was elbowing each other out of the way to get a good look at him when he was 'laid out'. All agreed that Jerry must have been 'Put back by the fairies because he made such a beautiful corpse; without a trace of a wrinkle or a line on his peaceful face'.

The morning after the wake, as is the custom, several friends of the family gathered at the house to bring the 'remains' to Leney Chapel. In the Chapel, the coffin would be mounted on the two black trestles in front of the Side Altar. Then the six big candles in their individual big black wooden candlesticks would be lit and stood around the coffin. Next, the Parish Priest would recite the Rosary, the mourners would give the responses and

Jerry Flynn in his plain, deal coffin would be left all alone in the empty church until the well-attended Funeral Mass was being said the following day. After that the cortege would walk slowly to the graveyard for the burial.

Leney Church is less than a mile from Flynn's and in those days a hearse was 'beyond the means' of poor people, so a kind neighbour offered to carry the coffin on his pony-drawn sidecar. The friends of the family coffined Jerry and carried him out of the house feet first, because we have a traditional belief that if a corpse is carried out head first there will surely be a second death in the family before the year is out.

They lifted the coffin on to the sidecar. The pony's owner gave the animal the signal to go, but for the first time in the pony's long life the normally obedient animal refused to budge a step. Everyone had helpful suggestions; one man even took off his coat and used it to blindfold the pony, but to no avail. Another suggested 'Take the pony out of the shaft and we'll pull the sidecar to the chapel ourselves'. Finally they took down the coffin, placed it on the ground and right away the fractious pony obeyed the slightest command. The pony was led a small distance from the house and the coffin put up on the sidecar but once again the pony refused to move one foot past the other. The same performance was repeated three times more — with the same result. Finally the oldest woman present had her say: 'It's plain to me that Jerry Flynn doesn't want to lave (leave) his home; you'll have to carry the poor sowl (soul) on ye're shoulders until you get past Flynn's little patch of land, then put him on the sidecar and he'll give you no further trouble.' She was right!

Here is a postscript to Jerry Flynn. In 1978 I presented my American friend Dr. Hannon to Marcella Finnegan and in the course of a conversation, 'drew her out' about seeing the fairies on Knockmorris. I was agreeably surprised when she reiterated her belief in 'the little people', but you could have knocked me down with a feather when after cocking a quizzical eyebrow at the Doctor I discovered that he shared Marcella's conviction that fairies really exist. I 'held my whist' as they say, but wished that he had fallen under the spell of my venerable friend John Brennan — the American would have learned more than 'a thing or two' about the hidden Ireland.

18. THE LEPRECHAUN

John Brennan was paying us his weekly visit and as usual we had everything in readiness to prolong his stay, because it is not every day you get the opportunity to exchange thoughts with a centenarian; especially one like John whose physical and mental faculties were on a par with someone half his age. Our children enjoyed John's company, particularly the times when, to my discomfiture, he related 'some of your father's kemares (antics) when he was a gossoon himself'.

John's memory bank was a repository for everything newsworthy that happened in our area, not only in his lifetime but in his parents' and grandparents' time. He was born less than twenty years after the Great Famine of 1845–47 which was a milestone and a tombstone in our island's sad history. Referring to the Famine, he said, 'Even if I tried my best to forget my parents' accounts of the Hard Times it would be impossible to forget one iota; because it must have been a terrible thing to see your own flesh and blood and your neighbours die from straight starvation and not be able to give them anything but a prayer.'

John was, as he said 'On the threshold of being able to say I've been around for one hundred years'. But in spite of that great age his conversation was completely lucid and his memory excellent. He glowed when our children coaxed him to sing one of his favourite ballads — ballads of interminable length. I'm afraid I didn't share my children's enthusiasm for John's singing. The content of the ballads interested me, but the 'rendering' of them as John called it, was hard on the ears. You see, I have it on good authority that at no time of his life did John Brennan have a singing voice, and I assure you, unlike a Stradivarius, John's musical tone did not improve with age.

For his era and background he was tolerably well educated; locally they said, 'John Brennan is no country ignoramus'. Actually he was, as he said, 'a finished product of the hedge schools'. Hedge schools were part of the Irish educational

175

answer to the Penal Laws which for centuries prohibited
Catholic education in Ireland. The schools were called hedge
schools because the master for safety's sake was obliged to
assemble and teach his pupils in the seclusion of the hedges,
forests, caves and other hiding places. The hedge school
curriculum was quite extensive, based on the three R's, and
usually included geography, history, book-keeping, mathema-
tics and surveying. Invariably the hedge teachers were scholars
of a high standard and devoted to the classics. It is recorded
that they turned out fluent speakers of Latin. I thought that
claim of producing Latin scholars was a bit far-fetched until I
remembered John Brennan's ability 'to spout Latin'. In John's
case he had, as it were, a post-graduate course in Latin due to
his lifetime association with the Friars and his daily participation
in their religious ceremonies, including serving Mass,
Benediction and so forth. In those days Latin was the language
of the Church.

John differed from the ordinary Irish story teller in that he
always stuck to the plain truth, but when he departed from
factual reporting, as it were, and told us stories of ghosts and
fairies I privately questioned his 'gospel truth'. Personally I
don't believe in ghosts, but because of the hair-raising ghost
stories I heard in my youth, there are places around here where
I'd hate to spend the night. John Brennan's belief in the
existence of fairies was shared by most of our people and as far
as I know, many of us cling to that long-held belief.

Irish tradition tries to explain the existence of fairies by saying
that they were some of the rebellious angels who were cast
down from heaven with Lucifer. They were the ones Michael
the Archangel pleaded with God to spare and stay His hand and
God stayed His hand; hence the angels who were already falling
to earth became the spirits of the air, while of those who landed
on earth some went to live in the Sidhe (fairy) mounds often
mentioned in early Irish literature, while others took up
residence in the fairy forts. The angels who fell into the water
continued to dwell in that element. John subscribed to the
commonly held belief that fairies looked somewhat like humans
and that they even participated in the same type of activities as
mankind. Fairies were believed to play human-type games and
on occasions even sought human assistance to win games and
contests. They held nightly revels; feasting, dancing, singing to
the music of their pipers and fiddlers.

Here is one instance of local lore. A couple of months ago my wife and I were gathering our winter supply of wild hazel nuts. She was admiring the abundant crop of wild blackberries in the hedges and remarked, 'They are very late, aren't they, but they look lovely and ripe.' I glanced at them and without giving it much thought said, 'You're a week late, you can't eat them now, Hallowe'en was last week and everyone knows that at Hallowe'en the Pooka touch the blackberries and no human safely eats them.' The Pooka were the fairies who played mischievous pranks and tricks on humans. I was surprised at the way the long-buried memory surfaced and she was amazed that I refused to even taste the apparently fresh, ripe blackberries.

When John got around to the subject of fairies I said, 'John when I was the same age as my youngest boy Kerry I heard you, around the fire in the old house down the street, tell about the time you spoke to the leprechaun.' John glowed. 'I'm proud you remembered me and the leprechaun; I well mind that May morning and me only fifteen years of age at the time. My family was early risers and were nearly always on foot when the Friary bell rang at six o'clock, day in and day out. My father sent me down to the field at the Bog Road to bring up our cow for milking. The road is only a hundred yards or so from our kitchen door and I started to trot down the smooth path in the bare ones. I left the path to run the rest of the way in the grassy field because there was heavy dew on the grass and when I ran my bare feet sent up spray that made little rainbows from the slanted rays of the rising sun. I must have had my head down watching my feet because before I knew where I was, I was almost at the gate and right forninst my two eyes was the neatest little man or gossoon you ever clapt eyes on and he perched as lightly as a bird on the top bar of our road gate. I was so taken aback you could knock me down with a feather. He was so small and dressed so well that I couldn't tell if he were a little boy or a full-grown dwarf. As well as I can remember his clothes were in a style of bygone days; I thought I'd seen pictures of old-time gentry dressed like him with his tall hat, his long green swallow-tailed coat, his tight knee britches, his stockings and his shoes with big, shiny silver buckles.

'I stood in my tracks with my mouth hanging open like a pike. I looked at the little fellow and he looked at me and I said, "Can I help you?" He answered me with a question, "Why?"

'Me: "Could you be astray, avic?"

'Lep: "How could I be lost or astray seeing I belong here?"

'Me: "I can't understand you atall, atall. I was born here, I know every bush and every blade of grass around the farm and I never clapt eyes on you in my whole life. And besides my father owns this place."

'Lep: "You said your people own this place. Don't you understand that a human can never *own* anything. No more than he owns time itself. Humans only have things and they have them on loan and even then only for a short time. Like the wild birds and the wild animals my people were here from the beginning of what your people call time; long before your race travelled over the wide waters and settled here. Before your people came, my people were here enjoying the freedom of the air, the fields and the forest and we never said we owned any of these things. Before your kind came and talked of *owning.* . . . "

'And he waved his little arms as if to take in the whole of creation.

'Me: "You didn't explain how come I never saw you before and why you put your come hither on me just now."

'Lep: "I didn't want you to see me although I sometimes watch you by the hour."

'Me: "Why?"

'Lep: "Because you are a bit like *us*, you love the birds and the beasts and on that account I feel close to you but I must go now. Good-bye and long, long life to you Johnny."

'At that split second my father up there at the house shouted for me and I spun around on my heel to answer him; I turned to our little visitor, but if the ground had opened and swallowed him he couldn't have disappeared any faster.

'I ran up to the house out of breath, told my father everything that had happened, except that I kept quiet over the little fellow calling me Johnny, because that was the private pet name my mother had for me. I was surprised that my father didn't doubt any bit of my story. He said "Johnny" — and it was the first time I ever noticed him calling me Johnny — "you're a Brennan alright; my grandfather that was your great grandfather was on speaking terms with a leprechaun." I could never make out why my father called me by my pet name because never before or after that did he use it.' John relit his pipe and continued: 'A few years after that, Father Dogget from the Friary was talking to me about several things and seeing that as well as being a priest of God he was an understanding and much travelled scholar and a barrister to boot I decided to tell him everything about me and the leprechaun. Father Dogget hardly breathed while I was telling it. Then he asked me an awful lot of questions and when I finished he spoke just three words, "I believe you". Then he muttered something to himself, something I couldn't make head or tail of — something about the pure of heart.'

I didn't tell John that the understanding Friar could have been referring to the Eighth Beatitude, which goes 'Blessed are the pure of heart, for they shall see God'. In fact, I believe John Brennan had the unique privilege of seeing and conversing with one of God's fallen — but spared — angels.

You will appreciate how much John Brennan's account of meeting and conversing with the leprechaun intrigued me and how I hungered for more detail. But eventually it dawned on me that John showed a marked reluctance to talk about his boyhood encounter. Actually he was a very private person and quite difficult to get real close to; besides I had no intention of prying into his 'rale sacrets' as he called them. My own boyhood was long behind me and John, like a game old thoroughbred was coming strongly towards the finishing line — the century mark — before he confided in me that he actually had a second encounter with the leprechaun.

We had been talking about birds in general and specifically about his goldfinches, that as John put it, 'As far back as I can remember we always kept a pair of goldfinches in a roomy cage in the brightest part of our kitchen. It'd take me an hour to count up the total number of 'finches we had, although some of them lived for over twenty years. As you can see from the pair in the big cage there in front of your eyes, the door of that cage is left open as often as it's shut.'

John was saying 'I still like to get up early in the morning but first I like to lie there and listen to the 'finches in the cage calling to the birds outside. They call and answer and join in the chorus of birds that always — rain or shine — welcome the coming of the new day. It's not everyone I'd tell this to but when the birds are at it they are surely giving glory to God and every morning of my life I join in with them in my own humble way in a silent prayer to my Maker.' Then almost sharply he challenged 'Do you listen to the birds?'. Without waiting for my hesitant answer he went on 'Avic! years ago you asked me if I ever saw the leprechaun again and I always avoided answering. Yes I saw him once more and that was the day after I was Confirmed, just before my fifteenth birthday.

'That second and last time I saw him, there he was perched for all the world like a bird on the thick arm of an oak tree and within a hundred yards of the house. I wouldn't have seen him at all except I already noticed something mighty strange about the variety of bird calls all coming from that same big oak tree. Ever since I was in petticoats I prided myself on being able to distinguish the notes of every single breed of bird in Ireland and they tell me that we have over 350 different species. So now what struck me as odd was that only one bird at a time was singing in the oak and then dozens of the same breed of bird would answer from everywhere within earshot.

'So I sneaked up close to the oak and there within twenty feet of me was my little friend straddling a thick branch and with eyes half closed playing the neatest little flute you ever saw. The second I clapt my eyes on the flute I knew the answer for the variety of calls coming from the oak. There on my hunkers I stayed stock still with my mouth hanging open — it could have been for half an hour — and my heart going out to the little fellow that was not only talking to the birds but had them answering back with their sweetest notes just as if they were up in front of God Himself and they showing off the miraculous gift He gave each and every one of them. In the middle of it all didn't the little leprechaun slip me a sly wink as if he were expecting me to admire his playing and to show me he well knew I was there all the time.

'Back there I asked you if you listen to the birds. I'll answer it for you — the leprechaun answered it for me when he finally put away his little flute and himself and me had a good long talk but I'll only tell you or my final Father Confessor one point the little fellow made very clear to me — a point that made a lasting impression on me. The leprechaun said that human beings don't really belong on this earth, he said they were latecomers and never fitted in. I asked him why and he answered that the animals, the birds, the insects and everything with life in it lived in harmony. But humans were different and foreign, they didn't even live for each other, each one only looked out for himself. They all had one thing in common, an obsession for possessions; each one putting all his energy into grabbing everything in sight and never saying "now I have enough".

'The leprechaun was sure that humans felt so threatened that they were even afraid of the open countryside. He remarked that they never stop "till they make stone houses, shut out the song of the birds, the other sounds of nature and the beauty of creation". Then added "And they never rest till they build more ugly clumps of houses they call towns".'

John went on 'By the time my little friend was finished I finally comprehended the wide gap between humans and the rest of God's creatures. The best way I can explain it to yourself is to confess that there were periods in my own life when my eyes and ears were closed to the songs of the birds and other sounds and sights and beauty of God's world. That was the last time the leprechaun and myself met face to face, but it was by no means the last time I heard his flute because back there under the oak tree I came up with the way to tell the difference of the notes of his flute and the real bird song. That's how all my life ever since I know for sure he is still around but unlike myself *he* didn't age a day.'

19. GHOSTS

If any of the children were within earshot John refused to tell ghost stories, so I asked him, 'Why are you so fussy now. When I was growing up, ghost stories were part and parcel of our cultural legacy and as well as I remember, no one hesitated to tell them with children around.' John answered, 'I myself never believed in telling yarns about ghosts to the childer. They will meet up with the ugly, dark things in life all too soon.' Even with adults, John, by making out to be a bit sententious and dogmatic, was unwilling to talk about ghosts, so I thought I'd get him going by declaring, 'Sure there's no such thing as ghosts. When I was growing up the old people would make your hair stand on end with stories of haunted houses and ghosts. But you never hear of anyone seeing any ghosts since electric light came about. Nothing like a good strong light to show things up. I think most, if not all, of the sightings were the result of poor lighting coupled with fear of the unknown and distorted by imagination.'

John rose to the bait. 'The electric light has nothing whatsoever to do with it, avic (my son). How about several people seeing *something* in the broad light of day?' I knew he was going to tell us about Johnny Blackhall, because it happened about the time I was born and many's the time I heard the peculiar story of the miller's ghost. John continued, 'I'll tell you what finally settled all the ghosts in Ireland; and you take a hand in it too every Sunday at Mass.' 'What do you mean John?' 'It's the Prayers After Mass that were written with that in mind. The part that goes: all the wicked spirits that wander through the world seeking the destruction of souls.' Triumphantly — 'That's what settled them me buchall (my boy)'.

John lowered his voice and we knew we were going to hear 'the plain, unvarnished truth'. 'Johnny Blackhall owned the mill that was within a hundred steps from the front door of the Friary. That mill had been in the Blackhall family for generations, but in his lifetime Johnny let it run down and about the middle of the past century the mill and it's machinery were demolished. Johnny Blackhall had a fine big farmhouse and close to a hundred acres of well-stocked land — land that his widow afterwards gave or left quite a bit of, to the Friary. Johnny often complained of having no children to leave the place to; but when the time came to leave it all behind him, he conveniently left his own flesh and blood out of the will.

'The Blackhalls were supposed to be the richest people around here and were classed as gentry. They always had a steady workman and never were without a servant or two. They hardly ever let the workman put his feet inside the door of the house but there were quarters for the servant girls. Sure, like all of their station, they never let a servant or hired man eat at the same table as them; but that was the way of things at the time.'

I thought John was rambling away from the ghost story, because even I remembered that the family name, Blackhall, had died out in our area. Johnny Blackhall and his wife were childless, and when her husband died Mrs. Blackhall never remarried. John Brennan put it very nicely with, 'But Mr. Blackhall had a love child and they say he gave the unfortunate servant girl the sack the minute her delicate condition was noticeable. There was quite a bit of bad feeling among the neighbours over it because the girl was young and innocent and came of respectable stock. But that was thirty years before Johnny Blackhall went to meet his Maker. And his body was hardly cooled off in the grave, when word got around that his widow couldn't get a night's sleep and that she changed a lifetime of habit and gave the servant boy (he was sixty years old) a room of his own in the house because she was afraid to be alone day or night. Soon the whole countryside was talking in whispers about Johnny Blackhall appearing not only at night, but in the full light of day.

'I could give you the names of at least four reliable persons that saw him. Twice he was seen — in the broad daylight — counting his cattle in the Currachs-marsh. That's the field on the south side of the bridge, just across the river from Martin Kenny's forge. To prove it wasn't imagination or too much drink taken, a complete stranger saw him and described him in such detail that if you had a slate and a piece of chalk you could draw a resemblance of Johnny Blackhall — right down to his walking stick and his swallow-tail coat.

'Of course Mrs. Blackhall went to the friars and to the parish priest and 'twas whispered that some of the priests even tried their hand at settling the wandering spirit, but that they weren't powerful enough.

'Then one of the friars who, they say, had a mighty unsuccessful tussle with the spirit, said to Mrs. Blackhall, "It's no use, we'll have to get Father — to tackle it, he was with Mr. Blackhall when he was dying and it was he that gave him the Rites of the Church. Father — is stationed in Rome, but I'll report the case to my superiors and I am sure they will do whatever they feel is necessary."

'Inside a fortnight Father — arrived at the Friary and you know how hard it is to keep anything that wasn't given under the seal of the Confessional from leaking out; it transpired that for three long nights and three long days, without any let-up, Father — with bell, book and candle did battle with something evil and he was put to the pin of his collar (equated with a horse hauling an overheavy load) but with the power that God gave him he managed to 'lay' the spirit.

'Father — was never quite himself afterwards. From being a strong, middle-aged, dark haired man, by the time he was finished with the miller's ghost his hair was white as the driven snow, the spring was gone out of his step and he had left his youth behind him.'

PART FOUR:
IN RETIREMENT

20. FINDING A HAVEN

I'll run like wildfire through that portion of my life previous to 1973, the year when we were so fortunate to acquire what my wife Eileen lovingly calls 'our little blue-grey home in the west'. My only reason for even touching on my life prior to 1973 is to enable you to grasp how people from another country and culture might cope if they came to live in Ireland.

Back in 1946 when Eileen and I got married we felt we 'wanted for nothing' because we had each other and had no financial worries as I had already served five pensionable years in the Royal Canadian Air Force. My Flight Lieutenant's pay was adequate for our needs and the Government provided us with excellent married quarters on their major Air Force Stations which had all the amenities for full, gracious — even luxurious — living. In 1960, after nineteen years of pensionable service in the R.C.A.F. I retired with the permanent rank of Squadron Leader. Six months prior to my becoming a civilian, my Canadian family, Eileen and the six children, sailed for Ireland, arrived at my native village, purchased a house and in a remarkably short time settled in. We call that *my* first retirement.

Somewhere else I mentioned how long it takes for outsiders — sometimes called 'blow ins' — to be accepted; but the villagers accepted my foreign-born wife and brood as readily as if they belonged in the parish: it must have something to do with what my friend John Brennan called 'continuity of the old stock'.

Without going into detail about those three full, worry-free years of our lives I will only mention how that short period in Ireland affected my Canadian-reared children. One of them — now an adult — recently remarked 'We didn't have to travel to Ireland to search for our roots, they were there alive and flourishing.' In those three years the children acquired a deep and lasting love for this land of their forefathers — a love few Canadians openly show for their country.

There was a 'bit of land' attached to the house we bought so

187

we decided like everyone else around to live off the land, and before long had our own miniature Irish farm and farmyard. I could give you a list as long as your arm of household pets — dogs, cats, birds, domestic fowl, commercial rabbits, pigs, pony, bullocks and cow — acquired by degrees. The ages of our family — three boys and three girls — ranged from five to fourteen and they took to the new life like ducks to water. Their mother and I could write a book on the way those three years of 'living the simple life' affected our children and in the fullness of time will surely affect their children. As if it were only yesterday they lived here, they can still tell you how to get to the best places around the village to pick fraocháns (blueberries), sloes, blackberries, hazlenuts, crab-apples, or mushrooms; they could direct you also to the many ideal places for picnics or hikes.

Now eighteen years later when either of us visit our children in Canada the talk always comes around to 'our years in Multy' and they vie with each other to recount their Irish adventures, exploits and escapades. I find it strange that they hardly ever speak about the periods when we all lived in various Canadian provinces including the Yukon and Northwest Territories. Instead they rhapsodize about the full life they lived in the village of Multy; as one of them said 'And without benefit of plastic toys or surfeit of T.V.' Their mother and I now appreciate that when they lived in the Irish countryside they required none of the mass-produced toys and other amusement aids or crutches designed to prevent or palliate boredom. This was because we were living on a part of this crowded, cluttered planet where grown-ups still cheerfully tolerate children and treat them as important individuals; also living in the country presents quite a challenge to city-reared children and even adults.

Our sojourn had an extraordinary influence on our eldest boy Kieran who was fourteen when he first came to the village. Up to then he was inclined to be withdrawn, shy and non-assertive although strong, athletic and by local standards big for his age. I remember him confiding to me 'I was never as happy as here; the days are never long enough and there is always something interesting to do; like working with you in the garden, rearing turf on the bog, playing with the other kids around, rowing the boat, riding the pony and especially milking the cow and looking after her heifer calf.' His mother attributed this rapport with Irish village way of life to the fact that up to that time we had moved immense distances every few years across Canada and our kids never had time to put down roots or make firm friendships. There is a lot of truth in that, but here in Ireland our children seemed to fit in almost overnight.

In 1963, for various reasons — none of them grave — we decided to sell out and return to Canada. One reason could have been that in the preceding twenty years we had become used to moving house every two or three years. So Canada — up near the Arctic circle — was our home for the next nine years, but we never lost sight of Ireland and things Irish. From then on one or more of us came back every year to the village on vacation. In 1972 Eileen and I in that order decided to come back to Ireland again and start our second retirement.

For years the whole family had lived with what they called Dad's dream of finishing his days in Ireland. Thus when the time came to make the big decision we held a family pow-wow and our three daughters decided to remain in Canada while the two boys, Michael and Kerry took the line of least resistance and muttered they would go along with us. The overall decision included a tacit understanding that eventually we would have a home in Ireland where our children could come for a holiday, or even for refuge, or eventually to live. In effect they said 'We'll live both in Canada and Ireland and have the best of both worlds.'

Shortly after arriving in Ireland we rented a house on the outskirts of Dublin, bought a good car, arranged for the continued education of our two boys and started hunting for our Shangri La. I won't bore you with details of our abortive 'place hunting' but it had one positive result: it taught us first-hand the geography of the country, because we travelled all the highways, byways and even the bohereens of the Republic. The distance to the furthest points of our irregular coastline from Dublin is only 200 miles; so from our base in Dublin, we were able to range the entire island daily and return each night.

When, with our children, we 'had a go' at settling down here in 1960–63, you could purchase a labourer's cottage and its acre of garden for one hundred pounds; but a decade later the price of such property had jumped to fifteen hundred pounds and very few cottages, let alone bigger 'places' were on the market at all. The 1963 price of one hundred pounds per acre for arable land had now quadrupled and for building purposes it had gone sky-high. Up to then we had felt we had enough cash to buy the place of our dreams — a modest house with ten acres of land. Eventually we decided to try for a non-residential farm on which we could build a house. To our surprise we failed to find one. Then — in desperation — we settled for having a 'dream bungalow' constructed on a site that belonged to our family for generations, in the centre of my native village.

It would take thousands of words to describe the delays and frustrations we encountered in trying to obtain planning permission for that bungalow and the difficulty of tying down a contractor to a firm commitment, coupled with the rapidly escalating price of labour and building material. And all the time we were paying what we felt was exorbitant rent in one of the 'housing estates' that like weeds are growing and proliferating around Irish cities and towns. Imagine our horror when we eventually realized we were trapped! Here we were, with our lifelong plans and dreams living in a rented place which was substandard — by any standard — and so far from Dublin that we were neither in the city nor the country. And to further complicate our lives we had previously shipped our Canadian furniture and belongings and they were now in storage in my native village, fifty miles from Dublin. Hence the more hold-ups that occurred with the planned bungalow the smaller and less realistic our life savings — and dreams — became.

No one likes to admit failure, even to their nearest and dearest; maybe that's why neither of us had the pluck to say to the other 'Let's face it we'd better return to Canada, write off our losses and relinquish our dreams.'

In the chapter on Céilé Houses in my previous book, *Ireland Where Time Stands Still*, I mentioned that one of the two remaining thatched houses in the village was Ned Malloy's. Well, our blue-roofed bungalow happens to be built within a stone's throw of the place once occupied by Malloy's thatched house; in fact we now own the little farm where Old Ned lived and worked on for close to a century. How we came to own Malloy's property is a long, complicated tale but suffice to say Old Ned and his wife reared a favourite niece Julia. Julia emigrated in her late teens to U.S.A., married her childhood sweetheart — my eldest brother Simon — and reared a family. When Ned Malloy and his missus died they willed the place to Julia, by then my sister-in-law.

'Good will' is an old Irish custom that goes back to the eviction
era when the 'Settler would sell the roof over your head'. The
custom was originally designed to ensure that property — if at
all possible — 'was kept in the family'. This good will means and
ensures that money alone will not guarantee possession —
peaceful possession. Malloy's property was 'put on the open
market', meaning widely advertised. Local people were
surprised at the unusual amount of competitive bidding —
taking into account that my deceased brother owned the
property; also that we already had the 'good will' for the
purchase in writing from his heirs in America. Financially
speaking, it put us to the pin of our collar to outbid the
opposition because it went at what was then considered a steep
price. But we were and still consider ourselves fortunate to have
gained possession of a small well-built bungalow and thirty
acres of potentially fertile farmland.

This might be an appropriate time to give a brief run-down on
farming. Ireland is essentially a country of small and
medium-sized farms. More than half of these farms are between
a few acres and thirty, only one tenth of them exceed one
hundred acres. Here in the Midlands more than half the farms
are over one hundred acres. It is worth remembering that when
land in Ireland could be bought — and that was even in my
lifetime — at fifty pounds per acre, one hundred acres was
considered a big farm. Farming land is now (1979) selling at
between three and four thousand pounds per acre.

Irish farming is mostly pastoral in character. The mild, humid
climate and the fertile soil conditions are less than favourable
towards tillage crops, but they do promote a year-round growth
of grass. Now that Ireland is a full member of the European
Economic Community which provides a vast market in Europe
for livestock products, the dominant agricultural pattern in
Ireland is one of mixed farming based on livestock.

Ireland has a variety of soils; but a broad distinction may be
made between the soils that have developed on the lowlands
from material derived from limestone, and those of the uplands
which are mainly from sandstone and granites. When drained
the lowlands are immensely fertile and suitable for agriculture;
the soils of the uplands are acid in character, poor in the essential soil elements and unfertile.

Although soil and climate conditions are suited to the
production of a wide range of crops, pasture occupies seventy

per cent of the total arable land, with about twenty-five per cent under hay and silage. The remainder is used in producing tillage, horticultural and fruit crops. Our principle tilling crops are cereals, potatoes, sugar beet, root and other green fodder crops.

A recent Farm Management Survey showed that sixty per cent of the Republic's farms are underdeveloped while their owners' living standard is 'far below levels accepted elsewhere'. Future prospects look bright only for 44,000 farms; and look dull for 27,000 more. The only hopes for the remaining 64,000 farms is to increase production. Thirty-two per cent of all farms have a family farm income of less than £1,000. The mainly drystock system (grazing) gives the lowest average return of any of the lowland systems both per farm and per acre; systems based on dairying prove the most rewarding. There are 27,000 small farms which because of their owner's age, ill-health or lack of a successor have no future in farming. In today's market, rural farming land costs up to £3,000 per acre, in fact its cost has gone far beyond its potential earning power.

As elsewhere, the scene has changed in rural Ireland. Fifty years ago you might see a solitary ploughman with a pair of horses and a plough; but today you can see £100,000 worth of up-to-date machinery harvesting a single field of grain. On all farms, both big and small, the horses have been replaced by farm tractors costing up to £20,000 each, pulling eight furrow ploughs and capable of ploughing thirty acres a day.

Now that we had our own little farm, we could have sat back, leased out our thirty acres, and it would have brought in a nice income — but. There is always a but. The first drawback was that our thirty acres had already been 'let' before we bought it and at that time 'letting' was based on pre-war prices. Of course as new owners we could "call an auction' in the hopes of getting the going price for letting our land either as conacre or on the 'eleven months' system. Conacre is a system of letting a portion of a farm for a single crop. The eleven months system consists of renting the land for grazing and is designed to prevent continuous occupation plus the danger of a renter establishing squatter's rights. If I chanced putting up our newly acquired land for auction while the renter had his cattle on it, word would get around that I was behaving like an English landlord. On the other hand if we continued letting the land, the Minister for

Local Government could and would step in and issue a Compulsory Purchase Order. Under that order we'd be obliged to sell the farm at the Minister's price and our land would be distributed to other small local farmers. Hence the only course was to farm the thirty acres ourselves.

Our farm has twenty acres of extremely fertile upland plus ten acres of poorly drained bogland. For a start we decided to 'graze the land'. Hearing that expression, a foreigner might envisage my wife and yours truly doing just that — ranging all over the little farm voraciously eating grass. Of course 'grazing it' means you purchase cattle at the fair or market, turn them loose on the grass and watch them grow and — hopefully — fatten.

To anyone who has not mullucked (Gaelic for a pig rooting in the mud) on an Irish farm, the farmer's life is the 'life of Reilly'. Like the Biblical lilies of the field, the grazier farmer toils not, neither does he spin; all the grazier has to do is drive small cattle into his verdant fields (hopefully well-fenced fields), ensure they have adequate drinking water, visit the cattle the odd fine day just to count and maybe admire them and when they are as big as small elephants, hire a truck, take the big fat·valuable cattle to the nearest fair or cattle market, sell them to the highest bidder and bank the winnings. From then on the carefree grazier watches the markets and when he considers that small cattle are a good buy he re-stocks the farm and continues the idyllic cycle. In practice it may not be all that simple; but there is a lot of truth in it and every locality has its share of good grass farms whose owners lead a lazy, indolent life and understandably are usually unpopular with their more energetic but poorer neighbours.

Maybe I had visions of myself becoming a grazier and with a bit of luck able to steer a midway course between an easy existence and sheer indolence; we decided to stock our thirty acres of grassland. I won't bore you with our struggle — not yet won — to drain and reclaim the ten acres of bogland that was 'run down' and neglected, or our ongoing battle to contain the whitethorn and briar jungle that a century ago started wild, unfettered life as fence and mearing ditches. Until recently, few farmers 'wasted money' on paling posts and barbed wire because they depended on their densely planted whitethorn hedges and high ditches. The standard procedure here is to stop gaps in field ditches by stuffing them with a few cut, thorny bushes and briars. I chuckle every time I see one particular 'gap stopper' — an old rusty iron bedstead — and wonder if any poet has made it the subject of a sonnet. Here it is, once an intimate piece of furniture that nightly served more than one generation, and now night and day still holds the fort.

Buying farm stock, that is young bullocks or heifers, is a risky business for a novice. I had first-hand and costly experience in the game when we tried our hand at farming in 1961. Then in spite of me being a country boy I discovered that my knowledge of cattle was poor and my knowledge of people, poorer. Admitting that I knew next to nothing about cattle I arranged with a local man who 'huckstered' (dealt) in cattle to buy and sell for me. He turned out to be a 'twister' and took me, as they say, both on the buying and the selling. So now eighteen years later we finally have a buyer who is knowledgeable with cattle and has integrity second to none.

Since he started buying and selling for us I suspect we are making a profit on the land. Notice I said 'suspect'; that's because we don't try keeping books. Maybe I should try to explain why we don't keep some kind of accounts. The main reason is that I dislike anything connected with bookkeeping, auditing etc. and watch like a hawk to avoid everything that might negate my retirement aspirations and trap me in a web of bookkeeping. I happen to have such a distaste for keeping accounts that if our stab at part-time farming and full-time grazing called for that kind of detail I'd be as well off to return to the old rat race. I heartily dislike bookkeeping. That dislike goes right back to my childhood, and peculiarly enough is connected with Tommy Gorman, our village baker, poet and philosopher.

*See Chap. 10. Tommy Gorman.

21. THE WEATHER

After my brief rundown on Irish farming I'll now slip in a few remarks about our climate, or 'the weather' as it's generally called.

Sunshine! Unashamedly, I am a sun worshipper. I have always loved the sunshine and as I got older this love affair grew and grew. But it became more intense after the ten years I worked underground gold mining in The Lakeshore Gold Mine in Kirkland Lake, Northern Ontario, Canada. The Lakeshore was then the deepest mine in the North American Continent — 8,000 feet deep. Imagine! eight hours a day down in the bowels of the earth; over a mile and a half of solid rock between your hard-hatted head and God's sunshine and His fresh air.

Regardless of my hunger for sunshine, if I were dependent solely on weather reports or data concerning hours of Irish sunshine I doubt if I would ever have chosen to return and make my home in Ireland; but then weather consideration was not the principal factor in making such an important decision.

If you try to study weather reports and data concerned with our Irish climate you will get more mixed up than the changeable weather itself. Before we came I made a weak stab at looking up some weather data to get some idea of the amount of sunshine Ireland is 'blessed with' and drew a blank. I would not go so far as to hint that there could be an official conspiracy or censorship on publishing information regarding Irish sunshine or that they are trying to cloud the issue.

After some research I did find something relevant and it *may* have been a coincidence, but it was in exceedingly small print on the back page of a newspaper. With the help of a magnifying glass I read: 'The mean duration of bright sunshine over the country for the month of January 1978 ranged from 2.9 hours at Roche's Point to 1.2 hours at Mallin Head. At Roche's Point it was the sunniest January since 1956. The most sunshine in any one day in this year was 7.8 hours at Roche's Point on the 26th January.' If you are the type of person who likes research and

195

wishes to pursue it further I suggest you get a map *and* a better
magnifying glass than mine and maybe you'd find Mallin Head
and Roche's Point. If a North American looks at the location of
Ireland on the map of the world he will see that Dublin is at the
same latitude as Goose Bay, Labrador, Canada. But if you feel
like visiting Ireland, don't let that latitude business lead you
astray, because Irish winters are mild and summers temperate.
February is our coldest month with temperatures averaged 42°F.
July and August are our warmest months with temperatures
around 60°F.

If this were my first visit to Ireland or I had not previously
experienced living in this country, I'd be puzzled and amazed at
the way people seem to be insensible to cold, damp weather. I
notice I have lost a lot of my original tolerance for extremes of
temperature as a result of my years in Canada, where a large
percentage of homes and public buildings are centrally heated.
Actually it's the lower temperatures in living quarters here that
cause me most discomfort. I find this strange because it's only a
few years since I lived, worked and enjoyed life deep in the
Canadian Arctic Circle. My wife still finds it remarkable that,
regardless of the weather, most country houses keep their
windows and doors wide open. As we drive around the
Midlands, through their invariably open doors, we see people
going about their normal household work while others casually
ramble in an out without every bothering to close a door. I think
that instead of trying to heat houses to accommodate bodily
comfort, preceding generations by a process of evolution must
have conditioned their bodies to tolerate lower than normal
temperatures.

Most houses depend solely for their heating on one solitary
fire which for practical reasons is located in the kitchen. This fire
can be on the open hearth, in an iron grate or in a stove. They call
the latter a range and the more sophisticated ranges are
designed for cooking and heating. Some of these ranges have a
water heating coil at the back of the firebox, and provide a
limited amount of domestic hot water. With the possible
exception of the fire on the hearth, few of these kitchen-based
fires appreciably raise the overall temperature of the kitchen, let
alone the rest of the house. The houses are not insulated and
even if they were it would not make much difference because in
the daytime most of the windows are thrown open, while the

doors are hardly ever closed. But when the day's work is done, the doors and windows are closed, the fire is stoked up and people sit around and relax. Of course when someone in the house is sick or too old to stand the cold and bustle of the big kitchen, there will always be a fire lit in the parlour or in a cosy room.

Since we 'settled in' here we have followed the local practice of keeping the bedroom without artificial heat, and winter and summer we sleep with our bedroom windows wide open. As a result, we feel immeasurably better. We do find it odd that so many visitors to our house never close a door behind them; but I think it's because our house is one of the few with central heating while in their own homes there is no appreciable difference between the inside and outside temperatures.

Our Friary church 'makes a stab' at central heating; there are about ten radiators spaced far apart, installed against the four foot thick stone walls. Maybe you could get some warmth from those heavy iron rads if you knelt close to them — the odd time the heat is on. Even if the rads were 'jumping' with steam (actually it's a hot water system), any heat generated or radiated would of course immediately head for the lofty uninsulated ceiling forty feet above. The Friars' heating man, my recently departed friend Brother Francis, knew what he was doing when he spaced those rads so far apart — about thirty feet — because although some previous heat-conserving priest or brother had installed self-closing gadgets on the church doors, most of the people attending church manage to leave the doors 'stuck' in the open position. On Sundays, Eileen and I go to ten o'clock Mass in the Friary and I always head for a certain non-drafty corner blessed with a radiator, because even if the heat isn't on, the cold rad provides a handy shelf for my wife's gloves, prayer book etc.

I'll admit that our Irish weather follows no fixed pattern. Take today for instance. It's still mid-winter, the noon Angelus has just rung and across the road two heavy tractor-drawn ploughs are working. I notice that the operators — one time they'd have been called ploughmen — are eating their lunch out in the open air instead of in the shelter of their car which is parked on the road outside. If I were in their shoes I'd be eating lunch in that warm car, but obviously they feel that an outside temperature of 50°F. is comfortable. On the other hand when the summer temperature goes to around 70°F. people universally grouse about the 'heat wave' and sometimes blame it on 'them Russians and their atomic bombs tampering with our weather'.

Discussing comfortable house temperatures with local people we think they sound slightly condescending. They look on it as a sign of weakness and poor health when anyone complains of cold weather. In my case they sagely say, 'Oh! being out in foreign countries does thin out a person's blood'. But then I get my own back when I 'trap' a visitor in our sunroom where even in winter, a sunny day raises the room temperature up to 100°F. Then, though on the verge of melting, I put on an act for the visitor's sake. Invariably the guest at first mutters a few kind words about the welcome heat, but before long he starts to show signs of wilting but is stuck *because* it's bad enough not to be able to stand the cold — but if you complain about the heat, the neighbour might show concern and remark 'You're not long for this world'. The length of time I suffer — a suffering heroically shared by the guest — depends on how much in the past that particular guest 'rubbed it in' by bragging how he could stand the cold; coupled with his gratuitous remark — 'Of course the older you get the less cold you can take.' By the way, when people here use the expression 'foreigner' it has no connotation of rancour, racism, intolerance and so forth; in fact people of other races or ethnic stock, visiting or living permanently in Ireland find that they are treated by the Irish people as equals — equals with an undefinable uniqueness.

I'll ruefully admit that since returning, we have missed many hours of glorious sunshine, but that's because we are too indolent to leave the bed before nine a.m. Many a morning even after nine, I ramble out to look the country over and not a cloud is to be seen; then half an hour afterwards it's not only cloudy but raining cats and dogs.

The summer of '76 set an Irish record for sunshine. Both Eileen and I independently arrived at the conclusion that a most attractive scenic factor of the Irish countryside is its variety and changeability which are tied in with our unpredictable weather. When the sun shone for lengthy periods we found that the scenery, beautiful and all as it is here in the Lake District, started to pall and become almost commonplace. Considering that Ireland's combination of mountain, hill and valley, sea, lake and river provides a world-renowned landscape of such immense variety, it sounds like sacrilege even to hint that Irish scenery could be branded commonplace.

Right now when I look out and with a photographic eye observe the masses of clouds, I realize that their immense diversity of shape, density and opacity so filter the sunshine that they act like a slide projector equipped with random infinite settings. Then I appreciate why so many visitors to our shores are never seen without cameras with which they capture and record the unending scenes of breath-taking beauty that appear to be perfection itself until a sudden shift in the wind or a stray sunshower acts like the flip of a picture projector switch; then the hitherto perfect scene not only changes but miraculously is enhanced.

People travel all over the face of the earth searching for what is to them beautiful, breath-taking scenery. I don't have to travel anywhere, anymore — I have arrived! Anytime during daylight hours and often on moonlit nights I've but to look out a window to see and appreciate what the author of one of our 'rebel' songs had in mind when he wrote:

'But sure the great God never planned,
For slumbering slave an isle so grand.'

I'm writing this in what we privately call the sunroom. Privately, because we live among people who are poor in regard to wordly possessions, but rich in spirituality and the things that money can't buy. In this regard strangers (which we are not) living here, would be advised to maintain a low profile at all costs, avoid 'putting on airs'. When we mention it at all to our neighbours, this glassed-in room which measures twenty feet by twelve, is 'just a handy space between the kitchen and the side of the garage that we covered in.' Usually we have two breakfasts: we first eat the North American-type breakfast, on-the-run with one eye on the clock; an hour or so afterwards we sit down, relax and eat the leisurely Irish breakfast — that's the one with the elbows on the still-cluttered table, 'with lashings and leavings' of time to talk.

So, one morning in mid-December, as we were on our third cup of tea I said to Eileen, 'here we are in the depths of an Irish winter; now if you were writing to your mother for instance how would you describe it?' No response: then hours afterwards she diffidently showed me part of a letter that she was writing to her

Irish-born mother, who by choice lives in Toronto, Canada. The letter in part went:

'I doubt if there is a more peaceful place on earth than this. They talk and rave about the rural life idealized by artists, poets and writers as being peaceful, simple and natural. When I look out our window I feel that it is all that — and more — it's alive, growing and productive.

We sit here leisurely eating and enjoying our second breakfast: only a few paces away I see our two bullocks grazing in the field as if they hadn't a care in the world. By the way we keep cattle around the place to try to stop the fast-growing grass from taking over. It is so cold out there that their breath is coming out like steam from a boiling kettle. Remember me telling you about the abandoned, starving collie pup that our friend Thomas Anthony Nugent rescued. Well, Rover is out there in the field marching around the bullocks as if he were desperately trying to strike up an acquaintance. Some of the cattle are staring strangely at us through the wall of glass. I feel they are gazing at us as if *we* were the occupants of a cage in a human zoo. One bullock has finally given up trying to figure us out and has collapsed in a heap. For a moment I thought he had fainted — then I noticed he was leisurely chewing his cud.

We had a light surface frost last night; it went to 30°F. which accounts for the heavy dew that's on the grassy fields. I notice that when the faint breeze gently shakes the grass, myriad droplets of dew on every blade, blaze like living diamonds. Hard to realize that it's almost Christmas and this little island village is a thousand miles nearer the North Pole than is your city of Toronto.'

22. ATLANTIC ADVENTURE

In 1963 we decided to return to Canada and agreed it would be best if I went on ahead of the family, find a job and arrange living accommodations. So in June of that year I boarded the S.S. Carmania in County Cork, bound for Canada.

The Carmania was one of the Cunard fleet of luxurious liners that included the giant Queen Elizabeth. The Cunard brochure made no idle boast when it promised that: on our ships you will enjoy the unrivalled service — friendly and courteous — and the matchless cuisine for which they are famed. The days will be lazy; swimming in the big pool and lounging around the sunny deck. The evenings will be filled with excitement and there will be dances, parties, entertainment and movies. These cruises are designed solely to make any holiday on which you use our ships, 'a truly memorable experience.'

I was not taking a trip as a holiday, rather I was returning to Canada after an absence of three years and would soon be faced with the problem of finding a job. Nevertheless this did not deter me from hoping to get my money's worth by having 'fun in the sun'. I was travelling 'tourist', which is a delicate way of describing second-class; but in this respect I can say from experience of several Atlantic crossings, one first-class and the rest tourist, that the latter is much the better way for the average person to travel, unless you happen to be a stuffed shirt or 'to the manner born'.

My stateroom slept four and although not exactly spacious it was comfortable. That first evening on board I was half asleep in my bunk (a top one) when I saw this head of long black hair on a level with my pillow and my first thought was, it's a woman! A second glance disclosed it belonged to a man of about forty who was to occupy the other top bunk. He was Polish and went by the name of Henry. We easily struck up a conversation and I resolved to become better acquainted as he had — to my mind — a most interesting background.

The third occupant was a young German emigrant who

spoke fair English, but spoke it in a rather laborious, pedantic fashion. His first name was Hans and superficially he was a prototype of the young war-time Nazi — big, athletic and blonde; he even wore his hair cropped short. The striking thing about him was that although the voyage was normally a time and opportunity to relax and enjoy, here was Hans — hours at a time — in our already cramped quarters, religiously working away on his portable battery of muscle-building gadgets.

In the tourist-class, passengers were advised to limit their luggage and have their bulkiest items stowed in the hold. The place of honour in Hans' corner of our crowded compartment was taken up with the most wicked looking, outsized chain saw you ever clapt eyes on. Out of deference to bare toes — especially mine — I remarked to Hans that the naked, sharp teeth of the exposed cutting chain reminded me of a wild wolf's bared fangs: he only shrugged. Then he said he was heading for British Columbia to work at logging and added, 'I intend to be Canada's number one lumberjack because I have the best chain saw in the world and I am an expert in its use.' In dead earnest I pointed out 'No matter how much muscle you pack or how adept you are with that brute of a machine, you'll go further if you become a salesman/demonstrator for the company that manufactures the saw.'

Sean, the fourth occupant, if you could rightly use the word occupant, did not use the bunk in our sleeping/living quarters; before the gangplank was up he had launched a shipboard romance, thus fulfilling the brochure's promise which hinted at such pleasant pursuits, with 'Cunard stewards have a sixth sense for knowing when you don't wish to be disturbed. You just lift a finger and your wishes are at once attended to.' He had other and I'm sure, more pleasant sleeping arrangements for the duration of the voyage and when I finally met him he turned out to be a young Dublin-born Jew and one of the most likeable and devil-may-care types imaginable.

Henry, the owner of the luxurious black hair, must have been hungry for an attentive audience — actually confidante — because he woke me early that first morning just to talk. I proved a willing listener as, like a torrent he poured out his life's story, starting from that tragic day in 1939 when the Nazis invaded Poland. From that day until the last Russian-run concentration camp in Europe was closed, Henry was in the 'thick of it'.

Actually he opened the conversation by pointing to a pile of paperbacks on his bedside table and made me welcome to them. He then picked up a particular book and suggested I read it and added that he had underlined some words and passages in it — he didn't explain the underscoring at the time.

Henry was a powerfully built man of around five feet ten inches tall and carried himself like a well-drilled soldier. His unusually pale face and sloe-black, sombre eyes reminded me of an artist or poet. When he casually walked from the shower or bathroom you could see a frightening number of scars that could have been from bullets or bayonets — or the bodily evidence of systematic torture. He never discussed his war wounds and I sensed that in that respect he was a very private person. But as far as I was concerned, Henry had what's called a one-track mind: night and day he talked about his marital problem.

He was in his late teens when the German blitzkrieg decimated the Polish army and blazed its way through that unfortunate land. Somehow he appeared vague regarding his loyalty or patriotism and seemed proud to have worked in internment camps both for Germans and Russians. Although claiming to have been an interpreter for both of those military powers he evaded my searching questions on their military policies and activities. When I pressed for details he changed the subject by talking about his wife and family. Before long I realized he was using me as a sounding board while he held forth about his marital affairs and this included some of his *own* peccadilloes!

He was a compulsive talker — in several languages. I had proof of his ability to express himself in English and French, while my Dubliner wryly admitted that Henry spoke more fluent Yiddish than did Sean's own parents. I had plenty of proof of his command of German. The only respite I enjoyed was when he finally trapped Hans; from then on he talked to me during daylight hours and concentrated on Hans after sundown.

Henry spoke for hour after hour about his background, his wife's background, and their courtship. The story as I pieced it together was that they first met in a concentration camp in German-occupied territory when she was about fifteen. He was not too clear whether they married or just lived together, but related how when the Americans liberated the camp the following year, his girl experienced a harrowing ordeal by being raped by a Negro American sergeant. He said that she appeared quite normal afterwards except that she behaved oddly if a strange male even looked at her. Henry firmly believed that by now she was a nymphomaniac and was unfaithful behind his back.

He admitted he lacked tangible evidence of her unfaithfulness and told me he was planning at the end of the voyage to rejoin his wife and their teen-age children, and then tried to interest me in a complicated senario he had 'dreamed up' to expose her unfaithfulness. He said he had lavished money on the hiring of detectives to shadow her — to no avail; with her consent he had had her hypnotized and had even hired gypsies to tell her fortune, hoping she would let down her guard.

After the second full day of hearing Henry's marital woes I got terribly bored and tried to give him a wide berth — did you ever try giving someone the slip on a ship? Daily as we came closer to Canada, Henry became more moody and tormented. He kept repeating 'I love my wife and I am going back to live with her but dread facing her as I know she is a lost woman.' Although I'm a heavy sleeper, my fourth night at sea I became aware that Henry was still talking — but this time to himself. This alarmed me, so next morning I went to the doctor's office. He was in naval uniform with a full breast of medals and when I gave him an account of my friend's behaviour and suggested that Henry might do something desperate such as committing suicide or running amuck, he callously replied, 'As long as he does not do it at night I don't mind, for I sure hate missing my sleep.' Not satisfied with the doctor's decision, I went to the Captain but he had already talked with Henry and assured me there was nothing to fear regarding the Pole's welfare. He kindly offered to move me to another stateroom, but I did not accept because I was ashamed of admitting that I was a worrier and a bit of a coward.

The following day was Easter Sunday and for the first time Henry brought up the subject of religion. He told me he was a Greek Orthodox Catholic and had a deep anxiety to tell his troubles to a priest. It wasn't news to me that he was a Catholic. Hadn't I already 'taken stock' of the mass of religious medals hanging around his neck. Why I noticed them in the first place was that they reminded me of a naive query I put to an American chap who served with me in the Air Force. He was one of those militant Catholics and like Henry he also sported a profusion of religious medals. One evening when he was exhibiting them I felt like taking a rise out of him. 'Flanagan' I said, 'surely you don't wear that anchor stone around your neck when you go swimming.' He took the bait and bragged 'I have *never* taken them off since I was confirmed.' 'But awhile back you were regaling us all with tales of your prowess in whore-houses; did the medals cramp your style?' I asked.

I heartily agreed with the idea of Henry's request for a priest because listening patiently and constructively to people's problems is one of their functions, and God knows! Henry's problem was rapidly eroding his sanity. I asked the ship's purser where I could find a priest and he explained that as it was the off-season they did not have their official chaplain around and added that this was one of the few trips when there was no Roman Catholic priest on the passenger list.

I told Henry the purser's answer and added, 'We will be in Quebec City in two days and then you can unburden yourself to a French-Canadian priest in your favourite language.' He was still upset so I suggested he come along to a Catholic lay service in the library in two hours time. Finally, I said 'It will be better than nothing.' He shook his head.

I went alone to the service and although I had plenty of my own problems I was so deeply worried about Henry's troubles that I thought I'd say a prayer for his peace of mind. Now I'm not much of a hand at praying; the best I could do was to try a bit of prayer mixed with long-distance telepathy and in a vague kind of way it went something like this: 'Please God, You know You seldom get around to answering *my* prayers but You do grant an extraordinary number of my wife's requests; I suspect it's because she *never* asks for personal favours; it's other peoples' woes she worries about. If I were in touch with her now she'd probably ask You herself. Henry is going through hell on earth: please do something for him — and quickly.'

Immediately after the short religious service I went to the library, got a magazine and found a quiet corner close to a big plate glass window. The window overlooked the rolling ocean who's vast expanse swamped me with a feeling of smallness and desolation. And I didn't experience any lightening of this sombre mood when — of all people — Henry sat down beside me.

It would break your heart to see how forlorn and miserable he looked and as usual he launched into his marital problems.

Now, I am cursed with a sensitivity and a strong disinclination
to hurt peoples' feelings — even when those people are
callously insensitive to mine, hence I resist telling them home
truths even when these truths are for their own good. I refrain
for fear it might hurt their feelings or injure their pride. But it
was the last straw when he said, 'Pat I love my wife but nobody
wants to help me with her problem.'

I knew then what I had to do. It would not be easy for Henry
to face the truth as I saw it. None of us relish the truth especially
if it questions our judgement — but Henry was asking for it! So I
steeled myself and said, 'Henry, we all have our troubles. I have
patiently listened to your troubles for four days and for four
nights over two thousand miles of ocean; I have even lost sleep
on your account and man to man, here is your answer: the
problem is *not* your wife, it's you. Jealousy has corroded your
brain so much that you have lost your grip on reality.' I
continued in this vein and surprisingly he did not seem stunned
or taken aback; I got the impression, instead of being angry or
embarrased that in reality he was relieved.

He and I then had coffee, followed by a brisk walk around the
deck and for the first time we conversed freely and easily about
unimportant things and eventually I rambled off alone to the
gymnasium. An hour or so afterwards I ran into Hans on the
main deck and he mentioned that Henry was below in his bunk
reading and that for a change he was silent, also that he had sent
Hans to the canteen for six packages of cigarettes. I recall
exclaiming '*Six*! but the canteen is open day and night and like
everyone else on board, Henry passes it a hundred times a day.'

A while afterwards I was standing at the bar when someone
asked the bartender, 'Has the boat turned around? The sun was
shining through that porthole a few minutes ago, now it's
coming through the one on the opposite side of the ship.' 'The
ship must have turned while we were talking', was the answer.

The bar was on the top main deck overlooking the swimming
pool and I went to the balcony and noticed a crowd of people
staring at a certain part near the stern where the guard-railing
was relatively low — about five feet. I asked the nearest person
'What's up?' and he said 'A man jumped over that rail a minute
ago.' Another bystander almost screamed 'He climbed up on
that rail and three other men tried to pull him down off it, I
thought they were fighting or horsing around. One man had

him by the leg but with his other leg he kicked the man, broke free, scrambled over the rail and hurled himself down into the water.' Another shouted 'About seventy feet of a fall; and now they're launching a lifeboat.' I recall muttering 'If it turns out to be Henry I'm his executioner. What a hell of an answer to a prayer!'

Without wasting a second I rushed to my quarters to check if Henry was there. Later I realized this had not been a logical move as there were over a thousand other persons who could have jumped — a thousand other places where Henry could have been. I hurried down to the lower boat deck from which they had already launched a lifeboat. A small storm was blowing, with waves about twelve feet high and within ten minutes the lifeboat was beaten a quarter of a mile to leeward because its crew seemed to be having trouble starting the engine and all the time the gap between it and the ship was widening. They must have lacked radio contact because the Captain on the Carmania's bridge was trying to direct them through some type of loudspeaker or hailer *and* he seemed to be more concerned about the lifeboat and the delay than with rescuing or finding Henry.

By now I was on shouting terms with the knot of crew members on the lower boat deck and looking over the rail I could see from the churned-up water that the ship's propellers were only turning over sufficiently to keep the ship on course. An English chap was just telling me he saw the man hit the water after his fall from the main deck — a fall of about twenty storeys — when right below me I caught a glimpse of something. The action of the ship's propellers had spewed up poor Henry. Yes, there was no doubt in my mind that it was Henry; I clearly saw his broad back and long black hair as he was tossed to the surface like a cork. Although he was face downwards, I recognized the hair and the wide shoulders that stretched the rather loud striped sports coat he invariably wore throughout the voyage. I yelled 'For God's sake throw him a lifesaver.' The response was rude — they were mostly former merchant marines and wartime Royal Navy types; also they correctly assumed he was lifeless and it would be futile to throw him a lifesaver. I'll admit no man in his right mind would consider plunging into the maelstrom created by the propellers in that rough sea and try to rescue Henry even if he were showing some trace of life. Within less than a minute he was churned under and did not reappear.

Meantime an anxious Captain was hailing his lifeboat to return to the ship and as the sky was darkening it looked to me as though Henry was being 'written off'. Finally the lifeboat was safely swung aboard and the Carmania's mighty engines resumed their customary deep throb.

A few hours later an announcement came over the P.A. system requesting the occupants of my stateroom to assemble there. The Master-at-Arms and his assistant asked us a few innocuous routine questions about our missing roommate. I did not mention my previous complaints to the doctor or Captain as I felt that they did their job 'as they saw it'. Needless to say, I kept quiet about my own 'sage' advice to Henry. As far as I could gather they wanted us there while they took inventory of the dead man's belongings. It seemed Henry's casebook was then closed. Incidentally I did not see any evidence in his luggage to give credence to a later report in a Canadian paper that he was a member of an international smuggling ring.

Later, Hans and I exchanged confidences. I learned two new facts: one was that Henry had tried to commit suicide a couple of years previous by jumping out a hotel window twelve storeys up in Montreal, and had miraculously landed unhurt in a mesh of telephone wires. The other was that Henry had confided in Hans that after due deliberation he was returning home to kill his wife and their two children.

My intervention — or was it God's intervention? — in Henry's plans to murder his entire family brought me up with a jolt. How do you apologize to God for making a snide remark especially when you feel He employed such an oblique — almost sneaky — way of answering a fellow's prayer!

23. WALK TO THE LAKE

One of the spin-offs of marriage — a successful marriage — is the sharing, whether by choice, pressure, boredom, or just plain old Love demonstrated by a desire to please, participate and share. My wife, thank God, takes a positive and active interest in most of my many hobbies.

Please don't ask, 'Do you participate in her hobbies?' A frank and truthful answer could be a bit embarrassing — for me. Anyway, the hobby or interest I have in mind, is my yen for the unspoiled countryside — and there is plenty of it in Ireland.

Since our return my most time-consuming interest lies in puttering around old forts, monuments, ruined castles, historic battle-fields, abbeys and the like. Certainly, without going outside the boundaries of this parish, an archaeologist could spend a fruitful lifetime pursuing his discipline. My wife had been reading one of the many books that recount 'The Fate of the Children of Lir', considered to be one of the most poignant and tragic of all Irish legendary romances,* so it was no surprise when she said, 'Derravaragh, our lake, figures largely in this story. Why don't we spend a day at the lake?' Her question could have been a rhetorical one, because luckily we have managed to become *free*. It did not require checking a Date Book (we haven't one) or cancelling any previous plan; or worrying about the hundred and one details that such a casual, split-second decision would have entailed when I was part of the 'rat race'. I said, 'We'll take the car; what road do you think we should take?' She replied, 'It is such a gorgeous day, why don't we walk to the lake and maybe go by Donore Avenue.' 'You know what?', I said. 'You know how I rhapsodize about scenes of my boyhood, and "vaporize" as my mother used to call it, about the good old times. It just occured to me that we are as tied to the car as when we lived in Ottawa or any other part of Canada. We even drive to Mass and it's only a few hundred

*See Chapter 31.

yards away. How about walking to the lake and instead of going by Donore Avenue, we can take the short cut by the Friary and down by John Brennan's.'

When we take the car to go any distance from base or to carry out any assignment, like most North Americans we load up with every conceivable bit of gear that we figure may come in handy; we bring along everything but the kitchen sink. Going on foot meant that we should travel light and take a minimum of gear. Although there are plenty of hotels and restaurants scattered around Ireland and most pubs serve sandwiches, we make a practice of bringing our own sandwiches and the 'makings' of tea. This entails taking along two large, one-quart thermos bottles of boiling water plus loose tea, sugar and cream. 'Travelling light' means that we dispense with the bottles and pack the 'billy can' for boiling the water over an open fire somewhere appropriate.

Strangers to Ireland are often 'sucked in' as regards weather. The sun may shine brilliantly early in the morning and coax the optimistic hiker to head for the open road, unsuitably attired for the 'sun shower' that leaves you 'wet to the skin' as my friend Tom Cassidy says, and then adds, 'And if your skin wasn't waterproof you'd drown.' I was born here and lived at a time before plastic or nylon waterproof clothing was invented, let alone in use. When we set out, the sun was shining and naturally we were suitably dressed for a warm day; but to be on the safe side we took along the usual nylon outfit.

At the foot of the village we crossed the bridge, turned left and headed down the beautiful tree-lined avenue that is the new entrace to the Friary. We passed to the left of the Friary and my memory bank unerringly led me to a certain corner of the Bridge Meadow where, almost obscured in the long grass, the age-old path which I had not trod for over forty years waited for me. Obviously that path had not been travelled for years but I realized that it takes more than a decade of disuse to obscure or obliterate a path that took a thousand years of passing human feet to etch deep into the living skin of Mother Earth.

We followed the path and a couple of fields further came to a branch of it which headed for Brennan's. Seemingly unchanged, the old 'ruckety' wooden stile was there and still performed its double function — a barrier to farm animals and easy pedestrian passage. I said, 'Let's sit on the stile awhile and

I'll point out the boundaries of Brennan's little place where our old friend spent his entire one hundred and two years.' The little place that once pulsed with life was now desolate, neglected and empty. Not the emptiness of a box or a room or even the emptiness of a robbed bird's nest — more the emptiness and forlorn appearance of a plane I once stumbled on, in a deep, nameless valley in Canada's Yukon. A plane that with its crew had disappeared off the face of the earth seven years before. Brennan's place had the same emptiness as that downed and desolate aircraft. The doors of all the stables and sheds were closed, the haggard was empty; not a trace of life around the place — not even a cat. The door of the house was nailed up and the little windows without drapes or curtains looked like the fully open eyes of a corpse.

Eileen said, 'I wonder what became of the two goldfinches John had in the cage hanging in the corner of the kitchen beside the window. Do you remember how proud he was of those birds. He'd whistle a few notes as a signal to the goldfinches and immediately they'd burst into song.' You know how women are! She then got dewey-eyed as she recalled the Easter morning when ninety-three year old John came with his gift. He said to her, 'A cushla ma cree (pulse of my heart) I've brought your Easter cludog.' It was a gift of a dozen eggs. I would like to have asked John about how the custom of the cludog originated; I know that the literal translation of cludog means Easter gift of eggs, but I never got around to it. I'm sure his gift of eggs was a continuation of one of the ancient practices or rituals connected with Easter — practices that were old long before Christ was born.

Eileen and I walked past Brennan's house and down the almost obliterated path to the gate that opens on to the Bog Road. It's the same old iron gate that the leprechaun perched on when he struck up an acquaintance with a barefoot gossoon called John Brennan.

Continuing our walk to the lake, Eileen and I went out Brennan's gate and on to what John always gave its full title, The Old Bog Road, The Bog Road must be one of the oldest roads in the area. Originally it was built level with the surrounding ground, but as a result of adding successive layers of road material, its 'wearing surface' is now around eight feet higher than the general area. Both sides of the road are paralleled by deep drains about eight feet wide which are always partially filled with sluggish flowing water.

As we walked along the road I pointed out various landmarks. Up there beside the old roadside stone cross whose writing is now almost illegible, are the ruins of Mickeen Ward's place. The little stone bridge beside the cross is where I fished for pinkeens when I was only an infant.

Next, we walked past Ryan's Ridge where a family of that name once lived. The Ridge is a narrow high strip of land that is part of Donore Planting. Locally it is called the Plantin because it is part of an area — hundreds of acres of bog and swamp — that was successfully planted with spruce, larch and beech trees over a century ago. We walked past Ryan's Ridge and came to the Rampart. The Rampart is also an extension of the Plantin but has a much heavier growth of trees; some of its larch trees are almost four feet in diameter. I don't know how the Rampart got its name.

On the east side of the road I pointed out an area that resembled a patch of tropical jungle and remarked, 'There was a house there one time.' I have no touble at all picking out places where once there was a dwelling — even if all the traces of the building have disappeared. The ordinary field ditch or even part of a ditch invariably contains trees, shrubs, briers and so forth, but if you see — for instance — a crab apple tree, or the odd shrub, bush or flower still blooming it is safe to assume that someone, sometime, planted, cultivated and maybe loved them because they were once part of a garden or yard attached to a dwelling.

'I remember now, that was where Johnny Tormey lived', I said. I've only a vague recollection of him, except that on Sundays he wore a hard hat with a very high crown — I think it was called a Homburg. Johnny and his wife Mary had no children and he was noted for his miserliness — I was going to say he was notoriously mean — but remembered he had to be that way to eke out a living from that five acre field over there; it was all the land they had. People whispered behind their hands that when the new potatoes were almost ready for digging, Mary had to sneak behind her husband's back into the garden and use a tablespoon to ferret out a potato here and there.

Both the Tormeys were noted for the tasty, and almost elegant clothes they wore on Sundays and on special occasions like

weddings and funerals. I remember when I served Mass on
Sundays and helped the Parish Priest take up the collection, I'd
always sneak a look at Johnny Tormey's suit and admire the
Homburg carefully held in both hands. Unlike the other men he
never put it on the floor under the seat in front of him for fear it
could get dirty or dented. His suit — even then — was a
museum piece. He said it was his father's, but older neighbours
claimed they saw Johnny's grandfather wear it — but wasn't it
tailored from Irish frieze made to last! Irish frieze was a thick,
heavy wool cloth with a shaggy uncut nap on one side. They
still tell stories of many a rack-renting landlord's life being saved
from a load of buckshot because he was lucky enough to be
wearing a stout coat of Irish frieze. Normally it took many,
many years of exposure to the elements before a garment of
Irish frieze showed signs of wear or lost its particular dark grey
colour. But Johnny's suit had been around so long that it had
turned a greyish green hue; yet it was without rent, tear or
wrinkle. Tommy Gorman used to say, 'Wearing Irish frieze you
might as well try to bend down in a suit of armour.'

In Johnny Tormey's time there was very little ready money
floating around and most people made a point of looking after
their clothes. Around here it was said that no one could 'hold a
candle' to Johnny Tormey when it came to getting the worth of
his money out of his 'best' suit. Yet it was his wife Mary who put
him in the shade in the making-clothes-last department. I heard
Mary's neat, perfectly fitting, hand-tailored suit likened to the
legend of Jesus' seamless garment. Tradition had it that He wore
a single cloak all His life; it fitted Him when He was an infant
and grew as He grew and still fitted perfectly in His full
manhood. I used to hear my mother and the other ladies —
maybe grudgingly — say, 'You have to hand it to Mary Tormey
for being the best dressed and turned out lady in the seven
parishes *and* the miraculous thing about it is the way Mary has
worn that identical tailored blue suit for a lifetime and it always
fits her figure like a glove; you can't tell me she hasn't taken it in
and let it out so often that it is a miracle it has held together this
long.' Mary was long gone to her eternal reward before it leaked
out that 'unbeknownst' to anyone — even her husband — every
four or five years she had a new suit made for herself and she
had it always tailored in the same cut and colour as its
predecessor.

The Tormey family, who were originally evicted from the upland part of Donore estate, wrung a meagre living out of the five acres of bog where we now stood. They could be the prototype of the very small farmer in the Ireland of the eighteenth, nineteenth and quarter way into the twentieth century. They had no income whatsoever. The only cash they ever handled was when they sold a calf, cow or pig, or when Mary sold eggs or fowl. Johnny took care of the scant income from the sale of these farm animals — scant when you realize that it takes a full acre of good upland to feed a single cow. It goes without saying that Johnny and his wife painstakingly cultivated and husbanded every square foot of their little farm.

As you drive around Ireland today, just observe that the tops and even the almost perpendicular steep sides of highest hills still bear evidence of our peoples' agricultural industry — or desperation. The evidence is there in the geometrically perfect furrows and ridges — relics of an era when, as Bill Barden would say, 'They were min in them days'. An era when small farmers tilled their own soil without ploughs as we know them.

Their plough was an agricultural implement called a loy. The loy is a type of spade with a six foot handle to which is attached a steel or iron blade about two feet long — a blade narrower than that of a modern spade. The sharp blade of the loy was used to nick or cut the sod which was to be turned — somewhat like a modern plough in the process of cutting and turning sod. Part of the wooden handle extended under the back of the blade and formed a protuberance which acted as a fulcrum to help lever up and turn the previously nicked sod. This is how it went: the loyman initially nicked or cut the sod to the desired width — in ploughing we call it the scrape; the loyman then forced the long, thin sharp blade under the nicked sod, levered down on the long handle and in one swift movement forced up and turned over a sod the full length of his blade. The loy may have been a primitive implement for ploughing, but obviously it was effective. In that era, Ireland supported a population of around nine million. In his 'deserted Village', Oliver Goldsmith expressed it:

'When every rood of ground maintained its man'

To get back to the Tormeys scraping a living out of their little farm, I'll try to describe how the average 'little farmer' including the 'cottager' with his one acre of land managed to rear a pig; it could give an idea of the state of our economy up to 1935.

For instance, we say 'he keeps cattle', he 'owns cattle' or 'has cattle grazing on his land', but when we talk about a pig, it's always 'rearing' a pig. In fact you could say the pig enjoyed special status in Ireland. You may even have heard the old Irish ballad that goes:

'For children not like pigs you know, don't help to pay the rent.'

Historically, not paying the rent meant certain eviction for the unfortunate tenants of the Settlers. The importance of the pig that often 'kept the roof over our heads' is lampooned by the English propaganda — cum sneer — of 'Paddy's pig in the parlour'. The 'peasantry' — a slightly disparaging and patronizing term employed by the Ruling Class — hardly ever could afford to 'kill their own bacon'; rather, they were often obliged to sell the pig for rent or for the bare necessities of life. Thus the pig often stood between them and destitution. People like the Tormeys in modest circumstances, usually killed their own bacon and thus could manage to eat meat at least once a week.

I know next to nothing about pig fattening or the best diet for those animals, but it was accepted as Gospel truth that pigs would — could — only thrive on boiled victuals. Maybe that helps to account for the ever-present pig's pot swinging from the massive iron crane over the Irish hearthstone fire in every home in Ireland — that's with the exception of the Settler's fine houses.

When full, the standard pig's pot required two strong adults to lift it on to the hanger of the crane. When loaded, the pot usually contained turnips, mangels, parsnips, carrots and poreens. Poreens is the Irish name for potatoes that are too small for normal use. Domestic vegetables for victuals were usually available when the pig owner had a bit of land; nevertheless many landless householders still managed to rear a pig. At potato digging time they traded their labour 'picking' for the cull of the potato and other crops; they also 'scoured' the countryside for 'greens' for the pig. Greens included brooklime, watercress, nettles and even dandelions. The pig's diet of greens usually was augmented by the fall from the house — meaning scraps of food, potato skins and other edible material.

Anything that looked like food or smelled of food was 'grist to the mill' and ended up in the pig's pot. Speaking of pig's pots, when I was a child I always imagined that the big bulbous pig's pot on the crane resembled a crushed-down black Buddha presiding over a votive fire.

Eggs were about the most important item in country peoples' fare. Every family kept domestic fowl — geese, turkeys, ducks, hens and when their egg-laying days were over they ended up on the kitchen table — cooked. Families like the Tormeys who lived close to the lake, river or sluggish bog drains always kept plenty of geese and ducks, which found all their food in the water and when evening came they unfailingly returned home. In our house we always had a large number of geese and ducks because we lived less than a hundred paces from the river. We were so proud of our big, ferocious gander, who every morning protectively marshalled our geese and ducks in a long waddling line from the yard down to the river and when evening came, like a fierce-looking drum major he led them home up the street and straight to their warm safe shed where they slept and laid their much prized eggs. We used to say 'God help the inquisitive dog, or the cur looking for trouble, if he crossed the path of our gander'. That fiercely hissing red-eyed gander would tackle a Mac truck and many's the challenging village fighting dog he put to ignominious flight.

Few families could afford the luxury of butcher's meat and if they didn't rear a pig for bacon they had to depend for meat on the rabbits and hares they trapped or snared. Abundant fish from the river and lake was always there for the catching and nearly every family had at least one fisherman — or woman — to keep the larder stocked.

After passing Johnny Tormey's place, Eileen and I crossed the Bog Road, walked over the 'kish' into the Plantation and were now on Donore estate, once the property of the Nugents. The kish is a crude bridge constructed by placing lengths of tree trunks side by side across a drain, river or swamp. Sometimes the travelling or walking surface of the kish is carpeted with 'scraws' to give a non-slippery foothold. Scraws are sods with their deep roots still intact and also retaining sufficient soil to continue growing when placed on the corduroy-type surface of the wooden bridge, Bare-footed youngsters avoid walking through patches of sedge because each blade of sedge has sharp serrated edges which cut like a razor when brushed by a bare foot or hand. It was with a blade of sedge we 'knocked out' our first musical notes when we were children. The trick is to loosely hold a blade of sedge — carefully moistened — longitudinally between the balls of your thumbs and then gently blow into the orifice between the thumbs. Later in life it occurred to me that such a blade of grass could have been one of mankind's first musical instruments — maybe it predates the classical Pipes of Pan.

We 'proceeded' — as a policeman giving evidence would say — through the Plantation, which is now a government reforestation site, but it still contains many of the larch and spruce trees that to my eye don't appear to have grown much in the half century since as a bare-footed, footloose boy I passed this way. I suggested to Eileen that we leave the beaten path that goes through the Plantation and travel a bit deeper into the more heavily treed area and pick a few 'fraochán'. Fraochán — an Irish word — is a species of berry resembling the Canadian blueberry, except that the Irish ones have more juice and contain less pith. When you pick the fraocháns you will find that no matter how gently you handle them, the riper ones burst and their juice will stain your fingers a dark blue colour almost impossible to remove. When you eat them, they stain your teeth and tongue and leave their mark for hours. But the taste! Each year since returning to live here we have placed a high priority on picking our winter's supply. Eileen preserves a portion of the fruit and with the remainder makes jam: jam that you'd get up in the middle of the night to eat. It was the last week of August and there was a great crop so we topped the billy can with the berries intending to eat them for dessert with our *al fresco* lunch. But the berries proved so delicious and tempting that we finished every one of them as we continued our walk.

Leaving the Plantation we crossed another kish and into the upland part of the estate which is divided into large irregularly shaped fields by unusually large well-maintained ditches. To most English-speaking people, a ditch is a shallow trench dug in earth to conduct water. In Ireland we use the term 'drain' to describe a deep channel (usually dug in boggy land) primarily intended as a fence or barrier to separate fields and farms. With us a 'ditch' is a continuous bank or ridge constructed of earth, clay and stone. Like our drains, ditches were built to separate fields; but they were also designed to provide shelter for the farm animals.

The unique factor of many of Donore ditches is that they are what we call 'double ditches'. When a double ditch was being built it was constructed thus: two rough low retaining parallel walls of large boulders without mortar were built to a height of four feet. Then trenches (must avoid saying ditch here) were dug outside each wall, and the dug material plus any loose stones, boulders, tree stumps, rubbish and so forth was packed between the walls. Then a row of young trees or bushes was set at the (inside) back of each wall. Next, more clay and earth were heaped up on the bank between the walls and you had your double ditch. Some of these ditches in Donore must be very old because until the timber scarcity (we never call it lumber here) in the recent Great War, those Donore double ditches produced ash and beech trees up to eight feet in diameter.

As kids in the bare ones we loved racing along the double ditch path that Eileen and I now sauntered along — also without a care in the world. The reason for our bare-footed preference for this path was the fact that the builders of the ditch did not include the whitethorn or the deadly blackthorn when they planted the twin rows of trees. May have occasion to mention those thorn-free ditches again in my experience of netting rabbits.

We had gone about a quarter of a mile when Eileen said, 'There's a body of water over there, is it the lake?' I marvel at the way my wife manages to lose herself less than a mile from the house. She, who without a map could and did unerringly find her way around in her native city Toronto, or in Montreal or even in New York, across the Canadian border. She wanted to rush down at once to the shore of the lake but I prevailed on her to come further along the path to see if I could locate the remains of an old house where myself and other fishermen used to shelter from the rain when I was a boy. We had no difficulty finding it because the remains of the walls supported, and were supported by a luxurious growth of ivy. As you travel around our country you will notice the extraordinary number of huge trees, old buildings and ancient ruins all garlanded with the evergreen ivy.

The type of ivy which thrives here in Ireland is common to most of northern Europe. Most of us imagine that ivy is parasitic upon the trees which support it: in reality it merely clings to them by its numerous holdfast roots which grow along the entire length of its stem and it is by constriction it eventually kills its tree host. Unlike a tree, a house is vunerable to the ravages of the hungry ivy because the ivy roots literally eat the very skeletons of the derelict buildings by feeding on the mortar between the stones. By the very nature of its construction, a mudwall house proves easy prey for ivy. It's incorrect to suppose that ivy always destroys buildings; actually in many instances the chain-armour-type network of ivy completely encases the defunct buildings and postpones indefinitely their ultimate collapse.

As we poked around the ruin I told her about Jimmy Blueman whose people lived there. Early in the nineteenth century the Bluemans were one of the fifty plus families evicted from Nugent's huge estate. The forefathers of these unfortunate people had occupied, owned and worked their little plots of land long before the first Nugents arrived here as part of the Anglo-Norman invasion around 1170. The Nugents, like the rest of the invading military leaders, received large grants of Irish land in payment for their military assistance, but the native Irish as a people *never* recognized the invaders' right to Irish soil. What makes it harder to stomach is the fact that the Nugents, a cultured and Catholic family, *professed* the same brand of religion their tenants believed in and followed.

Recently a friend of ours, Maggie Bardon, gave a vivid, stark description of an eviction her grandmother suffered here on Donore estate. She said 'The thing that stuck in my grandmother's craw was the bailiffs, supported by the Royal Irish Constabulary using the battering ram to knock down the chimney of the mudwall hovel *while* the unfortunate family was still inside cooking their dinner.' Maggie named more than fifty evicted families: like a litany the family names rolled off her tongue; Dougherty, Cox, Hopkins, Bardon, Brennan, Tormey, Ryan, Ward, Blueman, Kelly, Barry and the rest. She continued: 'They levelled our little house so that the view from the Big House would be unspoiled; that their visitors could come in the front avenue from the main road, visit the Big House and depart by the winding back avenue without seeing a single poor person's hovel.'

To give them their due, the Nugents were not as heartless as many other owners of large Irish estates. The Nugents did not evict their tenants, they just razed their little houses to the ground and moved the families to alternative locations on the estate. Unfortunately for their future occupants, the alternative locations were swampy, boggy lands which, as the locals have it 'wore out three generations of tenants and sent most of them to an early grave' before they managed to drain and reclaim their little holdings.

Around the middle of the nineteenth century the Settler Gentry were, I suppose, no more inhuman or callous towards their tenants and servants than were their counterparts in other parts of the world — either in the 'British Possessions' or in 'Mother Russia'. Our native Irish Gentry, and that included the Anglo-Irish estate owners on the whole, felt and acted as if they owned 'the peasants' (as they called them), body and soul. Most of the Ruling Class were reasonably kind and fair to their 'people'; the same type of 'kindness' that a horse owner displays towards his animals — as long as they do his bidding. But there was no doubt that universally the Gentry made a fetish of 'keeping the lower classes in their place'.

To give Eileen an idea of the way the Gentry generally behaved towards the native Irish, I gave her a shortened account of a well-authenticated incident that happened 'just over there at Coolure on that far shore of the lake'.

Coolure was a large estate owned by a Settler family — the Blacks. Major Black, a regular social visitor to Donore, met with a serious boating accident on one of his trips across the lake — on this occasion he was going to play tennis with some of the Nugents. A friend of mine who 'sclaved (sic) for the Blacks' gave me a version of the accident and I believe it spells out how the 'lower classes' were made to watch their P's and Q's. I'll try to tell it in my friends own words:

'Major Black's boat with its powerful in-board engine used to roar across the lake. It was just before Christmas Day and there was a layer of ice on the lough, maybe an inch thick; but it would take more than that to stop me bould Major. By the time he was out there in the deepest part, the boat was nearly sawed in two at the water line by the rough broken edges of the ice. Next thing the watchers on the shore saw was the boat goin' under and the Major's head sticking out of the ice and he bellowing like a bull. One of the labourers Jim Murtagh a tradesman himself when it came to handling a boat, rowed like hell out to where the Major was going down for the third time and managed to drag him into the boat and safe back to shore. And the mean bastard didn't even say "thank you" to Jim for his trouble in saving the army man from a watery grave. Then mind you! the very next morning at seven as the Major as usual has just finished ringing the big bell that daily warned start of work on the estate, didn't Jim Murtagh rush into the yard — as he himself said later "only about ten sthpes late" and the Major in the face of the whole work-force roared at him like he was a new recruit on a parade square, "Murtagh you're late and I'll dock you the usual half hour's wages; dont *ever* think that I'll make any exceptions in *your* case just because yesterday you had the privilege of saving *my* life".'

By all accounts, the tenants who worked at Donore were 'well treated'. Jimmy Blueman farmed a few of his own acres and also worked as a semi-skilled labourer at the Big House, where he enjoyed special status because he proved to be an excellent worker. One of his 'perks' was the annual privilege of getting as much hay as he could cut (with a scythe), in one full day, from a standing meadow. It was further spelled out that the standing meadow was a field of ripe grass not beat down flat with wind and rain; full day was from sunrise to sundown, on any one day of Jimmy's choosing. When Jimmy Blueman was originally given the 'full day's mowing', the Baronet must have been in an unusually benevolent mood; and he certainly forgot, or was unaware that Jimmy, in modern parlance, swung no mean scythe. In fact, 'every dog and devil in the country' knew that in meadow cutting competitions, Jimmy Blueman always finished half a headland ahead of the best scythe swingers in the business.

The first few years of Jimmy's 'buckshee' meadow cutting passed uneventfully and it was understandable that eventually Jimmy started to brag about 'getting the better of the Sir', because time came when everyone around would be keeping a weather eye on the calendar and the 'state of the weather' when the grass in Donore Big Meadow was at its best.

Eventually the Sir's sycophantic overseer — himself a tenant — alerted the Baronet and reported, 'Sir, Blueman is taking unfair advantage of your generosity'. When asked for details, the overseer complained that each year Jimmy was cutting an increasingly greater portion of meadow, although he (the overseer) on his own initiative and in the best interests of the estate etc. kept a personal watch on the entire operation. When the Sir bluntly asked if Blueman was 'breaking his end of the bargain', his overseer admitted that Jimmy was living up to the letter of the law; but, he added, 'I don't think it's fair the way he brags that he is besting you over the meadow cutting; he leaves no stone unturned to cut as much of your meadow; he even goes so far as to have not only one scythe but two scythes already sharpened the night before he starts cutting.' The Baronet, a good sport, said, 'Nevertheless Blueman is welcome to his day's cutting; a bargain is a bargain.'

But a younger son of the Sir felt that the Family was losing face — and meadow — plus being bested by one of their tenants. The young Master is reputed to have complained (mixed metaphors and all), 'It's one thing for us to play a trick on our own tenants, but it's a horse of a different colour when the boot is on the other foot.'

Finally the day came when Jimmy Blueman felt that conditions were ideal for 'his big day' and he was already in the meadow waiting for the sun to come up. A neighbour asked, 'how do you feel Jimmy?', and he assured him 'I'm fitter than a fighting cock: my wife has fed me on oaten bread and stirabout (porridge) for weeks — thar's no grub in the world that gives a man strength like the meal milled from your own oats. Look at what even one good feed of oats does to a thoroughbred horse. He'd jump over a five barred gate.'

From a sartorial point of view, Jimmy was stripped right down to essentials. He described his working togs: 'Stripped down to my shirt and trousers — to free my shoulders — I even took down my galluses and tied them around my waist for a belt. I even had prepared proper straps for my threeens.' The latter were string or straps which labourers in those days fastened around each leg of their pants a few inches below the knee. Their britches were usually made of heavy corduroy and I suppose the tying did tidy up the heavy pant legs. Jimmy could have mentioned that apart from his socks and brogues, the remainder of his clothing consisted of a shirt and as it has a bearing on my story I'll have to say a few words about men's shirts.

Up to twenty years ago, over here, a man's standard shirt

was long-tailed with the front of the shirt opening just large enough to permit the wearer-to-be to struggle his head through. The typical male shirt came down in front to about eight inches above his knees, while the back was about twenty inches longer; in fact it was designed to touch the back of his calves when it hung free. I would hazard a guess that the garment was not designed primarily with a view to modesty.

By the time the rim of the rising sun had cleared the horizon Jimmy Blueman had his scythe 'at the ready' and he briskly swung into action. Swung or swing is a very appropriate word to describe how an expert mower uses his curved blade. To me, a man with the knack of swinging his scythe is poetry in motion. Do you recall Milton's, 'Whatever thing the scythe of time mows down'? In the event that you belong to the younger generation you may have only a vague notion of what a scythe looks like, and a hundred to one you may never have seen a scythe being used to cut a meadow. In fact, pretty soon a scythe will only be found in a museum.

A scythe is a long, single-edged, pointed at one end, steel blade, about four feet long and three inches deep at the one end. This end is affixed to a wooden handle at right angles. This handle is about six feet long, and it in turn has two short horns or handles, each about eight inches long, set two feet apart and affixed at ninety degrees to the main handle.

If I were telling a native Irish person how to operate a scythe, instead of talking about the horns or eight inch handles, I'd simply say, 'The mower grasps the dorneens' and my meaning would be clear. That's because the word dorneen is derived from dorn, the Irish for fist. To use a scythe properly the mower first stands erect and easily rests the back part of the curved blade on the ground. Then he assumes the normal mowing stance. This is what we call a dhuck — meaning crouch, with the knees slightly bent and the upper part of the body tilted forward.

When the sned (blade) is set at the correct angle on the handle and swung in an arc parallel to the ground, it lops off the stem of the grass and weeds, leaving behind a smooth carpet of stubble. With the blade correctly 'whetted' so that you could 'split a hair three ways', it does not require much physical force to cut a swath of standing meadow. A swath is the space covered by a scythe's swing and a good mower covers a square yard of ground with each swing of his blade. 'Twas said that there were men in this parish who could cut three quarters of an acre in one day, but when he was under pressure 'your man' Jimmy Blueman could knock down an acre and a quarter in a single day.

When you see an expert mower swinging his scythe, you will appreciate my reference to 'poetry in motion'. In addition, the hiss of the razor-sharp blade as it slides incisively through the base of the tall, ripe thraneens (stalks) and the swoosh and sigh of the verdant growth as it topples before the merciless scythe is a sound and a sight to be treasured. Wrap it up with the smell of new-mown hay in an Irish meadow and you have a memory (when the mood is on you) which you will often wish to evoke.

To get back to our hero swinging his scythe. Conditions for slaughtering the meadow were ideal and before two hours were up, Jimmy had got his second wind and felt confident he was well on his way to a record. Another productive hour passed and he decided he'd rest and take a slug of the sour buttermilk he had left in the cool of the ditch. He was about to start on the buttermilk when an unexpected visitor arrived — young Master Nugent himself from the Big House — and he had a four-quart can with him. He said, 'Blueman! The cook sends her regards with this can of tea; she said she made it so strong that it should keep you going *non-stop*, till nightfall.'

As poor Jimmy never got tired of recounting, 'I swallowed a full quart of that tea before I noticed it had a damn bitter tang, but I put it down to the extra pinch of tea cook threw in — to strengthen it.' He returned to the cutting, but within minutes he had a 'sudden call of nature' and had to make a bunyog (the way a rabbit explodes out of cover) for the shelter of the nearest ditch. Within minutes Nature was giving Jimmy more than a call — a peremptory call, followed by a continuing series of calls. Then it dawned on him that the young Master had doctored the tea. In his heart — or further down — Jimmy Blueman realized the concoction was Jalap and he saw his dream of an acre or more of cut meadow go down the drain, as it were. Up to fifty years ago, Jalap, a cathartic medicine manufactured from the dried root of a Mexican vine, was widely used on humans as a purgative medicine. Unfortunately, it's quick-acting property made it a useful and often-used instrument for cruel practical jokes. In fact, it has an almost instantaneous purgative effect.

As Jimmy told it: 'After — I don't know how many runs to the gripe (shallow part of a ditch) — I felt like the unlucky traveller who had accidently walked through a patch of 'fear gorta'. His mention of fear gorta, which in Irish means hungry grass, is founded on the still widely held belief that in certain secret places in Ireland patches of the 'hungry grass' grow, and if a person comes in bodily contact with the grass it has the uncanny effect of robbing and draining his physical energy.

Jimmy described his progress — or lack of it — thus: 'Before the sun was at it's highest, I almost gave in (admitted) that the Jalap had me bet (beat), because there I was spending more time running like a redshank to the gripe and fustering (fumbling) with the galluses and my trousers, than at the mowing. Then in a last definite move to save time I made up my mind that there was nothing for it but to take both off and throw them on the headland. Then I put a neat knot in the tail of my shirt, blessed myself, swore I'd not stir a foot out of that meadow till the sun went down. *And* I stuck to my word. When the sun sank down below the rim of the hills, my last swath fell and I fell on top of it. After a short rest, I just left the scythe and all my belongings where they lay and staggered home and I must have been a quare (queer) spectacle with my shirt-tail knotted and me dragging my pants behind me by the galluses.'

I could describe Jimmy's race between the sun and the Jalap but I'm afraid it would be too earthy; because Jimmy used explicit expressions such as, 'my insides turned to water and I could shit through a thraneen' (hollow hay stalk). So the closest I'll venture to describing how Jimmy managed both operations simultaneously is to describe a mower's stance. A mower stands flat-footed with feet about twenty inches apart, knees slightly bent like a skier landing after a jump and the body at an angle, a position that Jimmy described as 'sitting on a high commode'. I'll leave the rest to your imagination.

Early next morning Jimmy was as he said, 'Dragging my weary bones out from under the quilt, when who should come to the door but Master Nugent himself and he looking drim and drew (down in the dumps) and he says to me "My father, Sir Percy, ordered me to come and say I'm sorry for dosing you with Jalap and to tell you to take a week's holiday with full pay and perks". I'm afraid I was speechless but my wife said to him, "We are grateful to the Sir, please tell him from us that we are real grateful". He said, "No thanks to my father, it's *me* that's paying your week's wages; he's docking it out of my pocket money."'

When Eileen and I left Bluemans old place and headed east, she suggested that we stop awhile at Doolin's wall. I had intended to walk along the shore and stop at the Big Wall but naturally I gave in when she said, 'You think I have a poor memory for the countryside, let me lead you to the *exact* place where you and I and the six kids had a picnic in 1962, one I have wonderful memories of' and unerringly she walked to the spot. It was the spot alright. Talking of total recall! She said, 'Let's have our lunch here'. Then as if it were only yesterday it all happened, she reminisced of that day seventeen years ago; the glorious sunshine, the six children and myself — all in the best of health — kicking the football around, paddling in the water and wolfing the SPECIAL lunch she had packed. If she only knew it, all her lunches for our outings were *special* — they were packed with love.

Recently when I was visiting our five (surviving) children now living in Canada, I was reminded of that particular picnic. How each of us react to memories of events and happenings! The five talked and talked about the three years of 'living a full life in Multy' and they vied with each other in recalling and evoking memorable incidents. They recalled our picnic at Doolin's wall and there in Ottawa, I, too, was transported back in time, especially when after a lapse of fifteen years, our youngest son Kerry, only seven at the time of the outing, broke into the conversation with, 'How could we ever forget that picnic; don't you remember how he (that's me) wouldn't give us the chocolate bars Mum brought for our dessert until we had eaten up that pile of sandwiches'.

Eileen and myself have another happy memory of an incident connected with that picnic. Somehow, no matter how hard I try to explain that incident the result appears — innocuous. We were on our first mug of good strong tea when we were joined by a Friar who happened to be passing by and without any fuss or formality he accepted my 'Would you care to join us for a drop of tea?' Then he casually sat down on the grass and within minutes was one with us — or we with him. When Eileen and myself recall that pleasant hour with the big, blonde, good-looking Friar in his ankle-length brown habit and bare toes showing through his sandals, both of us vividly remember how casually, informally and NATURALLY, he moved a few yards away and stubbed the butt of the cigarette he had been smoking — into a recently deposited cow dung! Both of us appreciated that there was nothing earthy or crude in the incident; in fact, Eileen and I often talked about it and both agreed that somehow it was a perfect part of an idyllic day.

The area in the vicinity of Doolin's wall, where we now sat down to eat our lunch, appeared to be unchanged in the seventeen years that have elapsed since we had our family outings there. Now tidying up after our little snack she made a gesture that took in — almost embraced — the entire Irish countryside. 'Today I'm enjoying this immensely, I was afraid it would revive memories, that in perspective, could spoil the present — our present. Now I find that it enhances memories of our family picnic and I realize it was just another of the countless "best times" of our lives.'

Doolin's wall is the western boundary of the ten acres of shoreline the County Council (Local Government Authority) purchased some years ago to create a public beach, camping ground, playing fields and so forth. This public area now includes the Big Wall and most of the ground once occupied by Donore House, gardens, orchards, cricket pitch, tennis courts and walks. I believe the Council purchased the property to prevent it becoming commercialized with all the attendant damage to the environment.

The Council has done an excellent job of levelling, clearing and grassing the land along a thousand yards of the shore. They have cleared and prepared acres of space for caravan parking and tenting with plenty of clear level grassed areas for children to play. In addition to providing other beach amenities they have also built a boat-slip that blends well with the natural appearance of the lake-front.

Eileen remarked, 'If this beautiful lake with it's almost unlimited shoreline, without a single dwelling site within half a mile of the water, were in any other country but Ireland, it would be crowded with visitors the year round.' I tried to explain the absence of visitors by mentioning that even the city of Dublin is in the same fortunate position in respect to public amenities. That large city is surrounded by open country, which is sprinkled with lakes and traversed by rivers and at least three canals; besides isn't it built on the coast of the Irish Sea, which itself has hundreds of miles of beautiful open beaches with easy and free access for the public.

The Big Wall is the local name for a stretch of shoreline that got its name from the gigantic size of the uncut boulders that went into the construction of the wall, spacious harbour, private beach and the Big Pond, all of which were once the proud possession of the owners of Donore mansion sited about a quarter of a mile away. Owing to the lower water level, the area of the harbour, once named the Big Pond, is now dry land. The Big Pond was built as a dock for the Nugent's yacht. As the craft was unique in our area, it was and still is referred to as The Yacht. Over a hundred years ago the yacht capsized and sank in a gale. Fortunately there was no loss of life because she went down in shallow water — in about twelve feet — a few hundred yards from Doolin's wall.

When I was a youngster out perch fishing, one of our favourite fishing holes was called The Yacht, because on a clear day we could just discern her outline on the level, muddy lake bottom. We were told that sixty years previously she was lying on an even keel just resting on the bottom of the lake. The lake floor in the area of The Yacht is a mixture of mud and marl, which explains why The Yacht has been slowly sinking deeper and deeper over the years. They still tell stories around here of the many unsuccessful efforts the Nugents made to salvage her — including yoking combined teams of horses to a long cable stretched to Doolin's shore. Now that the area of The Yacht is dry land and permanently higher than the present lake level, it's possible I'm one of the few around today who knows the precise location of that wreck.

Regardless of the changes to the shoreline which resulted from the successive lowering of the lake level, if you — a stranger — standing on Donore shore, were asked to pick an ideal site for a house or mansion, ten chances to one you would choose a particular area: an area that is *now* a wilderness of neglected giant trees and tangled shrubbery and so overgrown with briers and weeds that it is difficult to realize that below its surface lies the foundation of the Nugents' fine Georgian mansion which stood for over two hundred years. Stand now on the low plateau that once was their carefully tended front lawn and you will agree that from their second and third storey windows the view was superb and unsurpassed.

When we stood on what was once the site of the Big House, Eileen complained, 'It's a pity they demolished that beautiful Georgian mansion, especially as you told me it was structurally sound and built to last a thousand years.' 'So was Jerusalem in one A.D.' I answered. She queried, 'What's the connection?' Then I reminded her of something I had previously published which told of an incident that occurred when this century was new. About an elderly Friar washing his feet in the shallow water in the lee of the Big Wall and The Sir sending down his butler to 'Order that monk off our property' and the Friar's reply 'Thanks! Now I'll give you a message for your master. Tell him from me, that by the time half of this — the twentieth century — has gone by, his mansion will not have a stone left on a stone; and not one of his name will own one foot of ground where he now lords it over the poor.'

As we walked towards the lake I tried to reconstruct the layout of the orchards, gardens, walks etc., so eventually we ended up in an area of ruined brick walls which I recognized as the remains of the large greenhouse. Echoes of 'Upstairs, Downstairs', the T.V. serial depicting the two social extremes — the Upper Crust and the Underdog — rang in my ears because those relics of the greenhouse reminded me of an account that Jimmy Bardon, a schoolmate, gave me of how servants in the Big House were kept in line — and that was a bare forty years ago. Jimmy was working, he said, 'attending Lady Nugent in the big greenhouse at the end of the orchard when one of the maids knocked on the glass door, opened it, went up to Lady Nugent, curtsied and presented her with a telegram. The Lady imperiously drew herself up to her majestic six feet, kept her clenched hands at her sides and told off the unfortunate maid for "daring to offer *me* a missive in your fist". She then ordered the girl back through the muck and rain to get the silver salver, return to the greenhouse and go through the full rigmarole of delivering the telegram in style.'

The day was still holding up so we agreed to try and walk the length of the Gravel Walk. The Gravel Walk is the local name for that part of Donore shoreline that stretches from Doolin's wall to Ballinakill, a distance of around a mile and a half. Strange how the origin and history of a name is lost, even in a locality like ours where there is hardly any emigration and each farm and every little plot of land has been occupied and lived on continuously by countless generations.

My mother used wistfully to talk of the two Miss Nugents —
'Blue Bloods to their fingertips'. Then directing her attention to
yours truly, she'd continue: 'Every week without fail they had
their coachman drive them in their horse-drawn brougham to
the village, just to' and she'd pause dramatically, then sounding
every single syllable so as to give emphasis to the next word,
she'd continue, 'unpatronizingly come in to admire *you* in the
cradle. They said you were the most beautiful child they had
ever seen and look how you turned out!'

I don't remember ever seeing either of the ladies; as far as I
can find out, they were already in the autumn of their lives by
the time I was born. Years later I endeavoured to learn more
about them and all I could determine was that they were very
popular 'in their own set'; that they moved freely in high
society, followed the hunt, attended swanky society balls,
soirées etc., and enjoyed the normal life-style of the titled élite.
But apart from their normal social activities and in the seclusion
of their mansion and its broad acres, they lived very private and
quiet lives.

I was told that come rain or shine not a day of their lives
passed that the two Miss Nugents did not take a stroll from
Doolin's wall to Donore boundary at Ballinakill — and back.
Their favourite walk originally was along an ordinary country
path formed over the years by countless feet, animal and
human. This path paralleled the shore of the lake at a distance of
about two hundred yards from the water's edge. The path itself
was hidden from view because it traversed the thickly wooded
shoreline, but portions of it afforded a clear view of the lake and
the open countryside, northwards. Their brother the Baronet
had his workmen carry out improvements to the original
pathway and he issued strict orders to preserve its natural
identity and beauty. His men cleared obstacles, drained wet
areas, smoothed the surface of the path, and surfaced it with
gravel. So I suppose it is logical that — in time — the area
became known as the Gravel Walk.

My mother was not the only one who invested the Nugent
ladies with an aura of glamour and romanticism, à la Jane Austen;
in fact, out of deference to the noble ladies, during their lifetime
the entire area of the Gravel Walk was considered sacrosanct and
no local consciously trespassed. The Nugent ladies had long
passed away before the children of the village ventured to

explore the Gravel Walk. As children we considered it quite an adventure because the briars, weeds, saplings and other undergrowth by then were making a concerted effort to conceal and preserve the Walk. Our childish creativity likened it to the fairy tale 'The Sleeping Beauty'.

The original area of the Walk where it traversed fields and open ground is now difficult to locate because our damp climate and fertile soil cause grass to grow on every conceivable exposed surface and area. Each season's grass withers and dies and succeeding growths of grass build up layer after layer, which will and do eventually cover and bury even hard-surfaced areas like roads or tennis courts.

Once the Nugents were gone from the locality the Walk ceased to be recognized as a right-of-way, because as Eileen and I traversed it, we were obliged to crawl through barbed-wire fences where it met farm boundaries. If it had been accorded right-of-way status the boundaries would have been provided with stiles. In reality, those fences are erected in such a way that they present an impassable barrier to cattle but facilitate human traffic.

Parts of the Walk were perfect for foot traffic except where there were natural depressions in the ground; these were quite damp and muddy. You could see where originally there had been artificial drainage, but years of neglect plus passage of cattle on their way to drink out of the lake had returned stretches of the Walk to its primitive state. But we enjoyed walking along some fine portions without difficulty and Eileen exclaimed with pleasure when we came to some of the numerous vantage places, where in spite of the heavily wooded shoreline we had a perfect view of the lake. Part of the Walk goes through a maze of large and obviously very old hazelnut bushes. Some of the bushes must be sixty feet high. We noticed that there were several varieties of hazelnuts and although we failed to see any order in the grove, in ages past they must have been carefully planted and cultivated. The gigantic hazels must have been imported from 'faraway places'. Regarding heights of hazel bushes/trees: a Tibetan variety grows to thirty feet; Turkish (Colurna) seventy five to ninety feet; and Chinese (Corylus Chinensis) 120 to 140 feet. We promised ourselves a return trip early in November to collect a sack of nuts. Incidentally, years past we courteously listened to various local experts' tips on winter storage of potatoes, turnips and especially onions. We experimented by trying ALL the 'sure ways' to save them and then by trial and plenty of errors succeeded in having loads of sweet, ripe hazelnuts through the following winter. The way it worked out for us was to store them in shallow cardboard boxes at Canadian room temperature (around 70°F.)

Sooner than expected — as a boy I imagined it an endless journey — we were at the end of the Walk. We piled our gear on the sawn butt of a large beech tree, sat down on part of the trunk, relaxed, gazed around and only then appreciated the reason for the Walk. The path terminated at a level, circular part of the otherwise gently sloping forest floor and yet after generations of disuse and neglect the area gave the impression of a miniature amphitheatre. I gazed around and sensed that something — once important — was missing, then something triggered a long-buried memory and I said, 'Where are the stone seats and the slab-topped table with the lines of poetry chiselled on it?' Now I remember how myself and other youngsters out perch fishing used to land down there on the shore where the spring well flows into the lake. A stranger landing at the place now would never realize that the soggy area is caused by a long-neglected, overflowing natural spring well. I remember how the water used to gush up and out under a stratum of limestone that formed a natural shallow pool which retained enough water to give safe shelter to a shoal of minnows — and even the odd frog. Now, if you look closely you can tell the well's location by the heavy growth of watercress, brooklime and other plants that thrive in slow flowing spring water. Long ago, when we'd had a good drink out of that well — and we believed the hotter the day the colder the water — washed our hands and climbed up here to eat our lunches, we would then sit on stone seats at a stone table. That table was formed by a slab of stone almost a foot thick and measuring four and a half feet, by three feet. The slab itself was supported on four round legs or pillars each about a foot in diameter. The table top had ten lines of what we believed to be poetry chiselled into it and we used to compete with each other to see who could make out the greatest number of words. Even then the letters were difficult to read due to a heavy growth of moss and lichen on the stone and when we eventually made out the individual letters we found it difficult to decipher some of the words because sometimes the letter 's' was written as 'f'. Strange, the name of the place just now dawned on me — 'The Ladies' Bower'. The word bower was somewhere on the slab.

It was some weeks afterwards that Eileen and I found the lettered table top. Someone lacking sensitivity or just unaware of its history had moved the slab to the public beach where it was in imminent danger from vandalism, or even of being stolen by some unprincipled souvenir collector. Now I am happy and proud to report that on Good Friday 1981 the present Guardian of the Friary, Rev. Father Ulic Troy O.F.M. had the slab transported from the public park at Lough Derravaragh and given a permanent resting place — sanctuary — in the Friary grounds. He had an expert stonemason, Louis Shanley, build the slab into the wing wall of the old stone bridge that spans the River Gaine.

The slab now has an honoured place at the entrance to Via Dolorosa — the outdoor Stations of the Cross — and only a stone's throw from the Nugents' burial plot. The plot contains the mortal remains of a long, unbroken line of Donore Nugents spanning four centuries. It was here that the first Nugent of Donore was interred in 1603 and where Donore's last residents, Sir Walter and Lady Aileen Nugent were laid to rest in 1955 and 1957 respectively. Even in rural Ireland 400 years is quite a chunk of time!

A month later we cleaned the lettering on the slab and found that every letter and even the punctuation marks are still deeply cut into the stone and legible. In my youth I had the good fortune to have access to old books where the letter 's' was written 'f' EXCEPT when the 's' occurred as the first or last letter of the word. I find there appears to be some inconsistency in the poem's punctuation. This is exactly how the tablet reads:

> If Peaceful thoughts thy Tranquil Bofom raife
> To NATURES works and lov^d Hibernia^s praife
> Welcome approach MARIA^s penfive Bower
> Sacred to Retirement and friendfhips power
> From giddy Scenes the Cankring Mind to Chear
> HYGEIA Calls the feaft of Reafon's here
> Tis Here Reflection holds her happy Seat.
> Health Peace and Smiling Blifs united meet
> Free from the World its Tumults and its Noife
> To tranquilize the Soul for Purer Joys.

So far I have not discovered the author of these lines, but each time I reread it, it seems to give me a better appreciation of the Miss Nugents and the part the Walk played in their lives — and in mine — because I find that memories of the Gravel Walk and the Bower invariably evoke Wordsworth's 'That inward eye which is the bliss of solitude'.

We had not brought the binoculars along, but because I know the country around here like the palm of my hand, was able to point out many places of historic interest. From the Bower we could make out where the borders of Counties Westmeath, Cavan and Longford meet. In fact we could see halfway down into County Longford. A bump on the northern horizon we identified as the historic Moat of Granard, once the site of the royal residence of an Irish King. At the picturesque north-eastern end of the lake we could see the Hill of Knock Eyon rising almost one thousand feet sheer from the water's edge. About a quarter of a mile nearer than Knock Eyon and on the same shore we could see what appeared to be a square-topped cliff; it is the remains of the Old Court of Faughaltown. In 1682, Sir Henry Piers described Faughaltown in detail and spoke of the ruins of Mortimer's Castle. He wrote that it was the retiring place of Mortimer, Earl of March, who married Phillipa, the daughter and heir of Lionel, Duke of Clarence, third son to Edward III and an elder brother to John of Gaunt, the father of Henry IV. 'Mortimer', he writes, 'after King Richard (II) was deposed that he might be out of harm's way, with his princess, in whom, after the death of Richard without heir to his body, the right of succession remained, fixed his residence, as tradition goes, amongst us at this place.'[*]

The site of this Castle of Mortimer occupies three quarters of an acre of ground. A point of local interest: a family named Mortimer owns a farm in the vicinity of the Old Court but as far as I know the family claims no royal connection.

After looking around the country in general, I started to point out Big Houses and estates whose owners and occupants 'moved and belonged' in the same title stratum as the Miss Nugents. The Nugent family maintained close social and intellectural contact with their peers who lived in those mansions, the furthest of which was within an hour's journey

---

[*]*Annals of Westmeath*, p. 144.

by coach or on horseback. I well remember a very old man, who was coachman at Donore saying, 'All MY working days and my father's before me was taken up with being coachman in Donore and mind you we never drove without being rigged out in Donore livery — topped with the tall hat with the cockade in it. If I wasn't driving some of the family to the residences of the aristocracy I'd be as busy as a nailer looking after the coaches and horses of lords, dukes and earls that were always paying social visits to Donore.'

It must have been two full hours after our arrival that as we reluctantly bid adieu to the Ladies' Bower, Eileen remarked, 'From what you tell me about the Miss Nugents, they are surely in heaven, but I can easily imagine them often returning here — it's heavenly!'

About a mile beyond Knock Eyon you can discern Tullynally Castle still locally called Pakenham Hall. The castle is the seat of the Earls of Longford whose family name is Pakenham. The present Lord Longford, like several of his immediate family, is an established author. He is a relentless crusader in the war against the peddlers and purveyors of pornography in the British Isles and Ireland, as a result of which his adversaries in a futile effort to discredit, discomfit and ridicule, christened him Lord Porn. Seeing he's an earl, I suppose 'dubbed' would be a more appropriate word.

It is a bit of a diversion I know, but I can't resist including a tid-bit relating to the scene of Lord Longford's late-in-life christening. In 1971 Lord Longford became more than concerned at the growing flood — avalanche — of pornography in England. He started a one-man crusade. It carried him to Denmark to gather ammunition by studying a totally censorship-free society. Seventy-five newsmen and foreign correspondents were on hand when the lord and his aides arrived at a Copenhagen sex club where live acts of sexual intercourse in addition to what the newspapers coyly referred to 'as other things', took place on the stage. When the 'good' lord could take no more of the lewd acts he decided to leave the scene, but was intercepted by the manager with an anxious 'But Sir, you haven't seen the intercourse yet.' A reporter wrote 'The lord then delivered himself of the pronunciamento: 'I have seen enough for science and more than enough for enjoyment.'

Less than a mile from Pakenham Hall you can see the tower

and the remains of a little stone church where in 1806, Lady Catherine Pakenham was married to the Honourable Sir Arthur Wellesley, later to become the first Duke of Wellington, better known as the Iron Duke, conqueror of Napoleon. Maria Edgeworth, a famous literary friend of the Pakenhams, lived at Edgeworthstown five miles distant from Pakenham Hall. Maria (1767–1849) was a celebrated novelist and essayist whose prose fiction is credited with the cause of the rapid development of the Irish regional novel and short story. Maria Edgeworth was a regular visitor to Donore — she may have savoured the pleasures of the original Walk — and I even wonder if she could have had a connection with the third line of the inscription on the stone tablet. Students of English literature would be interested to learn that Edgeworthstown is within a stone's throw of 'Goldsmith Country' where various landmarks familiar to readers of 'The Deserted Village' may be seen.

The most politically powerful family in the area was the Grevilles. Lord Greville's residence, Clonhugh, was only a couple of miles from Donore and generations of the Grevilles were intimate personal and political friends of the Nugent family.

I realize that quite a bit of the foregoing reads like a chapter out of Debrett, who you may remember, in 1802 published *The Peerage of England, Scotland and Ireland, containing an Account of all Peers*. I touched on these famous people, not in a title-dropping sense, but to show that the Miss Nugents were not exactly 'flowers born to blush unseen . . . etc.'; rather, they were contemporaries, neighbours and possibly intimate friends of many of the illustrious literary figures of their era. Our next exploration took us into quite different circles.

PART FIVE:
THE DEEP AND RECENT PAST

24. ARCHAEOLOGY

I am blessed, maybe cursed, with more than my share of curiousity; curiosity about a lot of things, and though not a science fiction buff, I am deeply interested in anything connected with the discovery of possible intelligent life 'out there' in the far reaches of this boundless universe. But my interest in space exploration is small compared to my unbounded and insatiable curiosity about Ireland's pre-history and archaeology.

Broadly speaking, archaeology could be defined as a study of man's past based upon the evidence of his material remains. It is claimed that from these remains, a specialist can deduce much, but not all, of the living conditions of man, of his way of life and of his cultural connections. Unfortunately I lack the training to question honestly and intelligently many of the conclusions 'the specialists' have arrived at; but even if I don't accept all their findings, I am more than grateful for their efforts towards unlocking the secrets of our forefathers' way of life.

Over the years I have read avidly everything connected with Irish archaeology I could lay my hands on, but regretfully realize that in Ireland, archaeologists have barely scratched the surface. In fact it is conceded that to date much of the country is archaeologically unexplored. A few of the drawbacks to more widely prosecuted research are lack of concerted public interest, apathy on the government's part together with absence of adequate financial backing. The lack of public interest is difficult to appreciate because most of us Irish are immensely proud of our ancient cultural heritage; in fact too often we are accused of living in the past.

I can't speak for the urban dweller, but down here in the country it is almost impossible to whip up public or private interest in any of the countless, unlisted and mostly uncharted prehistoric sites that dot our Irish landscape. I doubt if there will ever be an upsurge of archaeological study and exploration; not even our late, beloved President de Valera — himself a man of action — managed to get any action on a prehistoric mound at

Bruree, County Limerick where he spent his early years, although it was his express wish the mound be explored. In his lengthy lifetime of ninety-eight years that was one particular dream he failed to fulfil.

The consensus is that man first appeared in Ireland nine thousand years ago. Experts appear to base this date on the results of archaeological excavations in the north-east of Ireland in County Antrim, as a result of discoveries in that area of large numbers of implements of characteristic shape; they gave the name Mesolithic or Middle Stone Age to the way of life of the users of these objects. The beach at Larne, county Antrim, disclosed a large number of these tools and weapons shaped from stone; hence their makers were given the name Larnian by the archaeologists.

The distribution of these implements has been traced by archaeologists to Sligo in the west and southward to Dublin in the east, but they failed to mention the possibility that these objects could have been in use in County Westmeath in the Midlands where I live. Here in my own garden in the more elevated area of this ancient historic village I have dug up dozens of peculiarly-shaped stones that originally were worked into shapes identical to implements now labelled Larnian. Without any stretch of the imagination one could credit that the artificially-shaped stones I found were dressed, hammered and chipped to produce what could have been crude fore-runners of our modern hammers, axes, knives and spear points. There is such a profusion of stone implements that it is conceivable our garden could have been the site of a prehistoric weapons factory.

It may not be true for other parts of the country, but locally I failed to arouse any interest, let alone enthusiasm, in getting anyone to give a second look at the stones which obviously were shaped by human hands and it dawned on me that if I pursued the subject further they'd undoubtedly label me a crank.

In Ireland, objects and artifacts of archaeological interest are found mostly by accident in the course of ploughing, quarrying, excavating for sand or peat, building ditches or drainage operations which lower swamp and lake levels; to a lesser degree they are unearthed by excavations of ancient areas containing burial sites, places of worship and centres of public assembly.

This entire country is dotted with earth and stone mounds, ramparts, monuments, tombs, burial mounds, cist-graves, court cairns, passage graves, ring forts, crannógs, ritual stone monuments, stone circles and Ogham stones. With few exceptions these earth and rock-built structures are unexcavated and unexplored.

Up to fifty years ago these structures and monuments were reasonably immune to vandalism or complete destruction. They suffered little if any damage from investigation, excavation or grave-robbery, mostly because of what could loosely be called superstition, or fear of what is unknown or mysterious. It has been suggested that they were protected and preserved because they were often associated with places of worship and burial that belonged to a people who worshipped strange gods whose magic powers still protected their sacred places, and thus were feared.

There is still a strong widespread feeling of superstition in the countryside and most people will give you a list as long as your arm of misfortunes that befell unfortunate individuals who wilfully interfered with fairy forts or desecrated ancient burial mounds or pre-Christian places of worship. Quite often you read accounts of the amazement and chagrin expressed by 'outside developers' (foreign companies) when landowners and local labour forces refuse to allow anyone to tamper with these ancient relics. Inevitably it results in re-routing roads, re-siting factories and housing estates to avoid demolishing or even disturbing the old sites.

Unfortunately the Modern Age does not always respect our ancient sites. Within the last few years the permissive society has gained a foothold even here in Ireland and a more broadminded, or less respectful attitude has developed. For instance, three years ago I noticed with dismay a local politician, who is also a large landowner, plough and take a crop from one of his huge fields that had a very large ring fort in its centre. He ploughed up the ring fort enclosure as thoroughly as the rest of the field; fortunately the outline of the denuded fort, though now somewhat faint, can still be discerned although the ten foot high banks that withstood the ravages of thousands of years of man and beast disappeared before the onslaught of a bulldozer directed by an individual who appeared to lack pride in our ancient common heritage.

Anyway I am thankful that whether due to superstition,

religion or what is more probable — respect — many of our monuments are as intact and undisturbed as when their last users departed the scene and that was long before recorded history. Time and the elements plus fair wear and tear have eroded them but they stand patiently waiting for the skilled archaeologist to investigate them and conceivably throw more light on phases of our country's history hidden in the mists of time. As far as I can determine the evidence unearthed by most of the relatively minor archaeological research and excavation carried out in Ireland was linked to that period of the Neolithic Late Stone Age accepted as 4,000 years ago.

Field monuments of all types and periods, Megalithic tombs, burial mounds, habitation sites, monastic ruins and so forth, are to be seen in remarkable profusion all over Ireland, yet the relatively small amount of excavation and research connected with them has yielded significant results. Fairly recent air reconnaissance shows that only a small percentage of the arable land in Ireland has been ploughed in modern times. This favoured the preservation of our ancient earthworks generally. In fact Ireland is the only country in western Europe where the corrugation of the surface representing man's activities is so clearly defined. Although few man-built structures have survived intact, aerial photography clearly shows a profusion of heretofore hidden earthworks and patterns of human settlement.

Prior to 1930, methodical archaeological excavations were rare, but in 1932 a five year programme was initiated by the Harvard Archaeological Mission to Ireland and from 1934 Irish archaeologists with the aid of state government were able to excavate some important and interesting sites. Further excavations have resulted in a changed picture of several periods and aspects of Irish archaeology but undoubtedly entire classes of monuments have still to be studied.

It is accepted that around 3,000 B.C. the inhabitants of Ireland were engaged in farming. This agricultural way of life brought about fundamental changes in the lifestyle of a people who previously were somewhat nomadic and resulted in an increase in population and more permanent settlement. It is agreed that the introduction and evolution of farming in Ireland and in other countries on the western seaboard of Europe may in many areas be accredited to Tomb Builders.

These Tomb Builders arrived in Ireland before 3,000 B.C. and are characterized as Neolithic tomb builders. They built their tombs for collective burial, constructing them of huge unhewn stones over which they built a mound of earth and smaller stones. The tombs are of various classes in Ireland; the earliest type is considered to be the 'Horned Cairn' in which various kinds of pottery and other grave furniture, including leaf-shaped flint arrow-heads, have been found. We also have the 'Court Cairns'. These were Megalithic tombs built in long barrows; barrows which average about one hundred feet in length and consist of long passages or galleries of huge upright stones roofed with stone slabs. Usually the galleries were divided into compartments. The broader end of the mound was a court of round or semi-circular shape, hence they were called Court Cairns. Over 300 Court Cairns have been discovered in Ireland, most of them are located in the Central Plain. Burials in these tombs were usually by cremation although unburnt burials are also recorded.

County Meath with its gently rolling, rich grassy farmland forms part of this limestone plain. Meath — or to give it one of its historic titles 'Royal Meath' — originally included my county, Westmeath. Royal Meath was ruled for centuries by pre-Christian kings and later by Christian kings. The entire Central Plain abounds in historic sites; to touch on only a handful, we have Tara, seat of the High Kings; the Hill of Slane where St. Patrick lit the Paschal Fire; Kells with its famous monastic ruins; the historic tumuli of Brough na Boinne and the now world famous passage graves at Loughcrew.

A few words about these particular sites: Tara of the Kings, or 'The Royal Acropolis' (the ancient name translated into English) was the religious and cultural capital of Ireland from the Druidic times right into the eleventh century A.D. It was here that our early Kings of Ireland were crowned and where one of them, King Cormac Mac Art (3rd century A.D.) founded schools of law, literature and military science. At the time of St. Patrick's arrival in Ireland (450 A.D) the Tara-based monarchy had been the most powerful of the (then) Five Kingdoms of Ireland. Eventually as Christianity spread, that monarchy only survived into the reign of King Malachi II who died at Tara in 1022 A.D. It was at Tara that the historic Feis was held every three years.

The Feis was the national assembly at which laws were enacted and clarified, disputes between rulers and other important leaders were settled and matters affecting the country *as a whole* were determined. The basis or yardstick used in settling disputes and promoting social harmony was the Brehon Laws. After decisions were handed down by the Brehons at the Feis, the King (Ard Ri), the Druids, the Princes and other dignitaries retired to the immense banquet hall in the King's palace. We are told that the palace at Tara was built in the form of a square with each side measuring 900 feet. It contained 150 dormitories in addition to the banquet hall which had capacity for a thousand guests at a sitting. Previous to the feast each guest seated himself beneath his shield which the heralds hung on the walls of the hall.

A brief account of the Brehon Laws may not be amiss here. Brehon was the name given to a judge or magistrate among the ancient Irish. Previous to Christianity, Brehons combined the offices of both judge and priest. Celtic society evolved a highly sophisticated legal system that became known as the Brehon Laws, which pictures a society presided over by priests (Druids) of elaborately graded ranks. The people were divided into free and unfree; commoners and nobles. Thus there were several distinct social ranks ranging from nobles to serfs. Every man had his honour-price which reflected his legal and social status and determined the validity of his contracts. This in turn guaranteed a highly developed system of suretyship involving pledges, hostages and honour-price.

Interestingly enough, most offences including murder, could be commuted by fines which were fixed with minute precision; because money was then unknown in our society, fines were paid in kind. It is probably news to many in our sex-equality-seeking society that 'under the Brehon Laws women were free to own property and to enter into contracts concerning it'.

Incidentally, the transmission of the Brehon Laws was not dependent on tradition, rather it was carefully written down in our earliest (surviving) manuscripts. Around 440 A.D. St. Patrick and other learned men revised and rewrote the Laws and carefully deleted what they believed were traces of heathenism. They renamed the Laws and formed a code called *The Senechus Mór*. This rewriting infers that a previous code written in the ancient Irish tongue existed at the time. Despite many ineffectual attempts by the British Government to suppress it, this Brehon Law as spelled out in the Senechus Mór was exclusively in force in Ireland until 1170. James I finally abolished it in 1605.

Until around the middle of the 19th century the Brehon Laws were cloaked in obscurity, but in 1952 a commission was appointed by the British Government to superintend the translation and publication of those ancient Laws of Ireland. Three years later an edition (in English) of the Senechus Mór was published in five volumes.

Kells, today one of Meath's principal towns, has the remains of a monastic settlement founded by St. Columcille as early as the sixth century.

The Book of Kells recognized as the most complete triumph of illuminated art the world has ever seen was created here at Kells around the eighth century.

Brough na Boinne, or 'Burial place of the Kings', is a few miles east of Slane village. It was on Slane Hill close to the site of the village that St. Patrick lit his Paschal Fire in the fifth century and proclaimed Christianity throughout 'the length and breadth of Ireland'.

Brough na Boinne is a series of Bronze Age tumuli located a few miles from Slane and stretching along the north bank of the Boyne River. The principal tumuli which are about a mile apart, are Knowth, Newgrange and Dowth. Doctor George Eogan, Professor of Archaeology at University College, Dublin, has been in charge of archaeological excavations in the area since 1962. When he commenced his research at Knowth the area gave the appearance of an ordinary green field with a small hill in the middle; but years of patient, expert excavations eventually revealed the remains of seventeen smaller burial mounds encircling the main one. A late Stone Age cemetery re-emerged which consists of a remarkably constructed series of stone-built burial chambers and entrance passages.

Speaking to a columnist, Professor Eogan said, 'If I were a Neolithic man here on top of this large mound, looking down on that bend of the Boyne River I would see before me a forested countryside. In the several clearings I would see farm homes with grassy areas for tillage and for grazing cattle. There would be a prosperous agricultural society, just as we have today, on some of the most fertile land in the country.' He says that the people who built the stone passage graves within the funeral mounds were part of a prosperous sophisticated society with a major developed cult of the dead. He claims that the engineering, agricultural and artistic skill needed to conceive, execute and embellish the monuments expresses the sophistication of their builders. For instance, the great mound of Knowth has two separate passages with leaders to individual chambers — one rectangular and one cruciform. The passages and chambers were constructed by using tall stones as walls, with flags or capstones forming the roof. Over the roof there are built-up layers of smaller stones and earth all of which form an enormous cairn. The whole area of the cairn is enclosed in a rough circle formed by huge decorated kerbstones.

Dr. Eogan concluded that the beautiful carvings on the various stones must have been done with stone implements since there is no evidence of metal instruments or tools on the sites. The carvings include circular motifs, spirals, partial circles and other geometric patterns. These carvings or markings are neither crude nor imprecise and have a variety of shape and texture which obviously required skill and a variety of tools.

When asked if the markings were of any other purpose than ornamentation, Dr. Eogan admitted he didn't know but would not totally dismiss any of the prevailing theories including those suggesting that the Neolithic builders had a unique (for their era) knowledge of astronomy and geometry. He added that some of the markings show a knowledge of sundialling and the existence of a calender based on the lunar month. Professor Eogan is proceeding to carry out a thorough investigation of this great mound of Knowth and hopes to complete the project in five years. Each step of the ongoing excavation reveals additional beautifully ornamented stones. One of those stones blocking a passage has just been uncovered. They call it the Guardian Stone because it appears to have great eyes and an owl-shaped body.

The Professor points out that Knowth contains the longest passages of any megalithic tomb in Ireland, Brittany or Spain. When opened, the chambers at the end of the passages each contained a stone cremation basin. So far Dr. Eogan has found evidence of at least twenty individual cremated bodies. Personal effects including stone beads and ornaments plus pottery ware were also found in the tomb chambers.

The most interesting theory connected with the 'mound mystery' has been propounded recently by a Mr. Martin Brennan, an American — who says, 'I am in fact a professional and my field is Visual Design Communication. I specialise in Neolithic rock inscription and have acted in this capacity for many years not only in this country but Japan and Mexico.' Early in December 1980, in a great blaze of publicity Mr. Brennan claimed that the three tumuli in County Meath, Dowth, Knowth and Newgrange are highly advanced astronomical observatories designed by Neolithic man as an elaborate calendar and *largely misunderstood since*. He said that three tumuli are astronomically aligned to the rising sun and were used by our prehistoric ancestors to fix the time of the spring and autumn — equal night and day, and the winter solstice — the shortest day.

Mr. Brennan claims that the beam of light which enters the chambers at Dowth is more precise than at Newgrange and that it definitely illuminates a fixed sequence of stone inscriptions. The American claims that his discoveries show the County Meath neolithic monuments to be much more complex and sophisticated than Stonehenge in England. He expressed surprise that this elaborate design had remained undiscovered until *he* came along.

An answer was promptly given in a newspaper report which quoted Dr. Michael J. O'Kelly, Professor of Archaeology at University College, Cork as pointing out that he and others had already studied the sunlight in the chamber at Dowth. Professor O'Kelly said that there was no doubt that the Neolithic community that built those mounds about the year 3,200 B.C. in the Boyne valley were quite sophisticated. Referring to the vast dimensions and complex construction of the burial mounds, the Professor observed that the Newgrange mound alone contains 200,000 tons of stone.

Regardless of what strange theories the savants and 'experts' express and argue about, the fact remains that there is an unbroken local tradition that those mounds long predate the Druids; that 'before the dawn of history' the Plain of Meath was a centre of pagan religious rites — including cremated burials. In fact the mounds owe their survival and preservation to the long held belief amongst Irish country people that the mounds are sacred. A venerable resident recently said to me, 'I've lived here all my life and generations of my family before me and we never had any doubt that our people built those mounds; that their ashes were buried there long before Adam was a barefoot boy.' Call it superstition if you will, but I hold that it is based on awe and respect for 'our own people' who lived and loved, worked and fought on Irish soil back in the womb of time.

Those mounds have been undisturbed for over 7,000 years, and we have scientific proof that this part of Ireland was inhabited 2,000 years before that. Thinking thus, it takes little stretch of imagination to give credence to the theory that something like half the genes in the Irish man or woman of today can be traced back to the Boyne valley Mesolithic settlers — long before they evolved into rock illustrators and tomb builders.

When I run out of interesting things to write up or a local rumour to run down, I make a bee-line for either Séan Weir's or Anthony Keogh's pub. Invariably there is a bunch of steady customers in for a pint and everyone knows everyone else; or as my friend Tom Cassidy would say 'I know every dog and devil for miles around'. So in a pub the other night without any trouble I drew the general conversation around to digging up long buried artifacts. Actually I'd have been foolish to have used the word 'artifacts' because of the danger of being accused of 'showing off'. Not that the average person around here has a limited vocabulary; in reality I envy the easy style and descriptive, colourful language they use. The 'boys' in the pub referred to artifacts as 'old relics' — but not with the religious connotation.

There are numerous reasons why our Irish bogs must be a virtual burglar-proof treasure-house of buried artifacts. Even today our bogs are the easiest place to dig or excavate, and the open bogholes from which generations have dug turf for domestic heating and cooking have always been an open invitation for burying dead animals or even disposing of human bodies.

In Ireland we meet two types of bog: the blanket bog and the raised bog. The blanket bog gets its name from the manner in which it blankets relatively steep slopes and even rocky surfaces. It's depth is comparatively shallow in relation to the raised bog.

Raised bogs are so named because they grow up above the general level of the surrounding terrain. There are nearly one million acres of this type of bog in Ireland and their depth varies from ten to thirty feet.

Thirty feet deep! How many years and how many layers of

vegetation did it take to build up that thirty foot mass of peat? A mass that is the sum total of innumerable layers of vegetation that yearly grew to maturity, ripened, wilted, rotted and in turn was compressed by succeeding layers. I am sure that scientists have the equipment and know-how to determine the age of each layer even in our deepest bogs.

Over five per cent of the surface of Ireland is bogland. Imagine! More than a million acres that undoubtedly contain tangible evidence of early animal and human habitation of this island. Hardly a month goes by but you hear of items being accidentally found or dug up in the bogs; items and artifacts that have been hidden, preserved (and to a great extent unimpaired) under protective layers of peat for hundreds, even thousands of years.

This preservation is due to acidity, low temperature and the absence of oxygen rather than to any specific preservative in the peat. In fact not only metal objects, but those composed of wood and even bone remain unchanged for an indefinite period. I often hear of local turf cutters finding firkins (kegs) of butter buried hundreds of years ago and to hear it told, 'If you wanted to chance it, I'm sure it still would be good to eat — I just tasted it and it was terribly salty, suppose the salt and the bog preserved it.' It's common to hear of corpses being dug up 'just as fresh as when they were swallowed up in the bog long ago'. Invariably the persons accidentally exhuming them hastily re-inter them, and *never* advise the authorities — a secretiveness which is possibly a hangover from the days when we 'carried the foreign yoke'.

Only a few months ago in a pub here in the village a local turf cutter regaled the customers with the account of a complete house he had uncovered in Clonave bog. The house, as he said 'Still had pieces of wooden furniture around a flat flagged hearthstone.' I asked him if any steps were taken to have the site examined by experts. He answered 'We were more interested in getting our turf cut and anyway it was twenty feet down in the bog so we bottomed the hole (dug the last layer of turf), let the water in and thought no more of it.'

Due to frequency and variety of 'finds' of prehistoric material and artifacts, the media seldom bothers to report them. Usually it is only when some editor requires stop-gap news that one reads about them.

The Midlands have been continuously served by newspapers

since the Westmeath Journal's birth in 1783. The present 'Westmeath Examiner Longford And Meath Reporter' appeared in 1882 with John Haydon as its editor for seventy years. Its next and present editor is Nicholas Nally. Fortunately 'The Examiner', as it's fondly called, gives historical coverage to most reported finds. Recently it reported a 4,000 year old burial.

An early bronze age burial place containing the cremated remains of a young person and a prehistoric vessel has been uncovered on the surface on the shores of Lough Ennel at Ledeston, Mullingar. A team of archaeologists from the National Museum in Dublin visited the site, made a report and added that this type of burial place was common enough in the Midlands 4,000 years ago.

Sometime previously, the *Examiner* had reported a discovery in and excavation directed by Mr. Michael Ryan of the National Museum. The finds included a number of areas in which stone tools had been manufactured. Over four hundred objects have been recovered including three polished stone axeheads, small blades and scrapers made from chert. Preliminary dating of the finds puts them in the period 6,000 to 5,000 B.C. — the Early Mesolithic Period.

I'll admit there *was* a small buzz of excitement in 1978 when an eighth century crozier turned up in a bog thirty miles from here. The crozier, accidentally dug up by a Bord na Mona turf cutting machine stands two and a half feet high — the top of it is missing. It comprises a core of wood encased in bronze which is ornamented with interlacing Celtic patterns, covered with silver foil. A knob on the crozier could have belonged to either St. Columbanus, St. Finbarr or St. Ciaran. This theory is based on the tradition that Bishops' croziers in early Christian times were made of wood. If Bishops became saints (after death) their croziers were encased in bronze and silver. Doctor J. Raftery of the National Museum is quoted as saying 'The bronze silver casing of the crozier is worn down as if thousands of pilgrims handled it over a period of time.'

An interesting footnote to the find. A few hundred pounds reward was paid to the finder! A friend of mine who unearthed a priceless sword in a bog a few years ago and 'kept quiet about it' said to me 'Now you see why no one but an idjit would report finding anything when they give such a measly reward as that.' The Director of the National Museum described the crozier as

'One of the first class objects of Early Christian Ireland, ranking with St. Patrick's Bell, the Cross of Cong and the Ardagh Chalice.'

Mention of those treasures beyond price will surely ring a bell with many of the millions who viewed the exhibition 'Treasures of Early Irish Art' shown in 1978–79 in a number of major American museums. But I'd like to say a few words specifically about the Ardagh Chalice.

Over a hundred years ago a boy digging potatoes near a ring fort at Ardagh, Co. Limerick unearthed the richest, to date, cache of Early Christian objects in Ireland. The find included one silver chalice, one bronze chalice and four brooches. The silver chalice, a beautiful eighth century two-handled vessel for dispensing wine at Communion is credited with being the finest piece of eighth century metalwork that has ever come to light. *The Oxford History of Technology* calls the chalice 'A supreme achievement of the goldsmith's art and probably in no other work in the world are the varied techniques employed in metal working more skilfully combined.' Experts added that the chalice was tangible evidence of the skill and spirit of our ancient craftsmen and bore witness to Ireland's eighth century richness in both senses of the word.

Finds like St. Patrick's Bell, the Tara Brooch and the Ardagh Chalice were recently overshadowed by a find of treasure trove in a Tipperary bog. It appears that a local building contractor using a four hundred dollar metal detector discovered the trove. The 'find' consists of a chalice similar to the Ardagh Chalice, a strainer and a large tray or paten together with its stand. The chalice is decorated with panels of gold filigree and amber settings. Extensive areas of its surface are gilt. The handles are elegantly ornamented. Panels of gold filigree and amber studs encircle the bowl immediately below the rim. The underside of the base is also decorated.

The strainer is made of gilt bronze. It is in the form of a ladle, the bowl of which is divided into two equal parts by a central bronze plate, perforated in a decorative manner. The handle terminates in a foil-backed crystal encircled by glass settings and is fitted with a ring for suspension.

The paten is a large circular plate or tray of complex construction. A band of delicate gold filigree panels separated by elaborate glass studs originally decorated the upper surface of its rim.

The sides of the paten carry stamped gold or gilded panels bearing interlaced and spiral motifs. The stand of the paten is a circular band, the outer surface of which is elaborately decorated with interlaced designs and magnificent rectangular glass settings with beautifully made complex silver grilles.

The basin which had covered the finds in the earth is made of beaten bronze. It is undecorated and in an advanced state of deterioration.

Apart from its archaeological significance a complicated human interest story is developing as a result of the find. It appears that the local building contractor who discovered the trove actually owns these wonderful pieces. Evidently the British Law concerning treasure trove was not taken over by the Free State when it gained independence — as the discerning lawyers argued in Court, an argument upheld by the judge — so the treasure evidently belongs legally to the discoverer. This appears to be the state of affairs at the time I write, and it seems that whoever owns the land has no claim. So the legal owner has a treasure worth something like £6,000,000.

To return to the travelling exhibition of 'Treasures of Early Irish Art', that exhibition contained a selection of sixty nine objects from the collections of three premier cultural institutions of the Republic of Ireland. The objects exhibited contain virtually all the major work that has survived from the three millennia before 1,500 A.D. and is a dramatic reminder of the high level of culture and civilization preserved in Ireland during the so-called Dark Ages.

The exhibition started with the genesis of Celtic art in the second millennium B.C. and focused on objects that form the very foundation of European art. Mainly objects of personal adornment, they exemplify a sophisticated knowledge of metallurgy.

The second and third sections were the focal point of the exhibition and included the world's greatest masterpieces of manuscript illumination: the celebrated eighth century Book of Kells and other noted works such as the Book of Durrow, the Book of Dimma and the Book of Armagh.

The final section of the exhibition concentrated on the Viking Period and its impact on Irish art during the Romanesque Period (tenth to twelfth centuries).

I would suggest to Americans interested in Ireland and things

Irish that if they did not get an opportunity to see the exhibition they should endeavour to obtain a copy of the catalogue published by the Metropolitan Museum. The 224 page catalogue is magnificently illustrated and contains essays by several writers who are experts in their particular fields and disciplines.

To buttress my plea for increased professional archaeological exploration and official preservation of our rich cultural heritage, I would like to quote from the catalogue's Preface penned by its author, G. Frank Mitchell, President, Royal Irish Academy who says, in part:

Only a very few of Ireland's early treasure survived, and almost all that have are included in the present exhibition . . .

The illuminated manuscripts owe their survival to having been jealously treasured in churches and monasteries; nearly all the other objects are of the noble metals — gold, silver and bronze — and so resisted destruction from both exposure to the air and burying in the ground. Those objects that did survive the attacks of nature had to face other constant perils in the course of Ireland's long and turbulent history; to be buried hastily without much chance of recovery: to be stolen and used to decorate the hall of a different lord or the altar of a rival monastery; to be plundered, broken up, and divided among a marauding gang who might mount the fragments as trophies; to be melted down and vanish forever in a pool of bullion metal.

Safe places for the conservation and display of the national treasures did not exist until comparatively modern times. (p. ix)

25. POLL NA gCAT

Sometimes I suspect the retirement I brag about is just an excuse for sheer laziness. When one of my pet projects gets 'sticky' I weakly say 'Oh, we'll have a go at it some other time.' Like the cave in the hill of Poll na gCat which I was so enthusiastic about opening and exploring in 1961.

When we were children a bunch of us would go for nuts to the Rock of Tyfarnham about a mile from the village, and when we felt like making a full day of it we'd continue on to Poll na gCat a couple of miles further, because it was supposed to have bigger and better hazelnuts. A trip there always held an element of adventure on account of the cave. The name Poll na gCat means the hole or cave of the cats. Our parents never failed to warn us about the cave and we in turn *never* failed to take at least a little peek in at its dark and forbidding mouth. Poll na gCat is one of the larger hills around here. The hill's western side and top are covered with grassy fields but the north-eastern side being too steep is to sustain a covering of grass, is a veritable jungle of hazelnut bushes. Out of the eastern slope of the hill and about thirty feet below its summit a huge rock face emerges. At a cursory glance it could be the face of a quarry except that the exposed solid rock is weathered; it has no workable layers which, previous to the discovery of explosives would have made it impossible to quarry.

It was common knowledge that at the beginning of this century the owner of the large farm that includes the hill, had the mouth of the cave permanently closed because some of his cattle disappeared and it was assumed they were lost in the cave. They say he eventually found one of his lost cows thirty miles away in County Cavan.

In 1961 I got permission to open and explore the cave and in June of that year my eldest son and I, equipped with shovel and flashlight, made a start on examining the cave. It was apparent that some time in the past, earth had been piled against the rock face at a certain place where we found traces of an opening in the rock. In this area the clay fill had sunk and it was possible with the aid of a flashlight to discern where the rock sloped downwards at about fifteen degrees and appeared to form the roof of a passage. This in turn seemed to branch into two more smaller passages.

We did a small amount of digging and in front of the opening in the rock came upon the rusted remains of a barricade of galvanized iron sheeting imbedded in the earth fill. This about verified part of the local tradition, although I suspected the sheeting could have been used to prevent foxes from entering the cave on the day of the hunt.

I had better slow up and explain briefly this business of foxes. As most people know, we have had fox hunting for hundreds of years in Ireland. As a matter of fact our (English) history books in school vaunted: 'Fox hunting has been carried out wherever we have established British rule'. Today fox hunting is still the 'in thing' with the gentry and the would-be gentry.

Personally I don't quite agree with the fox hunting fraternity's glowing description of 'the age-old mystique of fox hunting which evokes a picture of the hunt in full regalia, clearing banks, ditches and rough-built stone walls, with the hounds in full cry'. On the other hand I do not subscribe to that much-quoted sentiment expressed by another Irishman: 'The unspeakable in full pursuit of the uneatable'. There are two factors concerning the 'hunt' that bother me; first, the closing of the fox's burrow while he himself is out hunting for food, and secondly, the inevitable merciless kill. It disturbs me, although I have killed more animals than the next fellow — but *never* for the sake of killing, or under the guise or aegis of sport.

To ensure the day's hunt will not terminate too quickly or even draw a blank, it's accepted practice to stack the cards against the quarry 'going to ground' or escaping back into his own earth (burrow). Foxes invariably do their hunting in the wee hours of the morning, hence on the morning of the hunt, workmen plug or fill up the entrances to all the (known) fox earths in the area of the proposed hunt. Thus when the 'meet' goes into action and the fox hounds pick up Reynard's trail, he hastily heads for home; discovers that there is no welcome mat out for him; rapidly races to the next earth with the same result — no refuge; and tally-ho as the *sports* say, he is now running for dear life. Incidentally, if he finally found what he feels is a haven, a large rabbit burrow, a shore, or a road culvert it would do him no good. The baying, howling hounds would trail him and congregate at the entrance to be soon joined by the entire hunt. Next the fox terriers would arrive on the scene. Fox terriers, being much smaller than the quarry, can readily reach the cornered fox and 'bolt' him out to the ravening dogs. When the hounds have torn Reynard limb from limb the Master will award the 'brush' to the huntsman who was 'first in to the kill' and the latter will hang the trophy on a prominent part of his steed's gear. There is quite a ritual connected with fox hunting, *especially* the kill.

Now to get back to the cave; we returned to Canada some months after being confronted by the galvanized iron barrier but not before my son had extracted a promise that we would return some day and fully explore the cave.

Ever since I returned, that cave has been uppermost in my mind and every chance I get, I put out feelers about it. My enquiries led me to Cecil Gibson, well known sportsman and current world champion wet fly trout angler. Cecil, a nephew of the Mr. Gibson who originally owned Poll na gCat, told me that in his teens he went quite a bit into the cave but his stay was limited to the short life of the lit candle he carried.

Sir Henry Piers who lived at Tristernaght (three miles from here), in his history of Westmeath wrote in 1682 that the Rising of 1641 was concocted in the Abbey of Multyfarnham and in his account* of that event included:

'. . . Not far hence eastward, on the north side of a high hill, after you have ascended more than half the height, we meet with a great hollow or cave in the bowel of the hill, by the natives called Cat's Holle. The first entry is very low, so as you must creep on all fours, if you enter. When in this posture you have proceeded fourteen or fifteen feet, you may rise and walk upright, for here the cave is seven or eight feet high, and if you bring light with you you may behold a piece of nature's architecture, for as art is said in other things to imitate nature, so, here nature may be said to imitate art, so handsomely the vault seems arched. The first room that entertaineth you is pretty large, about twelve feet square, hence are divers narroe apartments verging east, south and west. Two of these, of the length of one or two perches, grow so narrow and incommodius for further travel that they give but

Annals of Westmeath, p. 130.

little invitation to a further search. The third towards the west admits a curious person to a further search. The natives say there is a subterrainean passage from this cave to Croagh Patrick, in Connaught, but very few believe it. In this cave, towards the latter end of the Civil War (Rising of 1641) the Chief Tory of Westmeath is said for a time to have lurked; but on better consideration, he abandoned the garrison, for although here one man might keep out a thousand, yet it was easy for one man without, the wind setting convenient, by a smoke to force a greater number within to surrender.'

In '79 the present owner, Mr. McClancy, kindly gave me permission to have a real go at the cave so for the moment I can't find any excuse to put off exploring it.

26. THE HILL OF BEALTAINE

A recent letter from Dr. Hannon, an American friend, says in part: '. . . don't forget the location of "our " hill, the low flat-topped hill about a mile west of Poll na gCat, as I hope to do an archeological study of it when I visit you this summer.' Sure there is little danger of me forgetting either the location, or the circumstances connected with my friend's interest in The Hill, because I can't look out my favourite window without seeing, at the southern end of the valley, that squat and flat-topped hill standing there accusing me of inaction. The hill is only a couple of miles south of the village; actually it is one of the lowest of the clump of hills that wall in the valley. From our house, on a clear day, it resembles a tonsured head because the bush-covered lower portion corresponds to the half-covered area of a monk's tonsured head, while the top is grass-covered and bald.

On Dr. Hannon's last visit I happened to mention I had never set foot on several of the hills we could see from our house. Within minutes the Doctor (who asked us to call him by his Christian name, Chan) and I were in his rented car and inside half an hour had driven a few miles of country road, turned down a narrow, winding muddy bohereen, and after opening and carefully reclosing several mearing (boundary between farms) gates we emerged on a newly constructed country road and suddenly were within a hundred yards of the flat-topped hill.

Where we parked the car there happened to be a few road maintenance men sitting around a little fire having their tea-break and I thought we might as well have a chat with them about the circular fort and other earthworks that are so numerous at the end of the valley.

Quite often I complain and grumble about the lack of public interest in the archaeological sites that are so widespread in Ireland. Then again, their profusion and easy accessibility could account for much of the disinterest or apathy. On second thoughts I'm the last person in the world who should complain;

here was I, at the foot of this historic hill which is within two miles of my birthplace and I didn't even know its name. We approached the 'road gang' and easily struck up a conversation. Over here, under circumstances such as these, no one has to bother with introductions or beating around the bush so I said, 'My American friend is interested in old forts, mounds, fairy wells, caves and such. Is there anything of that nature around here that might interest him?' Almost as if they had expected the question and without any preamble, one of them told us that two years previously when they were road building in the field next the hill they accidentally opened a mass grave 'that was filled to the brim with piles and piles of human bones'. We were more than interested, but I'm sure you could hear both our faces fall when another of them anticipated my next question with 'Oh! we covered it up right away and our ganger shook a few handfulls of hayseed on it. No one wants to get involved with government officials and their board of inquiry in this sort of thing'. As we walked away I remarked to Chan that if the same gang had uncovered still-warm bodies they would even more surely have kept themselves uninvolved. But then, what right have I to be critical, when in my heart I know that my own personal laziness will also prevent me from trying to have the burial site officially examined.

The present shape of the hill resembles a portion of a hard-boiled egg with its top cut off. In reality, ages ago, the original hilltop was removed and the resultant material used to build one complete and several portions of three concentric steep-sided earthen banks. Obviously the one-time steep banks had been built for defensive purposes. The almost flat top of the hill is roughly one hundred feet in diameter and must have been the site of a dwelling or citadel.

When we had partially examined and explored the hill and its man-made embankments, Chan was ablaze with curiousity. He drew my attention to a portion of the top outer bank where the grassy earthen cover had eroded and exposed an area about three yards square. The area was a pile of small, broken stones each of such a regular size, that they looked as if they had been passed through a sieve composed of four inch mesh. To me, the stones looked as if they had been exposed to fire and I hazarded the theory that they had been the contents of a lime kiln. Then Chan pointed out that there was an area of the heap of stones

where a small hallow or vortex had formed, as if the lower layers
of the small stones had leaked or poured into a hollow space
underneath. He wondered aloud if there might be a passage or
chamber under the stone pile. As we were not equipped at the
time to do any digging or excavating he reluctantly said "I'll be
back". Unlike ships that pass in the night, Chan has already
arranged to visit us this summer and it goes without saying that
the hill figures prominently in his planned itinerary. In the
meantime I'm toying with coaxing him into 'writing up' his
personal account of our little impromptu expedition to the hill.

Thanks to the American's avid interest I made some enquiries
locally and also did a bit of research on the hill's place in local
folklore and history. We were fortunate in mentioning the
problem to a longtime friend of the family, Frank Delemare, an
octogenarian who, as he said 'herded cattle in the vicinity and
for over sixty years lived in the shadow of the hill'. I asked him
to name the various hills in the area and as he identified each
one, their Irish names rolled off his tongue with the old, pure
Irish pronunciation even though that language has not been in
everyday use around here for nigh on 150 years.

Frank, like myself, learned a fair amount of Irish at school; in
addition, his normal conversation included a vocabulary of
hundreds of Irish words and phrases. For instance he usually
addressed my wife as 'a garahalla' (O girl!) or 'acushla ma cree'
(pulse of my heart). I asked him to pronounce the local name of
the hill. Slowly and clearly he said "Knocknabulteen' and agreed
with me that the word could mean 'Hill of the Bulteens'. In this
area we still use the 'old names' in countless ways and especially
for items and details connected with Irish country life style. The
word 'bulteen' invariably is used to describe a certain part of a
flail; in fact it is the only name we know for it. I assume you
alreay know that a flail is a farming instrument for threshing or
beating grain from the ears (of grain) by hand. It has a wooden
staff or handle at the end of which a stouter pole or club is so
hung as to swing freely. That short pole has an English name
'swipple'; the Irish word for swipple is 'bulteen'.

Pursuing my research further I procured a 1902 Ordnance
Survey of Ireland map that gave interesting information as to
location, altitude, roads and boundaries. This map spells the hill
'Cruckboeltane': thus this map gave me my second name for the
hill. The following notation on the map is also worth

mentioning:

Engraved at the Ordnance Survey Office Dublin, under the direction
of Major Leach E.E.
Surveyed in 1840 and published by Colonel H. James F.R.S. M.R.I.A.
R.E. Director General
Revised in 1898–99 and published by Colonel Duncon A. Johnston R.E.
Director General, 1902

Later I studied a 200-year-old map of the area around the
Gaine Valley and discovered that the map compiler had
obtained all the local place names from the Irish speakers in the
area. This older map gives the correct location of the hill but
spells its name 'Cnocnabaalteine'.

In realtion to this third and more ancient name for the hill and
from my own somewhat limited knowledge of our language, I
would say cnoc is the Irish for 'hill', na means 'of', Bealtaine is
the 'Irish May Festival', the 'first day of May', 'the month of
May'. Hence my partial choice would be Hill of the May Festival;
admittedly it is somewhat biased because I can visualize that hill
as the ideal setting for the age-old celebration of the pagan
festival of Bealtaine.

Recently I read a scholarly treatise* on the origin of Bealtaine.
In part it goes:

Gaulish 'Apollo' and congeners.

Like the classical god with whom he is equated in Gallo-Roman
sources and by Caesar, the Gaulish Apollo 'drives away diseases'. In
particular, he is the patron deity of thermal springs. His dedications are
more numerous than the status of his Roman counterpart would
warrant and it is obvious that the gods assimilated to the classical deity,
enjoyed an extensive and popular cult.

One may use the plural here with fair confidence, for of the fifteen or
more epithets applied to 'Apollo' in Gaulish inscriptions, there are
several which occur relatively frequently and are evidently separate
deity names. The commonest of these, *Belenus*, is attested — often
alone — in the old Celtic Kingdom of Noricum in the eastern Alps, of
which according to Tertullian he was the special deity, as well as in
northern Italy and southern Gaul, and there are also traces of his cult in
Britain. It recalls the Irish name for May-Day. *Beltene*, of which the
second element *tene*, is the word for 'fire' and the first *bel*, probably

Celtic Mythology by Prionsias MacCana. Hamyln, London, Peter Bedrick Books,
New York, 1970, p. 32.

means 'shining, brilliant'. This, together with the fact that he is equated with Apollo, suggests that Belenus had a markedly solar character.

When I next visited Frank Delemare and told him the older name of the hill I had unearthed, he agreed with my somewhat free translation of the Irish name, especially when I mentioned the layers of fire-scorched stones on the flat top of the hill. He said 'I know for certain that the land around that hill is the luckiest grazing land in Ireland.' 'Why?' I asked and felt he was sorry he had unconsciously divulged a secret. But when he realized I was not 'sneering' at the old customs and beliefs, he recounted his grandfather saying 'In my youth and from time immemorial, big bonfires were always lit on the level crown of that hill and people used to drive their cattle through the still smouldering fires and never a brone (sickness) touched any of the beasts for a full year.' I said 'Tell me Frank, did someone light that big fire at any particular time of the year?' As if amazed at my ignorance, he answered 'In the name of God what other time would they light it except at sunrise on the first of May!' He added 'The old people always spoke of that hill as one of the sacred places given over to the Druids.'

There is plenty of historical evidence that all Celtic peoples had a learned and priestly caste called Druids. However, accurate knowledge of the Druids and their religion is meagre due to their strict rule of not allowing their history to be written; their lore and rules were all committed to memory and their instructions only imparted orally. About the only recognized authentic reference to the Druids in Ireland dates from the fifth century. It is accepted historically that even up to the close of Saint Patrick's lifetime the Druids in Ireland wielded immense political and religious power. It is ironic that it was the Druids' sworn enemy — the early Irish Christian church — that recorded instances of the Druids' powers.

In addition to mastery of fire, Druids performed mystic rites that managed to impress the populace; the latter accepted that the Druids had magic powers, including the ability to foretell future events. It is known that the Druids practiced astrology and magic and were versed in mysterious powers usually attributed to animals.

The principal Druidic event was the annual Feast of Bealtaine, the great May Day festival. Besides religious celebrations, this feast was an occasion when the Druids promulgated their laws and held courts of justice. It was also a time for military displays, commerce and even matchmaking. The celebration of the Feast included lighting of huge fires on certain sacred hilltops. Our ancient Irish manuscripts provide evidence that fire figured prominently in many of the Druids' external religious rites and it is possible that further back in time, Druids gained the monopoly of producing, controlling and maintaining fire and used that knowledge to dominate everyone from king to slave.

The Druids were closely associated with the hill of Usnagh (Uisneach), known in ancient times as the navel of Ireland. Although the reputed centre of the country, it is logical to assume that 'navel' implied more than geographical location; Uisneach was credited with being the location of the primal fire and was also the centre of a fire cult. The Hill figured prominently in the annual celebration of Bealtaine and was also the site of a great assembly (Mordhail Usnagh). Less than five miles distant from Cnocnabaalteine, the hill of Usnagh, also in Westmeath, commands a clear view of twenty of Ireland's thirty-two counties.

Doctor Hannon's intense interest in Cnocnabaalteine was contagious. Later when Eileen and I made a thorough tour of the area we marvelled at the profusion and variety of circular raths, military forts and tumuli. Standing on top of the little hill and looking northwards towards Multy village we noted a relatively high ridge of ground, roughly shaped like a backbone stretching from the base of the hill in the direction of the village. We followed the ridge for a few hundred yards and it led us to a large field that contains a series of low, grass-covered mounds which at first sight appeared to be remains of partially eroded ditches or boundaries of unusually small rectangular fields. Close by there is a well preserved small circular rath or fort adjoining a field called the Bishop's Garden.

We spent some time trying to find out if the mounds followed a pattern — the spaces they enclosed were too small to have been fields, or even gardens. Eileen as usual gave me the inspiration. (By the way — did you ever notice that sometimes 'inspiration' is a marital euphemism — a polite, politic word for spur, or nag?) Now when I was stuck for an answer regarding the configuration and origin of the mounds she said 'Back to the

drawing board.' Me: 'Meaning?' She: 'How about the old map
or maybe Frank Delemare would have a clue.'

The old map from an early nineteenth century Ordnance
Survey was no help, but luckily I found a map of 'Monastic
Ireland'* which was published 'In an attempt to express the
geographical distribution and the character of the religious
houses from the time of St. Patrick in the fifth century, to the
end of the sixteenth century.' The map identifies the area
containing the grass-covered mounds as Tyfarnham. It
describes the site itself has having 'possibly no community after
the twelfth century'. Still following the 'inspiration' I went to see
Frank Delemare again and he volunteered to show me 'the ruins
of the old churchyard of Tyfarnham where they used to bury
unbaptized children up to one hundred years ago.' A few days
ago 'the wife' (as they say here) and myself, drove Frank to
within easy walking distance of the mounds. On the way Frank
explained why no one ever made any attempt to 'tamper' with
the ruins. He said 'In my young days this place was littered with
tombstones and a certain workman, I can't mention the mean
hound's name because his family is still around, was too
miserable to spend a penny for a whetstone so he took a sledge
and broke off a corner of an old tombstone to sharpen his scythe
on. The following morning he was stark raving mad and spent
the rest of his life in Mullingar Asylum just a few miles over
there on your right.' Frank had never heard of a monastery or
any other building being connected with the area but showed
me the acre or so of level land in the field beside the mounds
and said 'That field was always called "The Bishop's Garden".'

A year afterwards I asked assistance of a Board of Works
engineer and he gave me the correct geographical description of
the area: it is Knocknabealtaine and the entire monastic site is
shown on the Ordnance Survey map as Townland of Rathduff;
also called Staghfarnnan and Tyfarnham. They are on National
grid 428616. On the strength of that information I secured two
complete sets of aerial photographs of the entire area from
Oxford University, and gave one set to Dr. Hannon.

The present name, Knocknabealtaine, supplied by the
engineer is the fourth name I have already encountered for the
hill. It is noteworthy that the entire four are in the language of
our people. In a modest way I have further proved Rev. Paul

*Map of Monastio Ireland published November 1959 by Ordnance Survey,
Phoenix Park, Dublin.

Walsh's point which he makes in his Preface to *The Placenames of Westmeath.* He says in part:

The greater part of the placenames of the county, however, still preserve their ancient forms, some plainly, others in disguise, and their pronunciation by those who speak naturally and unaffectedly is, in many cases, as Irish as when the language was still in common use.

There is something else that is worth mentioning. Numerous artificial caves called souterrains have been found in the relatively few forts that have been scientifically excavated in Ireland. The souterrains examined so far were originally constructed so that their entrances opened from the floor of the house which usually was sited in the centre of the fort. Although to date many souterrains have been discovered their original purpose is obscure.

According to the material I studied on the subject, it is not considered that souterrains were constructed for defensive purposes, even though some were built with traps and snags, as if to hinder an intruder. Some obviously have been lived in, having ventilating shafts and chimneys, but these utilities could have been added and used at a much more recent date. It occurs to me that no matter how strongly one of those forts was defended, eventually the garrison could have been besieged and starved into submission; also I like to credit their builders with enough intelligence and foresight to provide escape routes. In fact many of the souterrains discovered to date have underground passages connected to other forts in the area.

Later I will give more detail of souterrains in general because I'm deeply interested in the subject and believe that some of them may contain artifacts that could throw light on the everyday lives of our remote ancestors; ancestors undoubtedly connected with the Boyne Valley civilization that built the great necropoli of Newgrange, Knowth and Dowth that are only thirty miles from Knocknalbealtaine.

The reason I mention souterrains at this time is that on the terrain in the vicinity of the hill, the Monastery ruins, the Bishop's Garden and the small fort are all situated on elevated ground connected by that backbone-shaped ridge.

To revert for a moment to the effect of the sun and wind on our scenery: this minute, I glanced from our sunroom window towards The Hill and it was just out there at the head of the Gaine Valley barely an Irish mile (2,000 yards) away and apparently so close that I could see the whitethorns in bloom and the yellow blaze of the furze bushes that form the hill's hairline. Then the gentle western, rain-laden wind blew a filmy, translucent veil of mist and rain across its face and like magic the hill appeared to be telescoped backwards in space, as far back as its history reaches into the mists of time. The very name Knocknabealtine conjures up much more than that hill's history; its Irish name reflects local tradition, legends and lore, religious beliefs and ritual that were old, long, long before the Biblical deluge. I consider myself very much 'down to earth', even pragmatic, but somehow that very hill touches and vibrates some atavistic chord in me. Oh! how I wish those fire-scarred stones on the flat top of that hill would, like the Biblical stones, cry out. If they could even whisper, I'm certain they would tell tales of Druidic rites and rituals ages before Saint Patrick's relatively recent Christianity clashed with that ancient pagan priesthood.

One thought leads to another: early in man's evolution, fire figured prominently in most religious rites and ceremonies. In our Catholic Church we have candles and incense; the latter as you know, is produced from the burning of certain gums and resins. In our ceremonies the priest sprinkles the powdered gum or resin on glowing charcoal contained in the thurible or censer. Then we have the annual ceremony of the Paschal Fire. The other morning at the Franciscan Abbey, a few hundred yards from here, I took part in the Paschal ceremonies and wondered as to how or when the Paschal Fire became an integral part of the Church's ritual.

The mention of Paschal Fire summons up thoughts of Easter, because Pasch, in various spellings, is another name for Easter. Then again, Easter is a convergence of three separate traditions. First: the word Easter is derived from the Norse Ostara, or Eostre, meaning the Festival of Spring at the vernal equinox when nature is in resurrection after the sleep of winter. Second: we have the Hebrew Passover or Jewish Pesach, celebrating that night in Egypt when the angel of death 'passed over' the dwellings of the Israelites and spared their first-born. Third: the Christian Easter which coincides with the Feast of Passover, when Jesus a Jew was crucified in Jerusalem and arose from the dead.

Every schoolboy — at least every Irish schoolboy — knows

by heart the well-authenticated account of Saint Patrick's confrontation with the Druids on the Hill of Slane where once again fire was much in evidence and the time was Easter morning, the Feast of Bealtaine. Patrick, the one-time slave pig-herder, had recently returned to Ireland to attempt converting the pagan natives to Christianity. At daybreak on Easter Sunday in the year of our Lord 432, Patrick and a small band of fellow missionaries climbed to the top of Slane Hill to light their Paschal Fire. Slane is only ten miles from Tara which was the site of the palace of Laoghaire, High King of Ireland. The top of Slane Hill may be seen from the summit of almost every hill in the Irish Midlands; in fact on a clear day it is visible thirty miles away from some of the hills surrounding my village.

Patrick's fire happened to coincide with the Druidic Feast of Bealtaine — The Festival of Spring — and that festival was officially opened each year by the lighting of the Druid's fire on the Hill of Tara. The honour of lighting the fire was the prerogative of the High King and it was explicitly forbidden, on pain of death, for any other fire in Ireland to burn before the Druid's fire was lit. Material for the Druid's fire was already in place and about to be lit, when ten miles away on the Hill of Slane, Patrick's fire blazed brightly. The Royal Court became a scene of confusion; the King demanded an explanation; the Druids held a consultation and then their Chief Druid declared 'If that stranger's fire is not extinguished this day, it will burn forever. It will consume our sacred fire and also destroy your kingly power.' Patrick's fire was not extinguished — the rest is history.

Incidentally, in many parts of rural Ireland there is still an age-old custom, also connected with fire. On the first morning of May, many people who still follow the 'old ways' refuse to light their domestic fires until midday 'when the sun is at its meridian'. Up to fifty years ago, in my own neighbourhood and before matches became plentiful and commonplace, it was normal for a householder to get a lit piece of turf from a neighbour to start his own fire. This neighbourly practice was never followed on the first of May because it was believed that the person taking a lit coal on that particular day would also be taking away the 'good luck of the household' with him and disaster would inevitably fall on the house from which the fire was taken.

27. SOUTERRAINS

A fair amount of significant professional work has been accomplished with the excavation and study of many prehistoric habitation sites, fortifications, places of worship, monuments and burial places including some 5,000 year old megalithic tombs, but somehow I can find only a limited amount of information about crannogs.

Crannog is the name given to what were artificial islands built in lake shallows or in normally inaccessible swamps. They were constructed by depositing alternative layers of tree branches, stones and clay within a rough circle of wooden piles. For added fortification, some of the sites were surrounded by wooden palisades and others had fences of pointed stakes with their tops just below the surface of the water. These islands thus provided a firm foundation for dwellings and a safe haven for their occupants. Most of the crannogs studied to date appear to belong to the Iron Age, or even later.

The greatest number of crannogs have been charted in Leitrim, Cavan, Fermanagh and Monaghan and some important finds have been made on a few sites in my county, Westmeath. Our own lake, Derravaragh, as a local bogman said 'Is plastered with crannogs' and a few years ago when the water level was lowered, three dugout canoes came to light. Experts from the National Museum concluded that the canoes were sunk about the time of Saint Patrick — that's over 1,500 years ago.

Another feature of our prehistoric forts, earthworks and early monastic sites that intrigues me is the prevalence of artificial caves or, to give them their official title, souterrains, that over the years have been discovered in every one of the thirty-two counties.

My recent research in public libraries disclosed that around the middle of the past century there was active public interest in locating and exploring souterrains; in most cases it was done by Government civil servants and members of the British Army stationed here, but interest soon evaporated, little or nothing of monetary value was discovered, or anyway reported and the hard work and personal danger involved in exploring the ancient passages was considerable.

Most of the souterrains discovered so far are in the vicinity of prehistoric sites and in many instances were constructed so that their entrances opened from the floor of the house or building. Many are elaborate structures with built-in traps, snags and puzzle passages. Some obviously had been lived in and contained ventilating shafts and chimneys, and even I know the location of one that has an underground spring well. Archaeologists generally say that the original purpose of the passages is obscure although a large number were superficially examined. As a matter of fact the few archaeologists I met have been rather noncommital on the subject; one candidly confided that they are too dangerous to explore. I even heard an expert hold forth on how the 'natives' tunnelled from one site to the next. The few souterrains I, as a layman, examined are simply underground passages built by roofing over two parallel stone walls with flat stone flags. I'm sure their builders were practical people who realized the logical way to construct such structures would be, first excavate a trench or ditch, then build butt walls; roof them with flags and finally cover over the structure with the excavated material.

Perhaps a few extracts from authentic reports might spark off some scientific study and initiate constructive exploration of what could be a veritable network of souterrains connected with some of our 4,000 or so prehistoric forts. I quote:

A rath near Ardfinnan, County Tipperary, described by the late Rev. James Graves, may be taken as a typical example as regards its souterrains. In the interior of many earthen forts and stone cashels there are often chambers and subterraneous passages, which vary in length as well as in breadth and height. These passages are built of uncemented stones, and are covered with flagstones, the extremities of which rest on the parallel walls; and whilst some are too low to stand erect in, and the explorer has to proceed on hands and knees, others are upwards of six feet in height, and of corresponding breadth. They were constructed not only for habitation but also for defensive purposes. The entrances to these retreats appear to have been concealed with great care. Their discovery is generally the result of accident.

In the Rath at Ardfinnan the souterrain lay a little from the centre of the enclosure and was approached by a regular flight of steps giving entrance to a small beehive-shaped chamber of an irregular circular form. It is about seven feet wide, by five and a half feet high, built of rough blocks of limestone. From this chamber a narrow passage, through which the explorer had to creep on all fours, led into another chamber of the same character as the foregoing, and from this a similar passage gave entrance to a third beehive-shaped cell of larger size than the preceding. The passages were square-headed and roofed with slabs stretching across from wall to wall. The jointing of the stonework was very irregular, no courses being perceptible, and the stones were rudely fitted to each other. In each chamber the beehive-shaped vault was capped by a single stone at top. What is very noteworthy, as bearing on the habitable nature of these souterrains, each chamber was provided with two ventilating shafts, placed near the top, and diverging in opposite directions towards the surface. That these structures were intended for the storage of valuables and for occasional places of refuge for the inhabitants of the rath, there can be little doubt. They would be unsuited for ordinary dwellings; but for that purpose they were not needed. In that area wattled, mud or stone-built houses served for the ordinary habitations of the chieftains and their followers, and it can be easily imagined how the entrance to these cellars might be concealed, so as to escape the attention of plunderers. That they were often discovered and rifled there is abundant evidence. 'In the Brehon Law, the law of distress contemplated the event of the distress being carried for concealment into a 'cave' and provided accordingly.' In fact these 'caves' were but the clochans or stone huts, so common in the west of Ireland, placed for concealment under the ground.

While a railway was in the course of formation, a most extensive souterrain was discovered in a cutting near Athlumney, County Meath. It consisted of a straight passage fifty-four feet long, eight broad and six high, branching into two smaller passages which run off at right angles from it, and ending in two circular beehive-shaped chambers, together forming the figure of a cross. The walls of this cave having risen to the height of about four and a half feet, they then begin to incline, and the roof is formed of enormous flagstones, laid across. These stones are all rough and undressed, and they are placed together with mortar or cement. Only a few bones of oxen were discovered.

T. Croften Croker gave a long and detailed account of numerous souterrains in County Cork, examined by him in the year 1835. Some had evidently been inhabited, for a considerable quantity of charcoal and fragments of a quern or hand-mill were found. He states also that his companion, Mr. Newenham, had 'been exploring underground chambers by the dozen'. In the course of an hour he visited five sets within a circuit of two miles. Some examples appear to have been

ventilated by small square apertures. They did not rise
perpendicularly but sloped upwards at an angle of about
seventy degrees. None of these latter were connected with
ancient forts or entrenchments.

The Rath of Parkmore, which contains a magnificent speci-
men of a souterrain, was defended by two concentric ramparts
and fosses, the diameter of the entire being 214 feet. The
ramparts were formed of high mounds of clay, faced with stone,
and having deep ditches. The opening to the souterrain is located
about the centre of the enclosure. The first gallery runs
in a south-westerly direction from the entrance. It is twenty-six
feet long, six feet high, and the same number of feet in breadth.
The side walls are formed of large stones, rudely put together,
and the roof is made of immense flagstones. At the end of the
first gallery is a passage about five feet in length, but only three and
a half feet high, by two feet wide. In order to pass through this
confined communication one must crawl on hands and knees.
When the end of the passage is reached it is found to be
terminated by a wall built across its breadth. The only way by
which to advance farther is by ascending through a square hole
overhead, the breadth only one foot nine inches. On emerging
through the opening one finds himself in a little chamber seven
feet long, by five feet broad, and four feet high. If desirous to
proceed further, one must descend through another square
opening, which is similar to that already passed, and creep from
thence, as before, through another low and narrow passage,
also five feet long, three and a half feet high and two feet wide.
This last-mentioned passage leads into another gallery which
runs at right angles to the gallery above described. It is fourteen
feet long by nine and a half feet wide, and six feet high.
Opposite to this another passage leads, as a kind of sally-port,
to the exterior of the inner rampart of the fort. The last
mentioned passage is five feet long, by two feet wide, and four
and a half feet high. The flagstone which was placed outside
against this aperture was four feet square. Thus, from whatever
end of the souterrain the inhabitants might be pursued, a fatal
resistance could be made. Flagstones stopped the holes (which
have been described) in the passages and their upper surfaces,
being even with the floor of the little apartment, a stranger
would have much delay and difficulty in discovering the
apertures they covered. In this little citadel a woman or a child

could arrest the progress of giants, for the instant one of their heads appeared at the opening, a blow of an axe or any heavy implement from above would prove fatal to him who was leading the forlorn hope, and his lifeless body would effectually block up the passage against those who followed. If the fort happened to be stormed, its occupants had a secret exit into the inner fosse by means of these caves, and, in case of friends happening to be pursued, and obliged to seek protection from the garrison, these intricate underground passages afforded safe ingress for friends but were impracticable to the enemy.

An interesting account is given of the exploration of a remarkable series of subterranean chambers underneath a fort on the townland of Doon, King's County, situated on the summit of a hill rising about 200 feet above the level of the surrounding country. These chambers were cleared out and appear to have been of great size, one of them being nearly thirty-four feet long and seven feet broad by six feet in height — the roof formed of enormous stones, some of them nine feet in length, and from five to six feet in breadth. The general architectural arrangements between this series of chambers and passages and the ancient entrances to the cashel of Inismurray are almost identical. The labour expended in their construction must have been very great, one stone in particular, forming the extreme eastern end of one of the chambers, being ten feet long, seven feet wide and two feet thick. Near Dysart, not far from Mullingar, in consequence of the rath under which they lay having been cut away, a complete subterranean village, consisting of upwards of ten beehive-shaped chambers, with connecting galleries, became exposed to view.

Souterrains almost similar in construction to those found under raths are often discovered in the most unlikely places, the means employed for concealment of the entrance to the one class being employed in the other, and, probably with the dwelling being erected over them.

One that was explored in County Clare consisted of three chambers of considerable size, two of them being about twenty-six feet long by seven feet wide and six feet high. In the innermost chamber a large flagstone was found resting on four upright stones that formed a kind of table; under this there were some bones.

Molyneux, in the year 1684, described a somewhat similar

object near a place he styles Warrington, County Down: 'In the middle of the vault were fixed, in the ground, four long stones, each about two and a half feet high, standing upright as so many legs to support a flat quarry-stone placed upon them. This rude stone table seemed designed by the heathen founder as an altar to offer sacrifice upon for the deceased. Under the table, on the ground, was placed a handsome earthen urn; it contained broken pieces of burnt bones.'

Both these souterrains may possibly have been built originally for habitation, as it is not likely that their architects would have erected such large vaults for deposition of the calcined ashes of only one individual. After the cave was abandoned as a habitation, it may have been utilized as a sepulchre or, though still inhabited, the innermost compartment may have been devoted to the relics of the dead.

In the townland of Mullagheep, County Donegal, there are small souterrains. When first entered, in the year 1854, in them were found traces of charcoal, together with the fractured bones of an Irish elk, seemingly broken for the extraction of the marrow. These bones were sent to the Royal Irish Academy, and were afterwards presented by the Council to the Royal Dublin Society, and are now, it is believed, deposited in the Museum of the Science and Art Department, Kildare Street.

The foregoing disparate accounts all follow a similar pattern and I believe them to give some idea of the prevalence of souterrains in Ireland. But I believe there must be an error or anomaly in reporting the bones of an Irish elk in the County Donegal souterrain. I was given to understand that the giant Irish deer (Megaceros giganteus), usually called the 'Irish Elk' became extinct before man first arrived in Ireland about 6,000 B.C.

Now, due to my avid interest in the subject, hardly a month passes but I hear about the existence of yet another underground passage. Only a week ago I learned that there is a series of souterrains a few miles from here at a place called Gaybrook. My informant says the passages seem to extend for miles, but added that over the ages several sections have collapsed and it could be dangerous to go in very far. I must take time off and visit the site — *some day.*

I pray that some day a thorough scientific program will be initiated to determine the extent of those souterrains, their origin and use. Our Old and Middle Irish literature preserves much mythological material; coupling it with beliefs and traditions handed down unbroken from generation to generation, I am struck with the possible connection between the forts with their underground passages and the mythological Tuatha de Dannan who are mentioned in *Leabhar Gabhala Erenn* (*The Book of the Conquests of Ireland*). This book claims to record successive invasions of Ireland since the Deluge.

28. MULTYFARNHAM ABBEY

Of the entire area around our village the focal point was and is the Friary. In fact from my earliest years and even in my declining ones the Friary exercises an extraordinary influence on my life. Locally it has several names: the Abbey, the Friary, the Monastery, and the Convent. Personally I think the Friary is the most popular local name. This could be on account of its association with the word Friar, which for Irish people evokes the monk, the anointed follower of St. Francis; the individual who takes, and keeps his vows of celibacy, poverty and obedience.

The word convent conjures up the presence of nuns, but my old *Webster's Dictionary* dated 1864 gives 'convent: An association or community of recluses devoted to a religious life; a body of monks or nuns', and my new *Webster's Dictionary* agrees with its older brother. It was news to me to discover that 'abbey' has the same meaning as convent, both meaning 'A monastery society of persons of either sex secluded from the world and devoted to religion and celibacy.' It adds, 'In the monastic building or buildings the men are called monks, and are governed by an abbot. The women are called nuns and are governed by an abbess.'

The exact date the Franciscans arrived in Ireland is not known but it's generally accepted by historians that the Friars had established themselves as early as 1226. We know for certain that they came to Multyfarnham in the year 1236 — ten years after the death of their founder St. Francis of Assisi.

Today the Irish Franciscans enjoy the freedom enshrined in the Constitution of our Republic which guarantees freedom of conscience and freedom of religious practice for all its citizens. Later I will give an account of vicissitudes this monastic foundation suffered, because the poignant and tragic history of Multy and the surrounding area since the thirteenth century was, and is, inextricably bound up with the everyday life and history of the Friary. The story and the often tragic fate of the

275

indestructible Irish Friars of St. Francis is also part of the story and epic history of the Irish people of that period.

Almost 400 years ago Sir Francis Shane, sheriff of Westmeath, who did his best — or worst — to impose the Reformation doctrines and practices on the native Irish, whilst faithfully serving his ruler, Queen Elizabeth of England, looted and put Multyfarnham Abbey to the torch. Although that was the gravest calamity the Abbey had yet suffered, it was not by any means the last of the trials endured by this historic foundation.

In 1975 the Friars at Multyfarnham published a booklet entitled *Multyfarnham Abbey Co. Westmeath*, which provides an abridged historical background of the Abbey and outlines the ongoing restoration work. This brochure, containing about 2,500 words, compiled by the then Guardian Pádraig O Gibealláin O.F.M., is full of diligently researched information, intelligently presented. Two years later Father O Gibealláin produced a second brochure *The Abbey Restored* and kindly made me welcome to either or both booklets telling me to 'Use them to your heart's content'. Gladly. Here are the opening paragraphs of the second booklet:

In the heart of the Midlands, about eight miles north of Mullingar in the Barony of Corkery, stands the Franciscan Abbey of Multyfarnham. There are many famous churches in the Midlands as old, if not much older than this ancient edifice, but they are all historic ruins. This Abbey, perhaps, is the only one in this part of Ireland which has continued to function as a Catholic church for more than 700 years. A mere glance at the captions of history set down here, will give some slight idea of the time-span which this Abbey encompasses, and of the depredations and burnings it has witnessed and thankfully, survived.

Founded for Franciscans, Multyfarnham Abbey had already become the spiritual powerhouse of the Midlands long before some of the great cathedrals of Europe were built and thank God the Franciscans still manage to devote themselves to the purpose for which this Abbey was founded, namely — to serve the spiritual and educational needs of the people, to preserve it as a place of prayer and contemplation, to retain it as a haven of study and recollection, not discounting the fact that it has been bedewed many times in the distant past with the blood of martyrs.'

Under the heading 'Foundation', the booklet gives dates and provides details of the Friars' arrival here, the founding of the Abbey and subsequent additions to the original building.

Under the caption 'Suppression' it lists the rigours of the Abbey from its suppression in 1540 by the Decree of Henry VIII, when at the risk of their lives, the expelled Friars remained in the vicinity of Multyfarnham and continued ministering to the local people; it traces the history of the Abbey through a period covering the following hundred years, including a long catalogue of events that were historical milestones sometimes bedewed with the blood of martyrs. The list depicts, even at that early date, Ireland's struggle for freedom, especially a freedom for her people to practice their own religion openly and faithfully as they had practised it at home and spread it abroad since St. Patrick in 432 A.D. brought the Faith to our shores.

Interspersed with the history of pillage, rapine and murder, the saga of the indomitable, tenacious Friars continues, as after each raid, after every disaster, 'they went underground' in the vicinity — like parent birds whose nest has been destroyed — returning, rebuilding and never ceasing to exercise their priestly functions, and the care of their flock.

The next subtitle 'Restoration' lists only half a dozen dates — the first is 1827, the last is 1975. During that period the Abbey was intermittently rebuilt. This change in the Abbey's fortunes came a scant two years before Catholic emancipation was granted and at a time when O'Connell 'The Emancipator' was at the peak of his career. The brochure spells out succeeding stages of rebuilding the Abbey. These included construction of a three storey Friary, Franciscan College and open-air Stations of the Cross. In 1973, a most significant project was initiated which called for the restoration of the main part of the Abbey church to as close a resemblance as possible to what it was before the Cromwellians sacked and partially demolished it. The brochure says 'Our dream is to reconstruct this edifice and make Multyfarnham Abbey the architectural gem it was 700 years ago.'

By 1972 my wife and I returned to Multyfarnham and were settled in — to stay. Before long I heard 'something big is going on at the Friary'. In my boyhood in Multy and long before that, there was always 'something going on at the Friary'. Even in my lifetime the fabric of the Friary and the grounds underwent many and sometimes startling changes, improvements and renovations. Generations of workmen and their families surely blessed current Guardians for the amount of employment the

Friary provided. The villagers only saw concrete evidence of the improvements and perhaps it is understandable that some of us imagined that each newly-appointed Guardian was indulging his personal taste and pushing his own pet project; projects such as harnessing the river and successfully producing electricity; building the gallery for the organ and choir; assembling the impressive Italian marble main altar and its two side altars; plastering over the entire interior surface of the Abbey's stone walls; installing terrazzo floors; constructing the Franciscan College; creating the open air Stations of the Cross, landscaping etc.

One of those pet projects that met with the unanimous approval of the village 'experts' was the electrical project. As you know, as far back as 1877, Niagara Falls had been harnessed to produce electricity in a small way. Around the turn of the century the Friars of Multyfarnham decided to try harnessing the River Gaine which flows through the Abbey grounds.

The operation was ambitious and included a powerhouse, turbine, new channel or branch of the river to the powerhouse, tailrace, together with hand-operated sluice gates. For that day and age the project the Friars undertook was more than progressive; it was a gamble. Possibly they were gambling on the electrical knowledge that two Brothers in their Multy community had somehow picked up. The tyro electrical engineers, Brothers Felix and Humilis, were always referred to locally as the German Brothers. The Brothers masterminded the operation and when the first electric light blazed at the Friary, full credit was given to them; in fact everyone agreed that 'When it comes to things electrical, no one can hold a candle to a German'.

The successful Friary electrical operation predated Ireland's first national hydro-electric station built at Ardnacrusha on the Shannon in 1929, and when our government called for tenders, it was no surprise to the Multy people when a German firm got the contract. In fact we knew the project was bound to succeed — wasn't the contractor, not to mention his engineers and technicians, all German!

Looking back now I appreciate that while there may not have been a positive pattern or plan for improvements during each Guardian's stewardship, every such steward surely made his mark before passing the torch — or the dream — to his successor.

So, in 1975, the current Guardian in that long line of achievers was the Rev. Pádraig O Gibealláin O.F.M. I had already taken stock of unusual activity around the Friary, especially in the graveyard which had been closed by local government orders in 1933 and allowed to become derelict. When I mentioned to my wife that they seemed to be cleaning up and rearranging the 'mixumgatherum' of monuments, crosses, tombstones and headstones in the old graveyard, she retorted, 'It's high time someone did something about the deplorable condition of Irish cemeteries in general; they are a blot on the otherwise beautiful landscape'.

I soon learned that cleaning up and rearranging the graveyard was only part of the 'something big' and I was keenly interested, especially as I had been professionally involved for many years in civil engineering and construction work, so who should I contact but my good friend Brother Francis.

About a year after the First World War a young man came to the Friary as a postulant. He was slightly over six feet in height and when a villager remarked, 'The new Brother carries himself like a trained soldier', someone in 'the know' answered, 'Course he walks like a soldier, the man is not long back from the trenches; he soldiered in the best body of men in the British Army — The Irish Guards — and he has a lot of war medals too. I hear he has a silver plate in his head because he got a shocking head wound in a bayonet charge.'

The young ex-soldier 'took' the Franciscan habit, the vows of Poverty, Chastity and Obedience and the religious name of Francis, the same name as that thirteenth century founder of three great religious Orders — St. Francis of Assisi. Nearly everyone knows something about St. Francis — peace lover, nature lover and animal lover. Keenly alive to the evils which even in his day threatened the very existence of the Church and society, Francis strove to counteract their baneful influence by establishing an Order whose members would vow to observe and practice absolute poverty and devotion to the Church. The goal which he aimed at, was to reproduce the ideal of the Divine life on earth, therefore neither he nor his followers were to possess anything temporal but were to go about the world doing good and preaching the Kingdom of Heaven to all the world. The three Orders he established were: The First Order — priests and brothers; The Second Order — Poor Clare Nuns; and the Third Order composed of lay people, including myself — a backsliding member. Incidentally members of the Third Order do not take the vows of celibacy, poverty etc.

Young Brother Francis not only fitted in to the monastic life in Multy, but before long became a jack-of-all-trades and for the rest of his life looked after the entire heating, plumbing and all other utilities of the Friary.

By the time I emigrated in the 'thirties I had only a casual acquaintance with Brother Francis, but every few years when I came home on holidays I made a beeline for the Friary and inevitably ended up making the rounds with the Brother. Now, as he and I went around the buildings and grounds his eyes would light up when I'd pass a remark like, 'You're a Friar alright. Every Friary in Ireland shows enduring evidence of the monk's passion for building in stone; I notice that with your own two hands you're still putting up solid stone walls and piers — enduring masonry work that will outlast us all.' Nowadays when I go down the Convent lane and my trained eye runs along the perfectly-constructed stone wall with its tasty coping and stoutly-built gate piers, I clearly recall Brother Francis, attended by Tom Cox, a classmate of mine, building this same wall. In my mind's eye I see both of them engrossed in the work; Brother Francis in his long, brown, well-worn, work-stained habit, with hammer and chisel dressing and expertly fitting every single building stone — none of your haphazard, jerry-built stone work about Brother Francis! I especially recall his hands — the hands of an artist — but calloused from a lifetime of dedicated manual labour.

So, early in that Spring of '75 I went to the Friary to see Brother Francis and found him working on what he called the graveyard project, and he took me over to the area we always called the ruined wing. Actually over the years it had become part of the already overcrowded graveyard. Both of us clambered through the weeds, briars, heaps of building stones, toppled and broken monuments and with difficulty we traced the shattered foundations of the historic Blessed Sacrament Chapel pillaged and destroyed in 1651 by Cromwell's soldiers. Standing there in the eastern end of the ruin with his back to the original altarstone of the Blessed Sacrament Chapel, Brother Francis said, 'Our new Guardian Father Pat O Gibeallain has already tackled the biggest job yet undertaken by any previous Multy Guardian; around you, you see what he has already

accomplished in this graveyard and we have made a good start
on restoring the Abbey Church. Now Father Pat tells me that up
above in Dublin he has got them all to agree to undertake the
tremendous job of building this entire wing — from the ground
up. When it's finished it's going to be *exactly* as it stood over 300
years ago.' I'm afraid I replied 'Hope he's a young man because
it'll take a lifetime to complete half the work you just mentioned.
They've been trying to restore that Abbey since my
grandfather's time.' With a quiet smile he said 'Wait 'till you
meet him.' Next thing I knew he introduced me to the new
Guardian.

If I'd been forewarned of the Guardian's academic and
scholastic stature I'd certainly have found myself at a double
disadvantage — physically and intellectually. I mentioned that
Brother Francis was six feet tall: well Father Pat, as he came to be
called, stood three and a half inches taller and was built in
proportion. (Later I found through accident that this heroic-
sized figure of a man has the right — rarely exercised — to put
M.A. Ph.D after his signature.) When I told the Guardian of my
interest in the restoration work, without any formalities he gave
me the 'run of my tooth;, suggested that I keep in touch with
Brother Francis and added, 'You're always welcome in any part
of the Friary'. From then on I'd go down every day or so to the
Friary, stroll around, watch the various stages of the restoration
work and exchange a few words with the building gang.

Before long I learned that the Franciscans had appointed an
architect to make certain non-structural modifications to the
interior of the main body of the Abbey, and also to rebuild the
wing that originally was the ancient choir, or Blessed
Sacrament Chapel. The architect specified that the new wing
follow the original architecture of the Abbey Church and that
the finished masonry match the parent building. This required
that the exposed face of every building-stone appear aged and
weather-beaten. It also called for a special 'mortar mix' so that
when it eventually dries and ages, it will match the age-old
mortar that shows between the courses of stone in the existing
building.

Space will not permit me to do justice to the 'building gang'.
Later in my capacity of 'Sidewalk Superintendent' my heart
sank when I saw the pathetic size of this work force that was
prepared to tackle such an enormous and complex operation as

the complete restoration of the Abbey. Not only did this involve construction of an entire wing that originally was the Blessed Sacrament Chapel and restoring the Abbey Church *exactly* to what it was hundreds of years ago, but the work envisaged on the Abbey Church proper, included removing the existing terrazzo and board floors of the Abbey and replacing them with flag-stones; stripping the wainscoting and plaster from the interior walls and pointing the joints between every stone with mortar that when dry would exactly match the existing mortar joints; removing the massive Italian altars and constructing a masonry curtain wall where the three altars once stood. Later when I saw that little work force in action, I appreciated that their lack of numbers was compensated by the all-round ability and skill of Noel Kirby — superintendent, foreman, overseer, master tradesman and sole stonemason.

For a start, the rebuilding of the entire wing would require old building stones. That is, stones not quarried or broken within the last few hundred years, because as you know, the surface of stones exposed to the elements, especially here in Ireland where the climate is normally damp, become grey and hoary with age. This greyish-green colour, or patina, which nothing but time — and plenty of time — can impart to the surface of building stones, is the stamp of antiquity that sets our ancient churches and cathedrals apart from their modern counterparts.

The history of Ireland's building stones would make interesting reading. In this part of Ireland, stones for building have always been quarried from one of the several layers of the abundant deposit of limestone which underlays our entire Central Lowlands. Until thirty years ago quarrying, breaking, dressing and shaping of building stones was done by hand and the stones transported by horse or donkey carts from quarry to building site. At the site individual stones were moved or carried by two men. Heavier stones were carried by a team of four men — even up a steep ramp — using a hand barrow called the contraption. This consisted of a sturdy wooden platform with four fixed handles, one for each of the four carriers. A cubic foot of stone weighs about eleven stone (154 pounds), so you can appreciate the difficulty of manhandling some of the building stones that are high up in the walls of our Abbey. Some of the larger quoins must measure up to fifteen cubic feet. Imagine the labour involved in the construction of even one of our smaller churches; the sweat, the toil, the man-hours. And the further back in time it was built, the greater the effort — the agony — that was expended on it, especially when we consider the primitive construction conditions complicated by inclement weather, poor food, worse clothing, bad roads and so forth. Just let your mind wander and try to envisage the superhuman efforts that went into the building of our thousands of places of worship.

Our stone-built habitations, fortresses, castles, churches, round towers have much in common. The stones of which they were built, unlike bricks or concrete, endure and are almost eternal. Here in Ireland for thousands of years individual, actual stones have been used, re-used and recycled. With that in mind you will understand why you never find a pile of building stones just lying around unclaimed. Recently the Garda were trying to run down the person or persons who stole a full hundred yards of an ancient twelve-foot demesne wall.

I am familiar with all the quarries for miles around and it is evident that very little quarrying has been carried out for the last hundred years; there were enough building stones always available — from unused, disused and demolished stone structures. Recently I witnessed a farmer bulldoze the high bank of an Iron-Age fortification and salvage building stones for his modern bungalow. The extraordinary thing about this cycle of the Irish building stones is that they have been used again and again. For instance it is well authenticated that on March 19, 1412, the King granted a licence to Maurice, son of John Delemare, to construct a castle over the bridge 'Multyfeanan'. The castle was built and occupied but not within living memory has a trace of it been discovered. Obviously the castle stones were used to build other structures, and it may be that the stones used to construct Multy Abbey in the thirteenth century had already been recycled more than once. Every time my eye catches a certain large stone that is part of the solidly-built Abbey tower I wonder about the significance of three well-worn holes chiselled deeply into the stone, each hole resembling a spud hole for hanging a gate.

All the stones used in the restoration project and the flags set in the floors of the Chapel and Church were donated by the people of the locality. Actually 'donated' savours of charity; I should say that the neighbourhood felt privileged to make stones available to the Friars. When the call went out for stones for the restoration work, as the song goes, 'everyone rallied round'. 'Everyone' included owners of many of the dilapidated and now empty Ascendancy-type big houses; in addition, caretakers and agents of vacant Protestant churches graciously, and in the very practical spirit of Ecumenism, donated stonework: slabs, door lintels, and window mullions from some of their own disused places of worship.

Maybe without delving too deeply into *our* history books I had better explain why those Protestant churches are disused. When the Irish Free State (which in 1949 became the Republic of Ireland) was established in 1921, the Protestant population percentage was drastically modified: the Protestant minority was reduced to 6%.*

This was concisely put in an article by our present Taoiseach, Dr. Garret FitzGerald in 1977 when Minister for Foreign Affairs:

'In the Republic too the division of the country created a somewhat different kind of identity problem. The exclusion of the people of Northern Ireland from the new State drastically modified its religious composition, reducing the size of the Protestant minority from 25% (?) to 6%. It is true that in terms of ownership of property, or the holding of key posts in industry, commerce and the professions, this Protestant minority was strongly over-represented for historical reasons.

Thus some years after independence they owned 28% of the larger farms (over 200 acres), occupied one-third of the employing or managerial posts, held from one -fifth to one-third of many skilled jobs, and occupied between one-quarter and one-half of posts in all professions. But this remarkable stake in the country held by such a small minority (which, incidentally, has largely endured to the present day) left this minority with a sense of vulnerability rather than of self-confidence.'

Further on, Dr. FitzGerald added:

'The new State went out of its way to protect the interests of the Protestant minority especially during the difficult period of the civil war of 1922–3 and the disturbed years that immediately followed it. Thus, for example, twenty-four of the sixty members of the first Senate were *not* Roman Catholics.'

---

*Garret FitzGerald, 'Ireland's Identity Problems' in *Études Irlandaises*, No. 1 New Series, 1976, pp: 35–142. Reprinted as 'A hope of solving Ireland's identiy crisis', in *The Irish Times*, 17 March 1977.

An impartial observer could hardly fail to note that the minority religion *appears* to get a 'fair crack of the whip' — including the fact that of our first four presidents, Dr. Douglas Hyde and Erskine Childers were Protestants.

In all fairness I had better also include Dr. FitzGerald's:

'While always scrupulous about not intruding upon specifically Protestant rights, the new State became increasingly insensitive to the cautiously unexpressed feelings of the Protestant minority on such matters as divorce, contraception, censorship of publications, etc.'

The decline in the number of Southern Protestants resulted in such a falling-off of attendance in their churches that within thirty years after the founding of the Free State, you could not fail to notice the unkept and unattended conditon of the average rural Protestant Church; the padlocked, rusty iron gates and unused driveways leading to the grass-covered thresholds of those buildings.

The Settlers' Big Houses, stately and imposing buildings towering in the middle of vast, fertile acres, always sited in commanding and picturesque locations and for centuries the abode and hallmark of the Ascendancy, had reached the end of their tether and nearly all of them had gone to rack and ruin. Most of these Big Houses were occupied by generations of a Ruling Class slavishly following the policies and the official religion of Britain — their racial homeland. During the 1920–22 'troubles' some of the Big Houses were burned down and their owners did not rebuild, but in many cases sold the estate, moved to the North of Ireland, or emigrated. Large numbers of them then 'rented out' their land, lived abroad and became absentee landlords.

Every individual stone in the newly-restored Blessed Sacrament Chapel and in the restoration work of the main body of the Abbey was hand-picked, shaped, dressed and mortared in place by one master stonemason — Noel Kirby. One day as the new wing of the Friary was nearing completion I made an effort to compliment Noel by mentioning that I marvelled at the tremendous effort and skill he put into the work; he replied that he felt privileged to be part of God's plan. 'What plan'? I queried. He answered, 'I'm rebuilding this 700 year old Abbey with stones that were part of a Protestant church; but to build that church these same stones were originally looted from our own desecrated, demolished churches. Some of our own stones may just be coming home.'

Brother Francis and myself hoped the restoration work would bring to light artifacts and maybe records that could fill in many of the blank pages of the 700 year history of the Abbey and he became almost excited when he learned I owned an electronic metal locator; he begged me to use it to check every inch of the excavated area. In the long run, we located only a few unimportant metallic items but the search satisfied him that we missed nothing worthwhile. He was a bit disappointed though, with our fruitless testing of every square inch of a hitherto hidden chamber that was exposed when the plaster was removed from the inside surface of the Church walls. This perfectly-constructed room was formed in one of the massive walls of the Abbey Church. The original purpose of the recess which is about ten feet high, seven feet wide and eight feet deep is uncertain. It has been suggested that it was once a Confessional and other authorities even say it was a leper chapel. From an examination of its construction, I'd say it was built as part of the original wall and not created at a later date.

One day when Noel Kirby and his men were removing an old floor in a room thirty feet behind the location of the main altar they discovered an entrance to a cave. Noel told me that one of his workmen then got a lighted candle, climbed down into the passage opening and followed it for about one hundred yards until he came to a place where the roof had caved in. Before long Brother Francis and myself were examining the opening and making plans to explore it on the following morning. When I went to sleep that night I entered a nightmare world. Nightmares connected with being trapped in the bowels of the earth and in the dark are no strangers to me. This is the result of working several years in the world's second deepest gold mine, the Lake Shore Gold Mines, in northern Canada. Being young, and I suppose reckless at the time, I was a voluntary member of the mine rescue squad during a three-year period when that mine held the unenviable record of being the most dangerous mine in Canada.

Brother Francis worried that there might be gas in the cave but I did not worry about the workman carrying the naked flame — even if it were not a blessed candle. As for the danger of the tunnel caving in on me I tried to comfort myself that the roof of that tunnel had held for hundreds of years and was unlikely to choose that moment to collapse and bury me.

Next morning bright and early the Brother and myself were on the job, equipped with two flashlights and a tape measure. I lowered myself through the opening the workmen had made in the floor and slid down a pile of debris that lazy workmen of a bygone era had shovelled under the rug, as it were. The bottom of the passage is about twelve feet below floor level of the Abbey. This floor is of hard-packed clay but I had no implement with me to determine if a wooden or flagged floor lay under the clay. The cave or passage is formed by two parallel stone walls roofed over with stone flags and I had little difficulty exploring it because it has a head clearing of around five feet and is almost four feet wide. Many of the building stones in the walls of the passage weigh over half a ton each and the average roofing slab is one third as heavy. The side walls, as well as I could determine, were built without mortar but the large stones are so well fitted that none of them have slipped out of place. The edges of the roofing slabs fit closely enough to prevent loose material from trickling through.

The passage goes in a north-westerly direction for eighty-five feet and then for twenty-three more veers towards the west, gradually getting slightly smaller. At the end of this twenty-three feet I came to a dead end where the roof had caved in. Later when I climbed out of the hole in the floor Brother Francis was eager to get my account of the interior of the cave and suggested that we should have another go at it later and determine its exact location in relation to the surface.

The following day, carrying surveying equipment and flashlights I went down the hole again and this time Noel Kirby 'spared me' one of his men named James. James and I went down into the cave and ran a traverse; then we climbed out and duplicated the survey on the surface. The first hundred feet of the cave runs inside the building line of the western face of the Abbey; then the final thirty feet turns westward towards the Gaine river and clear of the building line. At a point some yards from the hall door we marked the precise location of the cave-in.

On reflection, the Brother and I agreed that maybe it is fortunate the cave is blocked, especially if it happened a long time ago, for it still guards its secret. Due to the high priority of the reconstruction job no further work was done on exploring the cave, but Father Pat had a well-constructed permanent trap door installed to facilitate future inspection.

I was gratified to find that once the cave cleared the building site it headed in a certain direction, because in that direction lies Lacken which has ruins of an Abbey erected by St. Cruimin in the fifth century. We learn from Tirechan's Life of St. Patrick as preserved in the *Book of Armagh* that: 'The church at Leacan was erected by St. Patrick in the territory of Raoidhe (the present barony of Corkaree). Over it he placed Cruimin who lived to the very old age of 108 years. . . .' The Saint's name is perpetuated locally; our new village school with an enrolment of around 200 was christened St. Cruimin.

Countless legends and old customs have been forgotten or allowed to lapse due to the so-called enlightenment of this twentieth century, but around here it is universally accepted that a cave connects Multy Abbey and the old ruined church at Lacken. In fact, only a few years ago, a local landowner carrying out bulldozer work a quarter of a mile from the old church and in a line between it and the Multy Abbey exposed a portion of a flag-roofed passage. Surprisingly enough he was advised to close it up again and he did.

Personally I like to assume that the ancient Irish monks whose monasteries were such a booty-rich target for marauding Norsemen and later, Henry the VIII's minions, had sufficient intelligence and foresight to build escape routes. Hopefully, the Multy Friars' escape route — the cave — was built large enough to permit them to carry away, or maybe store their sacred vessels, books and other treasures.

When I speculate on that Friary cave I'm reminded of old John Brennan often speaking about another hidden passage or chamber opened at the Friary in his time. He told me of the discovery of three skeletons but 'Neither hilt nor hair of even one skull.' 'Why no skulls John?' 'Sure avic (son), everyone in the seven parishes knew that on one of their raids on the Friary, Cromwell's troopers managed to ketch (sic) three of the Friars; they tied each poor priest's heels to the tail of a mounted trooper's horse; each trooper put spurs to his terrified steed and the three murdering scoundrels galloped 'till they were only dragging the headless bodies of the martyred friars behind them.' I think it is peculiar that there does not appear to be any written record of the event — could it be that it was then considered commonplace?

. The official seal of approval was placed on the restoration work 11 May, 1977 when the completely restored Blessed Sacrament Chapel was solemnly blessed by the Minister General of the Order, Rev. Father Constantine Koser. If I list the salient features of this famous Abbey as it is now restored — reconstructed — stone by stone in its original 700 year old setting I'm afraid it won't read any better than a mail-order catalogue. How does one go about trying to describe a sense of antiquity or the feeling of history plus the thousand and one ways that this Franciscan Abbey and its Friars was and is part and parcel of our history, our culture and our everyday lives?

I wonder if I can coax you into taking a stravaig, as we say here, down to the Abbey; it's only a few hundred yards from the heart of the village. Actually we all consider the Abbey to be Multy and vice versa. Let us stroll down the main street of the village, linger awhile on the centuries-old stone bridge which spans the River Gaine; follow the wall of the bridge and after a few paces stand in front of the semi-circular walls and piers which support the blacksmith-fabricated ornamental gates that embellish, rather than guard, the entrance to the Friary's tree-lined avenue. Ramble down this evergreen, cedar tunnel and within moments you are out of this world. Momentarily you may linger to admire the Lourdes grotto constructed of wave-worn stones carted from a rocky portion of nearby Lough Derravaragh; stones that I like to think could have been trodden by the hapless Children of Lir in both their human and their swan-like forms.

Stop awhile at the graveyard and maybe try to decipher the inscriptions on some of the older tombstones — the ones with 1600 A.D. on them: the oldest are illegible because the writing on them has long since been wiped clean by the hand of Time. When you come to the front of the Abbey — that's the side facing west — don't go into the Church yet, just stand there and take a long look around you at the ancient Abbey itself, its adjoining grounds and some distance away, the outdoor Stations of the Cross.

The grounds, over twenty acres surrounding the Abbey and the College, are so beautifully and so realistically landscaped that nothing appears contrived or artificial. Here where the rich fertile upland meets and mingles with the lush growth of the bogland and 'far from the madding crowd', is a place surely designed by nature for peace, relaxation and contemplation.

Now follow the sign 'Via Dolorosa' that points the way to this unique and famous Way of the Cross which straddles both banks of the river and occupies a generous portion of the Abbey grounds. One unusual factor about the Stations is that when the artist created those heroic-sized figures he used contemporary individuals as his models. Some figures resemble certain well-known villagers, others carry a likeness of key members of the Franciscan community, and two of the figures bear the facial characteristics of Hitler and Mussolini.

I admit those outdoor Stations tug at my heartstrings. After a recent visit to the Friary I wrote:

It was early evening of Good Friday and the crowds of penitents had departed. Alone I did the Stations and at Station number twelve — The Crucifixion — I, who consider myself somewhat cynical and even pragmatic, lingered long at this Station. This replica of the Hill of Calvary is about forty feet high and the three crosses with their pathetic burdens stood starkly silhouetted against the backdrop of the already darkening western horizon.

And an article entitled 'The Week We Call Holy' by a Father Joseph Menton came vividly to my mind. He wrote,

'On a small spot in this immense universe and on one definite day on the infinite calendar of time, The Great God Himself wearing the drab dress of humanity, was lifted on a giant cross in the golden April sunshine and then amid a swift, sudden darkness dropped His head and died. So He atoned for the multitudinous sin of a planet and for the guilt of its sovereign creature, man'.

When you finally tear yourself away from the area around the Stations I hope you'll have plenty of time to visit the Abbey itself. Visit this historic building and regardless of how insensitive you may be to 'atmosphere' you, also, will feel the strange impact of this hallowed place. Go in by the main door and once your eyes become accustomed to the subdued light level, you are in another world, especially if you come from the other side of this world; then you will miss the fine marble, polished wood, chrome, ornamentation, central heating and even the ubiquitous foam-rubber covered kneelers. The only concession to modernity in our Abbey is the up-to-date sophisticated lighting — only turned on for special occasions. I have had the privilege of *trying* to pray in churches and cathedrals in many parts of the world, and to each his own, but no matter how often I go to the Abbey, the moment I cross the threshold I feel that this is one place where I belong; this old church is the archetype of the church where my people for fifteen centuries have given public expression — in their own way — of 'the faith that is in them'.

On entering the main west door your gaze is trapped by the distant flickering red rays of the sanctuary lamp that flanks the tabernacle, then travels to and focuses on the splendid window at the far end of the Blessed Sacrament Chapel. I think we could commence our tour of the Abbey at this window of the Chapel. The window itself is unique in that it is wrought from hand-made glass. Starting from the base of the window the following features are portrayed: the old Friary going up in flames on the night of October the third, the eve of St. Francis' Day, 1601. Above the burning Abbey we look at a new setting — it is the figure of a Franciscan priest who, having been hunted from the ruined Abbey, is offering Mass using a rock as an altar under the open sky and surrounded by his flock. The Friar is holding the Sacred Host aloft and from the Host, rays of light are shafting obliquely down on the Franciscan scribe on the left and on the Franciscan preacher on the right. These two Friars symbolize the ancient motto of the Franciscan Order 'sanctitate et doctrina' — sanctity and learning. Beside the scribe on the left is the famous dictum in Irish 'For the glory of God and the honour of Ireland'. Beside the Franciscan on the right, with crucifix in hand, is a sentence from St. Paul's letter to the Colossians 'This is the Christ we proclaim'. Above the head of the celebrating priest are the Latin words — 'Hoc est Corpus Meum' — 'This is My Body', which contains the whole meaning and central point of the Christian liturgy. At the top of the window there is what is called a folium, depicting the coming of the Holy Spirit in the form of a dove; while on the folia on either side we see rays of light ascending from the Sacred Host.

We now move to the focal point of the whole chapel — the tabernacle. Of an unusual and unique design, it is formed by a wheat stalk with the ripening ear, symbol of the bread of life, which seems to grow through a two hundred year old millstone. This tabernacle itself is formed of thin leaves of copper bonded together in a process called patinating. The millstone was used for many years to grind corn for the farmers of Sligo, Leitrim and Donegal.

The front panel depicts a white oval shape, representative of the germ or essence of life — the kernel of the seed. This wheat germ is surmounted by the Greek Christogram 'XP', meaning 'The Christ'; to the right of this are the symbolic tongues of fire representing the Holy Spirit present in the Church and in the Sacraments.

To the left of the tabernacle is the sanctuary lamp. This lamp is symbolic of the Burning Bush, indicating the presence of God. The stem and branches are from a single solid bronze bar, cut and wrought to form branches and roots, while the flames are constructed in sculptured and enamelled metalwork; the whole related both symbolically and materially with the tabernacle.

Before you reluctantly walk out of the Chapel and back through the Abbey Church be sure to study the four beautiful side windows. Personally their central motif — four swans and a reference in Irish to Lough Derravaragh — intrigued me immensely, because the windows depict the ageless and poignant legend of the Children of Lir. I was amazed, even intrigued, to find this pagan tale given such prominence in a Christian Chapel; in fact, I felt it savoured of a 'marriage of convenience'.

Father O Gibelláin's brochure *The Abbey Restored* answered my query about this 'mixed marriage' and answered it in language that evokes memories of our early Irish literature of which it has been said, 'The best of its prose has a simplicity and directness that is hard to equal outside the Old Testament'. The brochure says:

This story is dear to the heart of every Midlander and hence we thought it proper to perpetuate in stained glass in this Chapel, the poignant story of the Children of Lir in the place where Aoife turned them into swans but left them their gift of speech, and she also said to them in her fit of rage 'You will be singing the sweet music of the Si (fairies), that will put the men of the earth to sleep, and there will be no music in the world equal to it, and your own senses and your own nobility will stay with you, the way it will not weigh so heavy on you to be in the shape of birds.

On reflection I realize that enshrining this legend* in the Abbey — itself a living legend — is a touching example of an ability to blend our rich legacy of pagan culture with our viable Christian faith.

*See Chapter 31.

I have only touched on some of the highlights of this work of restoration, but trust I included enough to whet your appetite to visit it some day. My own feeling about it is this: all my life I knew every nook and cranny of the Abbey so I can appreciate the extent and significance of its restoration; a restoration that bears the imprint of Father Pat's reverence for Irish culture as witnessed by the emphasis on unearthing and preserving the rich historical character of Multyfarnham Franciscan Abbey.

29. FAMILY TREES

A few years back when Alex Haley's *Roots* was the rage, it inspired a fad for searching into the family past almost everywhere in the English-speaking world — except Ireland. The reason so few of us here display curiosity or even interest in the family past as it's called, is that our past, present and future is like an unbroken chain — it has no missing links.

When someone comes up with impressive data listing the number of people of Irish descent now living abroad, we shrug it off with 'Sure everyone has an Irish ancestor: so many American Presidents appear to have had Irish blood in their veins it's surprising that any of our people at all stayed home.'

Roots did increase the normal volume of overseas enquiries directed to the Genealogical Office in Dublin Castle. I am told that if you are of Irish stock and desire to establish an accurate family tree, the Genealogical Office will give you expert guidance. In a published article an officer in that department wrote: 'Our office is like a consulting room where a need may be ascertained and defined and the needy advised, directed and offered assistance should they not be in a position to search for what they require.'

Here are a few tips if you wish to dig for your (Irish) family history. The first step in researching your background is to gather information concerning the names of ancestors plus relevant dates, addresses, occupations and religion. Some of the principal sources of information are available at the Office of the Registrar General in the Custom House, Dublin.

Some of the best sources of family history are the Parish registers. Many Church of Ireland parish registers were destroyed in the Four Courts fire in 1922. The bulk of Catholic registers date from about 1820. Another fruitful source is *Griffith's Primary Valuation* drawn up between 1848 and 1864. That document lists each occupant of each house or piece of land with the name of the immediate lessor. It is available in the National Library, Genealogical Office and the Public Record

Office. Tithe Appointment Books are available in the Public Record Office. They range in date from 1823 to 1832 and list the occupants of land on which a tithe was then payable to the Church of Ireland. The Registry of Deeds, Henrietta Street, Dublin, gives useful information on middle-income groups such as merchants, gentry and substantial farmers. The Registry also contains records of property transactions stretching from 1708 to the present.

Early in this century a dozen volumes of tombstone transcriptions were printed; the Genealogical Office plus the Irish Genealogical Research Society are now endeavouring to transcribe every tombstone inscription in the country. The earliest surviving census is dated 1901 and it is available in the Public Record Office. Additionally the 1911 census tells how long a woman had been married and provides a clue to the date of her marriage in the Civil Record.

When and if you have exhausted the above sources — and yourself, I'd suggest you try and tap another source: try human contact. If you have narrowed down your search for 'family' to a particular locality, why not combine business with pleasure, get into the holiday spirit, relax and mix with the people and tell them of your quest. If you happen to be of Irish stock, the truth of the old saying 'blood is thicker than water' will quickly prove itself.

If your Irish ancestor emigrated from here inside the past two hundred years, you stand an excellent chance of getting positive information. Although Ireland has a long, sad history of emigration we have few instances of entire families emigrating, therefore there is every possibility that some branch of your family is still living in the area.

This brings me to one of our living traditions, you could call it folk memory as it includes traditional beliefs, legends, sayings, customs and accounts of happenings worth telling and retelling. Our folk-lore is a living, pulsating linkage of memories stretching into the past, and the fact that our people have stayed rooted in their own particular environment, practically ensures that any important event is faithfully recorded in the local memory bank.

I'll just touch on a couple of instances which could point up the viability of this reservoir of local lore. Recently our village Tidy Towns officials decided to 'dress up' the village graveyard, called St. Andrew's, because it contains traces of the foundation of a very ancient church of the same name. So far, no local individual has been able to find any historical record of the old church; in fact we have been unable to locate any record of the building date of the new St. Andrew's church which is about 100 feet distant from the village churchyard. It was proposed to clear the growth and accumulated rubbish from the almost invisible foundations of the old church and then rebuild the complete outline to the height of the bottom of the original windows. In the course of clearing the site, a vast assortment of human bones was exposed. Then the rumours started to fly; the source of the skeletons became the consuming subject for local discussion. The most logical and plausible theory expressed was that it was a typical Famine burial.

This was a reference to the Great Famine (1845–48) which decimated the countryside, and the point was made that the starving, stricken survivors were too weak to bury their dead the accepted depth, six feet. Luckily, folk memory helped solve it — for me. I learned that my grandfather who was born around 1830, which would place him in his teens at the time of the Famine, often spoke of the Rising — meaning the Rebellion of 1798.

The Rising, an historical watershed in Irish history, aimed at separation from Great Britain and the establishment of an Irish Republic on the French model. The French, then glorying in the success of their recent revolution sent military aid to Ireland. But only a limited measure of that aid reached Ireland; it also proved completely inadequate. After widespread bitter fighting between the Irish rebels and the English yeomanry plus other military units, the rebellion was crushed and harsh reprisals became the order of the day.

Historically our local interest in the Rebellion centres on the Battle of Wilson's Hospital. I mentioned the mound of bones to a member of my own family who has a wide-ranging interest in our history, culture and Irish heritage. She is blessed with the ability to store a phenomenal amount of interesting information and to repeat verbatim tales told long ago around the family fire, happenings 'handed down' and information 'passed along' by preceding generations. She effortlessly recalls my grandfather's account of the disastrous Battle of Wilson's Hospital and how the piles of Rebel dead were carted to St.

Andrew's graveyard to be buried in a mass grave. No tombstone was ever erected to mark the spot: at the time, the size of the resultant mound was considered an everlasting grim reminder.

By a coincidence the 'face-lift' for old St. Andrew's took place a few months after a film company shot part of the film, *The Year of the French* at Wilson's Hospital, just on the outskirts of our village.

That film soon to be released, is based on Thomas Flanagan's 1979 best selling novel *The Year of the French*.

30. IRISH IDENTITY

Last year my favourite newspaper *The Irish Times* ran a competition entitled 'In Search of Irish Identity'. I had the best of intentions to have a go at it myself but never got around to it. I read and studied the winning entry and all the published runners-up because it's a subject near and dear to my heart.

Reading the entries, especially the one that was the first to be printed, left me with a feeling of bewilderment because some of the essayists seemed to be writing about a people and a place foreign to me — *and* them. My first feeling was, they can't belong! If they only sojourn in Ireland they have my sympathy but I would suggest they try to get rid of some of their bias, take the blinkers off; get around and endeavour to mix with, what they would term, the common people.

The title of one of the winning entries was 'Discovering Ireland' (*The Irish Times*, 22 October 1977) but reading it, the only discovery this Irishman made was that Noel Griffin's slip was showing. I marvelled at the temerity of a national newspaper in publishing that essay especially when a generous proportion of their subscribers come from the ninety-three per cent Catholic population. The essay's main and space-consuming theme apparently devoted to denegrating that age-old whipping boy, the Catholic Church. Its publication proves at least that the 'stateling', as the essayist calls the Republic of Ireland, does not muzzle its miniscule religious minority.

The author makes a list of what he terms 'ascriptions' that we Irish are guilty of. They are 'stage Irish', 'priest-ridden', 'lazy', 'devious', 'garrulous', etc.

Out of his long list of our failings I thought he'd surely give 'priest-ridden' first place — but that might prematurely spotlight his bias. He then mounts his hobby horse with 'The Ireland that emerged fifty-odd years ago lacked two essential ingredients: modern ideas and a tolerant and enlightened church.' He even includes the old hackneyed statement: 'The second element (the church) might have done better for not

298

having existed at all. . . .' He goes on: 'The Irish Catholic Church with all its age and constricting ivy did much to harm the youthful spirit of that new democratic stateling in ways too numerous to mention; suffice it to say that the Irish male inherited a kind of psychological castration which still persists today.' The essayist takes up more space with, 'And this leads us to the nerve centre of Irish life. In an educational system that teaches that we are Catholics first and Irish-men second there can be no coherence.'

I re-read this entry thinking it could be one of those tongue-in-cheek articles written to spoof naive readers. Then again he could have written and slanted it with a calculated and cagey eye on the possible 'party line' of the adjudication committee, or deliberately to get a lot of his readers very annoyed.

I quote from that essay *not* to show up its author — because I'm sure he was writing from his heart. I used it to show several things, not the least of which is that while I may be one of his psychologically castrated males, I'm at a loss as to why he spared the gentler sex, because surely the Church had and has more influence on them and they in turn on us.

The essayist's resentment of the Church, as enunciated in 'Discovering Ireland', is an echo of the voice of imperial-minded Britain which understandably blames that Church for preventing, over the centuries, a British take-over — militarily, intellectually and culturally. That Church is still doing its level best to protect and cherish our culture: Faith and morals *are* an integral part of that culture.

Now that I've got that off my chest it behooves me to say *my* piece about Ireland. If someone asked me what I like, or love about Ireland I'd pour out a list as long as a late breakfast. At random it would go: the people, the unhurried way-of-life, the clean unpolluted air, the scenery — and I could go on and on. Imagine! regardless of living abroad for years in a country that 'has everything' and amongst a people who are the salt of the earth, I still love Ireland best; its people and most things Irish. But how can one explain it on paper? How can I evoke for the reader the fragrance of new-mown hay on a balmy June evening or even the smell of a turf fire?

As far back as I can remember I have been tremendously proud of 'being Irish' and acutely aware of my country's rich cultural heritage and am not ashamed to admit that like the majority of my countrymen I have a strange and mystical love for this land of ours. I'm sure anyone worth his salt feels something special when he hears his National Anthem; but there are those unique occasions when the National Anthem touches a chord deep in your heart. Recently I experienced such an occasion — at the All-Ireland Hurling final.

Hurling has been described as a fierce, fast and furious field sport. Actually strangers to the game have been known to mistake it for a free-for-all donnybrook. For the people in most of our southern counties, roughly these are the counties south of a line extending from Dublin City westward to Galway Bay, hurling is a way of life. It has been said that the game of hurling, or hurley as it's often called, is a part of the soil we work for a living; that for generations hurling has been a veritable art form in which the players dedicatedly use their skills.

Typically a senior hurling team is composed of fifteen bigger than average men. When the referee throws in the ball, those apparently awkward giants suddenly are transformed into virile athletes. To an 'outsider', hurlers in action seem to be committing mayhem, even to a 'native' on the sidelines, the participants seem to play a reckless, dangerous game; one almost expects to see murder committed every time one or more players 'pull on a ball' that happens to be dangerously close to some other gladiator's head. Actually, serious injuries are few and far between because they play 'close to their man' as they term the particular opponent they are 'marking'.

Years ago before hurling became what its critics call a more civilized game my personal hurling hero, Andy — was universally idolized by 'our side'. On the other hand, opposing players invariably referred to Andy — behind his back of course — as 'The Scourge' on account of his wild, almost murderous style of hurling. I once asked him, 'Andy, how come you never seem to get injured on the hurling field?" "Sure that's the job of me hurley; to defind meself with; and the same goes for the innimy (opposing players); they carry hurleys too and if *they* can't defind themselves they have no right taking the field with rale min.' Maybe I have already explained that when we are solely among friends, we invariably relapse into old style speech. Among other peculiarities, the letter 'e' becomes 'i', hence ten men comes out 'tin min'.

Admittedly the game has become more 'civilized' but it's still

not effete by any means. In Andy's time I recall an occasion
when Andy, who was a substitute for that day's game, was sent
out on the field to replace an injured team-mate. Recalling the
incident later, Andy said 'I wint into that game to revinge our
man that was knocked out.'

The hurling field is 140 yards long by 80 wide. Goals at ends
of the field are indicated by posts twenty-one feet apart connected
by a crossbar at a height of eight feet. The object of the game is
to drive the ball between the opponent's goal posts. A goal is
scored when it goes under the bar, but a point is recorded when
the ball goes over the bar — regardless of the altitude of its
flight. It takes three points to add up to one goal.

The object of the game is to drive the ball into or over the
opposing team's goalmouth. The leather covered ball — in
Gaelic *sliothar* — is about the size of a cricket ball but does not
have a perfectly smooth surface because of its raised seams.
Traditionally the hurley is made from hand-picked ash saplings.
When the wood is well seasoned the new hurley is then
manufactured and usually 'shaped to the taste' of the individual
hurler. The Gaelic name for hurley is *caman*, literally curved or
crooked. A hurley resembles a field hockey stick except that the
portion next the ground — the boss — is much heavier, much
thicker and has two almost flat, striking faces. A hurley could be
a formidable weapon; a blow from the boss could crush the
skull of an ox. It's not uncommon for a player to drive the heavy
sliothar through the air well over a hundred yards *and* with
unbelievable accuracy.

Historically, the Irish cling tenaciously to hurling; even during
the centuries of war, invasion and in more recent times, through
British occupation when hurling was outlawed by successive
English Kings. I have read well-authenticated accounts of
hurling in the Penal Days. In counties the Cromwellian planters
had already subjugated, the planters would on occasion permit
the peasantry to play their ancient game. The Landed Gentry,
like royal spectators in the Roman Coliseum, would watch as
the 'mere Irish' fielded out sometimes 200 men a side. At times
the 'Elite' condescendingly applauded the gladiators as they
wagered golden guineas on the outcome.

In reality hurling goes back a long way in Celtic culture. Our
ancient annalists went so far as to claim that the Celts were
playing hurley when the Grecian gods were still young. Hurling

crops up again and again in our oldest mythologies and definitely plays a major role in the tales woven around our beloved legendary hero Cuchulain. Regardless of his prowess in the chase, or in battle, none of our ancient heroes was accepted as a true champion unless he excelled at the game of hurling. According to legend the very possession and ownership of Ireland itself was decided on the Plain of Moytura in County Mayo when the invading Tuatha de Danann — 'The people of the Goddess Danu' — defeated the indigenous Firbolgs in a bloody, lethal hurling match; and don't forget that Moytura abounds in megalithic monuments. The rules of that prehistoric hurling game at Moytura were decided mutually beforehand: 100 men on each representative team and the possession of Ireland to the side that had any survivors at the termination of the match.

A few Sundays ago I was one of the 70,000 spectators at an All-Ireland Hurling final in our National stadium in Dublin. The finalists were the Kilkenny hurlers versus the men from Cork. People from every county in Ireland and from all walks of life were there, from President Hillary to the standing room only spectators on Hill Sixteen — the latter aptly named after another battle ground in the First World War. Our Prime Minister Jack Lynch, himself a Corkman and a holder of one All-Ireland football medal in addition to five All-Ireland senior hurling medals was there, flanked by Church dignitaries both Catholic and Protestant. I mention the medals because an All-Ireland senior medal is without doubt the most coveted award in Irish sport.

Our internationally famous bands — the Garda Siochána and the Artane Boys Band — were out there on the field playing martial airs. Then the men from Cork and the stalwarts of Kilkenny marched onto the field, each player carrying his hurley as if it were a shining sword. And the crowd exploded in applause, the band played the opening notes of our National Anthem 'The Soldier's Song', everyone stood to attention and by the time the anthem came to the line: 'We're children of a fighting race . . .' you'd have a heart of stone if you hadn't felt in every pulse of your body the fierce fervour and pride of race that engulfed the mass of spectators and the millions of our race following the spectacle on television. Personally, I felt a strange mystical oneness — a sharing — with the hurlers on the field and the crowd, and could feel atavistic pulsations sent out, from back there in time, when our race was young.

You may ask what makes an Irishman? It could be an amalgam: language, literature, art, drama, religion, sports, music and education. In the case of Irishmen of my own and preceding generations, I'd say that religion comes first in forming our Irishness. History could run it a close second; maybe we could sum it all up in one word — culture. A fair definition of culture might be 'the total intellectual and institutional heritage of civilization'.

I recall being at a party when an English guest was holding forth about Camelot, King Arthur and the Knights of the Round Table. A fellow countryman of mine jumped into the ensuing discussion and regaled us with a lecture. At the time I thought he sounded condescending, even disparaging when he said 'It's a pity ye English have so little in that line; I'll grant that ye have the Saxon Chronicles, the medieval Morte d' Arthur and the British Museum, but we have abundant and unparalleled early literature, surviving antiquities, legend and history that go so far back that . . .' and he paused, more from a loss of breath than for words and proof.

I'm a little leery of history — as written — giving us a true picture of the past, because even when it's backed up by all the modern technical aids for following, reporting and assessing events, the resultant report or account is seldom incontrovertible; fortunately our Irish history is not dependent on, or confined to the written word. Countless ages ago, long before their people had mastered the art of writing, our ancient Celtic bards learned by rote and transmitted from father to son, the lore, epic poems, legends and the songs of our race.

It is safe to say that today we have a history that's 'alive and kicking' simply because that history has been handed down from generation to generation by survivors and eye-witnesses who personally lived, felt and suffered it; they recounted it to reputable persons who in turn faithfully passed it along.

Anyone reading some of the historical books recently published in Ireland had better be prepared for the new image promoted therein. This new image holds that Irish History as taught in our schools 'under the thumb' of the clergy, has not only fomented violence in the North of Ireland but was the prime mover of that violence, because history so taught unjustly blames England for Ireland's past and present ills.

Scholars agree that although there were and are several Celtic languages, there is no such thing as Celtic literature. We know that Irish literature in a form that could be attractive to the modern world existed long before Christian missionaries introduced writing here in the fifth century. The Celtic peoples had a learned and priestly caste — the Druids. This caste was subdivided into seers, historians, bards and poets. These four passed oral tradition from one generation to the next 'by the joint memory of the elders, by the passing from one ear to another, by the chanting of the poets'. It is claimed that this chanting had a rythmical alliterative style and was in the form of a language which was so archaic as to be unintelligible to the masses. But it did contain elements that justifies its acceptance as a kind of literature. The highest grade of poet was able to recite up to four hundred poems, stories and songs from memory. But they did not commit their material to writing, for to do so might not only eliminate their profession altogether, but lose them their honoured place as part custodian of Ireland's cultural heritage.

Irish literature as we now know it, owes its existence to the arrival in Ireland of Christianity and to the Latin alphabet. Around the fifth century Irish monks, fearing that the pagan stories of heroic Ireland might be forgotten, began religiously to put the stories into writing. Thanks to the labours of those early monks much of our ancient Gaelic literature is preserved for us on folio-sized vellum and contains a miscellaneous collection of poems, verse, history, legend, hagiography, medical and legal tracts, bardic poetry and much else.

As far back as the fifth century most of the Irish, including kings, Druids and priests accepted Christianity but they still clung to much of their pagan custom and belief. As a result, even down to recent times, there have been two distinct streams of tradition in Ireland: the Christian and the pagan. Unfortunately no literary manuscripts previous to the eleventh century survive and we depend for our knowledge of earlier literature on the antiquities of the eleventh and twelvth centuries and the great collections called *Leabhar na h Uidhre* and the *Book of Leinster*, whose prose have a simplicity and directness that equals the Old Testament, matched with literary skill of a modern kind — including the flashback.

Apart from the many ancient histories and annals that to date have been translated, we have a mass of literature, most of it in manuscripts, such as no other nation in Europe possesses. It consists of history (legendary and real), narrative poems and ballads, prose, historical tales, mythological and other imaginative tales, lyric poetry, satire, religious literature, law, science and various translations from other languages. The most important collections of Celtic manuscripts are housed in the libraries of the Royal Irish Academy and Trinity College Dublin; the Bodleian at Oxford; the British Museum, Louvain, and the Vatican. There is also a significant number of manuscripts in various other continental and home libraries and in private collections. Altogether the unprinted literature of Celtic Ireland would fill 1,500 volumes of vellum, among which are the *Leabhar na h Uidhre*, or *Book of the Dun Cow; The Book of Ballymote; The Book of Lecan;* the *Leabhar Breac*, or *Speckled Book of Duniry;* and *The Book of Fermoy*, all of which may be seen in the library of the Royal Irish Academy. But perhaps the most valuable of all the books of manuscripts, from a literary standpoint, is the twelfth century *Book of Leinster* in the library of Trinity College.

Ireland is indeed fortunate in possessing the world's richest mythology; a mythology in which scholars have discovered traces of the ancient Irish pantheon — the world of the great pagan gods. A world full of fantasy, magic and exaggerated flights of fancy; a bewildering other-world of wonder, dreams and magic.

The number and variety of tales and sagas in that mythology is immense, and they are related under many headings: Destruction, Cattle Raids, Courtships, Battles, Cave Stories, Voyages, Tragedies, Adventures, Banquets, Sieges, Plunderings, Elopements, Eruptions, Visions, Love Stories, Hostings and Invasions. Regardless of their scholarly classifications my favourite stories all belong to the Mythological Cycle. To this cycle belongs one of the best known and best loved of the old tales — 'The Doom of the Children of Lir'.

31. THE CHILDREN OF LIR

To generations of Irish, the young and the old, the poignant story of the Children of Lir was and still is real — or on the threshold of reality. We believed it when we were children and even as we grew older some of us hoped there was a grain of truth in it. After all, the locations, the place-names and the very atmosphere — meaning a deep understanding of, and a sense of being part of the same unique ancient culture — still prevail. Maybe we just *want* to believe it.

Apart from its claim to antiquity, the Tale of the Children of Lir is so popular and so widely known that there are few students of Irish mythical lore unacquainted with it. I'm sure most of us from our school books easily recall the lines:

> Sorrowful is my song,
> Of songs most sorrowful,
> The song of the doom of the Children of Lir.

The tale of the Children of Lir is set in the era that marked the close of the Tuatha de Danann rule, and the accession of the Milesians to sovereign power in Ireland. After their disastrous defeat at Teltown, County Meath, the Tuatha de Danann voluntarily retired to pleasant hills, caves and caverns where, from then on, they led a mystical and concealed existence. In their new environment they still formally adhered to the titles and claimed the privilege of rulers. They were not adored as gods but were accepted as supernatural beings endowed with great magical powers who occasionally interfered in human affairs. Undoubtedly many of our fairy stories are based on the legends woven around the once powerful de Danann.

This tale of Lir's lonely children begins when, under their altered circumstances, the Tuatha de Danann assembled to elect a High King. Bodb Dearg was elected, an election disputed by a once powerful chieftain named Lir. Nevertheless Lir and Bodb Dearg remained close friends. Later a great misfortune befell Lir — his wife died and this preyed greatly upon him. On hearing

306

the sad news Bodb Dearg assembled his people and said 'If Lir choose, my assistance and my friendship would be useful to him; for I have three maidens of the fairest form and the best repute that are in Erinn namely, Aoh, Aoife and Ailbhe — my own three bosom nurslings.' Hearing the King's kind offer, Lir begged assistance. Later when the marital preliminaries were over the account goes: And the three daughters were on the same couch with the Queen of Tuatha de Danann. Then Bodb Dearg said 'Take your choice of the three maidens oh Lir.' 'I do not know' said Lir, 'which is the choicest of them but the eldest of them Aoh, is the noblest and it is she that I had better take.' And Aoh was united with Lir that night.

And in due time after this his wife became pregnant and she brought forth two children at birth, a daughter and a son; Fionnuala and Aodh were their names. And she became pregnant again, and brought forth two sons; Fiachra and Conn were their names and she herself died at their birth. And that preyed greatly upon Lir; and were it not for the greatness of the love with which his mind rested upon his four children, he almost would have died of grief.

Bodb Dearg said 'We grieve for that girl (Aoh) on account of the good man we gave her, for I shall give him her other sister as a wife, namely, Aoife.' Eventually Lir espoused her, took her with him to his house and Aoife felt honour and affection with the children of Lir and of her own sister. It was said that everyone who should see those four children could not help giving them the love of his soul because the beauty and symmetry of their form was a joy and delight to all who beheld them.

But in time the black dart of jealousy stabbed into Aoife the stepmother, and she soon regarded the children of her sister with hatred and enmity: 'Dumb on her bed a year, nursing her heart's cold snake.' Eventually she perpetrated an act of hateful treachery, as well as of unfaithful jealousy, against the children of Lir. She endeavoured to have her people kill 'the four children of Lir for whom my love has been abandoned by their father. . . .' But her people answered, 'They shall not be killed by us; it is an evil deed you have thought of, and evil will it be to you to have mentioned it.' She drew her sword to kill and destroy the children but her natural cowardice and the weakness of her mind stopped her. And so she ordered her charioteer to drive herself and the four children: Fionnuala, Aodh, Fiachra and Conn westward to the shores of Dairbhreach – literally the Lake of the Oaks, now Lough Derravaragh in County Westmeath.

Arriving at the lake their horses were halted and Aoife said 'Go in and bathe'. As the poet puts it 'And naked in delight the children ran and played in the cold mere'. Then the stepmother raised her witch wand in her hand and smote the children and they were seen no more; but on the lake four swans beheld their plumes amazed. Fionnuala said to her 'Evil is the deed thou hast done this day; to ruin us without cause.' Then Aoife relented somewhat and said, 'In the feathers of swans 300 years shall ye float on deep Derravaragh: on the Sea of Moyle a like period: with wild and lonely curlews of Erris Head (Co. Mayo) shall ye spend your final 300 years.' And finally she said 'Till the bell rings in Innis Glory I curse you: 900 years.'

In all the various tellings of this classical folk-epic, the most articulate of the four swan children was Fionnuala. In fact a study of her role would give Women Libbers something to think about. So now, Fionnuala weeping said 'This is a mighty curse, O mother of our tears, unmothered, comfortless, cold through the age-long night!' And moved, Aoife answered

> A boon, a boon I yield you
> Ye sorrowful Children of Lir!
> Man's reason shall breed within you
> Sweet words in the tongue of men.
>
> Sweet, sweet be your voices,
> Ye mournful Swans of Lir!
> The sad, sweet moan of your music
> Shall comfort the sick with sleep.

Next we hear of Lir getting word of his childrens' plight and 'Rushing in flames of wrath by Derravaragh Lough'. The Swans beheld their father and with a human wail of song over the water, called the name of Lir. Hearing that heart-breaking cry 'Lir ran all trembling to the shore and bent in ruth to kiss the piteous feathery things and fast, full and hot fell the tears of Lir on the feathers of the Swans.' The striken parent recognized each child: he gently stroked Aodh's snowed golden head and stroked Fionnuala's neck 'writhin to meet his touch', and stroked Fiachra's wings and the downy crest of Conn.

Then Fionnuala told her father of how 'A cruel witch for our mother has given thee swans for children' and went on to tell the full story of the 900 year curse that would only end 'when the bell rings in Innis Glory'. And Lir with his children four, lay down that night and with the Swans he made his bed by Derravaragh's rocky shore.

Lir then rushed to inform Bobd Dearg of Aoife's vile deed. The High King summoned Aoife and Lir confronted her: 'Wearily still she smiled, I have done it; let me die.' In wrath Bobd Dearg asked her 'What vile shape is most abhorred by thee?' 'A demon of the air', she moaned. Then with his magic wand Bobd Dearg smote her 'And her blue eyes grew white as dazzling leprosy. Her hideous body seemed the snake-fiend of her heart, and she burst forth on dragon wings.' So howling on the blast, fled from the face of men, Aoife for evermore.

Lir dwelt on Derravaragh's shores for the remainder of his life. He never lacked human company because 'By the lake dwelt peace, and all men — even mortal enemies — sat down together for comfort of the songs of the Swans'.

When their 300 years on Derravaragh was up, the spokesman — Fionnuala as usual — said 'Sweet brothers our age here is ended for tonight our flight must be'. So they spread their wings and headed north. Loud was the Swans' lament and loud the grief of Lir. The Swan children bade farewell to Derravaragh: 'To the gulls and the curlews, fly the Children of Lir.' And soaring high the four swans headed north and eventually lit on Sruth-na-Moyle. This was the ancient Celtic name for the tideway between Ireland and Scotland.

I won't endeavour to cover the Swans' 300 years sojourn on Sruth-na-Moyle that commences:

Now sang the shrill sea-wind through the feathers of the Swans,
And cold round their white breasts the brine of Sruth-na-Moyle
Boiled in the bitter surge; and bitter was their lot,
Tossing unsheltered on the tides of Sruth-na-Moyle.

Listen to this brief description of the pitiable condition of the Swans after a storm:

Hoarse o'er the hissing waves howled Oifa in the blast,
And dreadful through the night the chill glare of her eyes
Gleamed in the dazzling snow; and through the Swans the surf
Shot arrows, burning cold, barbed by the stinging frost.

In spite of my attempt to make a long story short I can't resist including part of Fionnuala's lament in the cold: 'Behold us on the rocks featherless, cold, we print our steps in blood.' Also:

> There they dwelt, with the seals, the human-hearted seals,
> That loved the Swans, and far followed with sad soft eyes,
> Doglike, in sleek brown troops, their singing, o'er the sea;
> So for their music yearned the nations of the seals.

(Seals occupy a special place in Irish mythology, folk-lore and superstitions.)

The course of their second 300 years being run, Fionnuala said 'Swans your flitting time is come again.' Then the four Swans soared high and swiftly to the west and flew 'till they reached Erris Domnann — possibly Erris Head in the present County Mayo. There for the first time in their long lives they first 'knew the ocean without shore: and in their ears all night boomed on with solemn sound the thunder of it's waves.'

When their thrice 300 years were up the Swans wearily winged their way westward and 'Under the eyes of dawn, flew home to the halls of Lir. And found that but a heap and a desolation there dwelt and a tongueless grief as of a harp unstrung.' They found their home a heartless home, without fire, without joy, without a harp, without a hound. No talk, no laughter, no sound of song. Sadly and wistfully Fionnuala said 'A lost dream to us is our home.' Then forlornly the four Swans flew westward to the wild western sea and made their home on Innis Glory — an island on Mayo's rocky coast. There they dwelt in peace until the coming to Erin of the Faith — 'Till holy Patrick's feet blest Erin's faithless fields.'

Eventually a priest — a cleric named Mocholm Ogue — came to the island of Innis Glory and built his church of rude stone. And like the wild birds he lived, 'no better than the birds; but more lonely.' Introspective and questioning God, Mocholm the monk asked, 'why am I wasted here: Aloof in peaceless peace: Shall I feed the fish with praise, birds of the air with the Bread of God?'

Then one morning the Swans heard the ringing of the cleric's bell on Innis Glory 'As far, faint from some dim alien world the bell's mysterious tone.' And Fionnuala told her brothers 'That is God's bell — the bell that brings us ease,' and through that day and the following night the Swans 'praised with sweet fairy music the great God of Heaven.'

The next morning Mocholm Ogue went to the 'Lake of the Birds' and seeing the four Swans he enquired 'Are ye the Children of Lir?' 'Indeed we are.' Then the cleric knew why he came — or was sent — to 'this island, beyond every other island in Erinn.' And he entreated the Swans to put their trust in him and he'd 'separate them from their sins'. And there they dwelt with him, 'four weary things at rest'.

The Swans' travail was not ended. As Deoch, wife of Liargnen, King of Connaught heard the account of the Swans she became seized with deep affection and love for the birds. She told her husband if he did not procure the four Swans for her, 'Empty shall be thy bed.' Then Lairgnen the King, came to Innis Glory and demanded the Swans of Mocholm. The cleric refused: 'Liargnen arose and seized the shuddering Swans. A pair in either hand, he dragged them from the altar with 'Here woman take thy birds!'' ' But immediately Deoch laid her hands on the birds, a wonderous thing happened:

Suddenly from the swans,
Slack fell their feathery coats, and there once more they stood,
Children; yet weird with age, weird with nine hundred years
Of woe: four wistful ghosts from childhood's daisied field.

It was then that Fionnuala said 'Come baptize us, O Cleric for our death is near; and afterwards shalt thou dig one grave and O friend thou shall lay us: one sister and three brothers: at my right hand Fiachra; and Conn by my heart and Aodh in my bosom.' Then were the four baptized and with the Blessed Host houseled. And praising God that night they sang their souls away. And keeping Fionnuala's word the cleric laid the four in one grave. And many Masses for their souls the cleric said and wrote he their names in Ogham on their gravestone. And in his church he hung the four white shapes of Swans.

The Bardic tale ends there — or does it? If the original teller of the tale could have looked forward to the present year of our Lord he might truly have written his postscript thus:

And a full fifteen hundred storm-tossed years will sail one after another into, *or out of*, the shoreless, bottomless, sea of infinite time. Then another cleric, a Friar himself who also off Erris Head in his native Mayo long heard the lonesome cry of the wild curlew, will see fit to hang in another stone-built church 'the four white shapes of Swans'. The four white Swans shaped in leaded glass, today adorn the four side windows of the rebuilt Reformation-ravaged Blessed Sacrament

Chapel in The Abbey in my native village Multyfarnham. And within a curlew's call of Derravaragh's oak-lined shore!

Of all our Irish wild birds and animals the swan — back beyond the memory of man — was held in most respect. This respect, almost amounting to veneration, is as old as the hills and undoubtedly is rooted in, or connected with the age-old legend of the four helpless children imprisoned in swan garb.

The Brehon Law, itself possibly rooted in Druidism and certainly pre-dating Christianity, was codified in the eighth century and it stipulated 'no swan in Ireland shall be killed'. To this day there is a strong belief that if you purposely kill a swan you are inviting a disastrous run of bad luck; and plenty of people will give you facts and figures to prove it. Another of our living traditions is that at the approach of its natural death, the swan sings its own death dirge in notes plaintive as the banshee's wail. I believe that all this — and more — is reflected in the poignant tale of the Children of Lir.

32. EPILOGUE

Early in May 1981 Eileen, with her old typewriter, pecked out
Finis to our four years of work on what we privately call our
Roots. My reason for tackling the task was to depict Ireland
and the Irish as seen and experienced by a mature individual
reared in the school of hard knocks who, still retaining his
Irishness and on his own terms was accepted in countries and
by cultures foreign and even inimical to his own. Please bear in
mind that the picture I paint is not coloured by childhood
memories when I knew not the wide world beyond the Irish
Sea, or the broad Atlantic; neither does it reflect the nostalgia of
a lifetime exile or an inhabitant of a dream world.

Researching and typing *Roots* was done while we were at
our busiest: rebuilding the bungalow and utilizing the farm to
best advantage. Eventually it dawned on both of us that
somehow our long planned retirement was, in military
parlance, becoming a retreat bordering on a rout. Taking stock,
as they say, we realized our workload had imperceptibly
increased and we not only lacked leisure, but the challenge, fun
and excitement had vanished.

Next I asked myself why was I getting so little pleasure from
gardening and how come the boundary hedge seemed to be
stretching a bit more every year than its actual length of 500
yards. From time to time Eileen suggested we hire help to do the
bulk of the manual labour and with less conviction than usual I
remonstrated that we didn't get into this bit of light farming to
make money and there's still that old matter of paddling our
own canoe. In 1977 we decided to let the land.

Before renting out the little farm we resolved to stock the land
fully, so contacted my good friend Cecil Gibson, the best judge
in the county of an animal, and finished up with twenty-four
prime bullocks. Two years later we sold them 'fat as snails' in
Mullingar Cattle Mart at 500 pounds sterling a head. Then we let
the farm minus the two acres around the bungalow in the
village. Letting the land resolved some of our problems but

before long I discovered that my interest in the condition or
even ownership of the land we had rented out, had not only
dwindled, but that I had gradually lost the desire to even visit
our once 'proud acres'. The winding down operation took away
some of the strain, then out of a clear sky I woke up to the fact
that somehow I had become involved in writing a book.

Around 1980, my itchy feet syndrome, that's worse than the
seven year itch, started showing signs of life. Sensing the
symptoms, my wife said 'It is almost two years since you
visited the kids in Canada'. Neither of us had ever hesitated to
catch a flight to Canada from Shannon and visit the family for an
indefinite period; we had usually made those trips separately. I
mustn't have shown much interest in the subtle suggestion of a
holiday because she astutely enquired 'Is it Sharry's boreen
again?' To explain that reference to the boreen I'll need to
backtrack to 1963 and an apparently minor incident that
significantly altered all our lives. In 1960 my dream had come
true when we had moved in style to my native village with our
half dozen children. We purchased a substantial house in the
village and now, in retrospect, appreciate that the years we lived
there were the best and most fruitful of our family's entire life.
In Multy our children not only recognized and embraced their
roots, they revitalized them. Now when they all get together,
the talk inevitably centres on the three years they lived in what
they call Dad's village. The surprise is that Multy memories
seem more real and interesting to them than the longer period
they spent in Canada's ten provinces and equally long periods
in the Yukon and Northwest Territories.

For the first time in our (then) sixteen years of family life
Eileen and I felt we had finally put down roots; a house with
plenty of elbow room, large garden, and for a modest rent,
about five acres of Sharry's farm to graze our donkey, pony,
milch cow and several calves. Sharry's boreen is a short sunken
road connecting two parts of their farm and even in dry
weather, due to lack of drainage and years of the leisurely
passage of cattle, it had become a veritable sluggish river of
mud. A certain morning after milking the cow, there was I in the
boreen, gingerly picking my footsteps, trying to keep the full
can of milk from spilling and I up to the top of my knee-high
rubber boots in sticky mud that contained a generous helping of
cow dung. Being pretty agile in those days I kept my balance

and my composure, saved the milk but left one boot stuck in the mud. Luckily it was early morning and as far as I was aware, I reached home unobserved by the neighbours; then I got cleaned up, secured proper equipment, rescued the 'wellie' and returned home. Some time later Eileen remarked 'You're terribly quiet this morning.' 'I am. Can you get your hands on a good map of Canada?' Six months later I was in New Brunswick with a newly built house to receive the family and start another life.

'Another life' included eight future years employed in the Canadian Civil Service. In 1964 I got a job as Regional Engineer for the Northwest Territories and found myself in charge of 1.3 million square miles of ice-bound wilderness. My family and I moved to Fort Smith which is about 470 miles north of Edmonton, Alberta. We lived three years in Fort Smith and during that period, as a result of a medical doctor's botched operation, our eldest son, Kieran, at seventeen met an untimely, lingering death. We shipped our boy's body home to Multy.

In 1967, still in the Civil Service and accompanied by the family, we moved to Ottawa where we lived until my retirement in 1972. On my retirement from the C.S. I was awarded a certificate of tribute signed by Prime Minister Pierre Trudeau for 'Over 26 years of faithful service'. In 1972, with our two remaining sons, we returned to Ireland.

By the time *Roots* was completed, 1981 had rolled around and Eileen appeared to have contracted a mild case of my wanderlust, so we decided it was high time we talked things over.

The talking over disclosed that out of several options, two seemed reasonable: sell the farm, retain the house and its two acre site in the village and continue our frequent Canadian visits. The drawback to this was that the upkeep of the house, garden and grounds had become the proverbial albatross. The other option was a home each side of the Atlantic to suit our modest lifestyle and commute according to our whims. We decided on the latter and in June 1984 put up the entire place for public auction.

The events leading up to the auction had all the ingredients of a Le Carré novel and contained intriguing material for a playwright. I was already aware of the average Irish farmer's grád (love) for acreage, so enjoyed my ringside seat during the

foreplay and at the auction itself. We realized a handsome profit
on the sale of the farm; *The Examiner* quoted it as 'a record price
per acre'. We turned down the highest auction bid for bungalow
and grounds. I phoned Dr. Hannon in Florida, U.S.A., and over
the phone we agreed on a mutually satisfactory price. The
Doctor and I have been in constant touch since, and he
continues to be enthusiastic about returning (physically) to his
roots — his people hail from County Clare.

The dozens of times I departed (not left) the village, I had
never said individual good-byes, not even a lifetime ago, when I
got my mother's blessing, picked up my cheap valise, threw
back my shoulders and stretching to my fullest inch (66)
marched out of our kitchen without even a backward glance,
or a moist eye — on my part. Years afterwards I was told
that my mother, with a touch of pride diluted with wistfulness,
had whispered 'There's a cool boy gone out.'

In passing, I had better say a few words about 'the
neighbours' around Multy. I could easily fill a book describing
that community we had the privilege of living amongst for those
fifteen years. While living in Ireland we consciously avoided
giving the impression that we expected, let alone needed special
consideration; yet somehow, quietly, unobtrusively and
without any expectation of remuneration, our neighbours
looked after both of us as if we were something special. Ireland,
even in the rural areas, is rapidly becoming modern and kids
will be kids the world over; in the fifteen years of our combined
stays there, we never suffered from vandalism, not even on All
Hallows (Hallowe'en) night when the 'go boys' are up to their
tricks; like the time the unpopular Mr. — returned in the small
hours from a pub crawl and found his harnessed horse fully
yoked between the shafts of a cart in his already cramped
kitchen.

Just two months after our auction we arrived in Canada's
capital, bought a house that suits our modest needs and also
took delivery of a huge shipping container packed with the bulk
of our well-worn, much travelled furniture, fixtures and other
personal effects. Now less than a year after leaving my native
village we are already planning an Irish holiday for a lengthy,
indefinite period: a vacation designed to suit the ongoing
carefree pursuit of our dreams.

At this point I'd like to put on record that within living

memory, and further back, the minority religion that founded, owns, and operates Wilson's Hospital and Preston School in Multyfarnham has long enjoyed peace and genuine respect in our community. Before the word ecumenism was coined, our twin parishes of Multy and Leney enjoyed an unbroken tradition of harmony between the two religious groups; close pastoral and social ties always existed between our incumbent Parish Priest and the current Warden of Wilson's. The following is from the Prospectus given to me some years ago by the then Warden Rev. James McKeon B.A. H.Dip. Ed.

Wilson's Hospital, Multyfarnham, Co. Westmeath, was founded by the benefaction of Andrew Wilson of Piercefield, Mullingar who gave his lands and hereditaments in trust to the Primate of all Ireland, the Archbishop of Truam, the Bishop of Meath, and the Bishop of Kilmore, to build a hospital for the care and maintenance of Protestant male children with a school house attached thereto for their education. Suitable employment was found for the pupils on leaving school, and noted in the early registers of the hospital. The school has been in continuous operation since 1761, and closed only during the Battle of Wilson's Hospital in 1798, when it was occupied for a time by the rebels.

At the end of the chapter on Poll na gCat I promised to return and explore the cave. Some time before the auction, with the able help of several of my table tennis partners, we managed to enlarge the cave entrance, but only stayed long enough to examine the interior and take some rough measurements. Piers' particulars as quoted in the Annals of Westmeath proved amazingly accurate, except that our measurement showed the floor level now is many feet higher than the elevation Piers reported in 1641.

The boys and myself spaced our working visits over several weeks; it happened to be in the autumn and the colony of badgers that obviously inhabited some adjoining areas of the cave had been engaged in changing their bedding. On each of our trips, there were piles of freshly pulled grass and about an equal amount of semi-rotted vegetation strewn around the entrance and in the cave itself. From the almost over-powering stench in the cave we concluded that the rotted bedding had gradually accumulated on the floor of the cave and so raised its elevation many feet higher than the level recorded in 1641. At present only the tops of the openings into the three branches (described by Piers) are visible. To permit further exploration the silt floor will have to be lowered. The Cat's Holle (sic) beckons.

About our future plans: I have more plans than time. Who said 'Man's reach exceeds his grasp?' Apart from taking sufficient exercise to keep in shape I will try to avoid physically demanding tasks. I have an urge to try my hand at an offshoot of *Roots*. This is a result of my driving curiosity to follow up questions posed by souterrains, the ancient monastic site in Tyfarnham, the passage under the Friary, the cave in Poll na gCat and *especially* that unmarked grave connected with the historic Battle of Wilson's Hospital.

I have a personal interest in that 1798 tragic event so will try and explore folk memory in relation to the Battle of Wilson's Hospital; especially its effect on local families and descendents of the losers. I would then try to strike a fair mean between their collective verdict and Piers' detailed and (apparently) historically accepted report of the battle. Piers' report calls it '— the battle, or rather massacre of Wilson's —'

Sir Henry Piers, born in 1629, was a writer of considerable repute; his published works include the *Chronographical History of Westmeath*, which was published in 1770 by Colonel Charles Vallancy.

Piers' report in the Annals of Westmeath about the battle covers many pages. Apart from the content of each chapter, the very titles of the chapters sound melodramatic: the titles go:

The Battle of Wilson's Hospital — Cruelty of the Yeomanry — No Mercy — The Wounded and Prisoners Butchered — Numbers of United Irishmen Burnt to Death in a Farm House — The Reign of Terror — Reilly, the United Irishman, Almost Flayed to Death — Retribution, the Wild Justice of Revenge.

I recently had a letter from Dr. Hannon and he radiates enthusiasm when he unfolds his plans for a (possible) return to Ireland. His answer to a friend who asked 'Why Ireland?' was 'No person can pick their birthplace; but they can choose a place to live — I chose Ireland.'

Many of my future plans coincide with the doctor's. For instance his intentions include positive follow-up of our mutual desire to promote archeological research in Ireland; also to interest Irish-Americans in what he calls the Real Ireland. In that respect here is a sample of our correspondence on the subject. He writes:

I have also felt a deep sense in my bones of being 'home' each time I have stepped from a plane onto Ireland's sod. There is a quickening in the heart and spirit and the softness of the speech captivates the ear. Where else on God's green earth can one ask directions to Clonmacnoise in Kilbegan of an elderly lady walking her dog and thirty minutes later part company with knowledge of her brother's serious ailment, the dog's pedigree, an opinion on Garret Fitzgerald's Fine Gael party, the restoration project at the site of the old distillery across the road and the danger of so many motor cars on the Irish roads, all told with intense interest and the most captivating style and charm in words strung together like pearls on a necklace. In the future it would be well to have a pocket tape recorder equipped with a buttonhole microphone to capture such moments of pure literature.

And when friends ask 'Why Ireland' I say 'Where else!' There is to be a Christmas party at my house in Multy in 1988. The invitations, most of them that is, went out with Christmas cards sent in 1985. They went all over the world — to Canada, Africa, South America, the States, Europe and of course, the people in Multy. The party is set to begin at noon on Christmas Eve and is planned to last until New Year's Day.

Usually I try to avoid sentimentality but admit both my wife and I are old fashioned and religious: my religion has a Celtic flavour of superstition. Living as we did, only forty yards across the road from St. Andrew's churchyard, I never had to examine my palm to recall *Memento Mori*. Over the years both of us 'broke our backs' wrestling with and hacking the ivy, nettles and other strangling growths invading the Nevin plot.

Actually thoughts of death, even our own, are less awesome in the context of Ireland and the semi-spiritual hold it has on me. Both of us have an abiding interest in St. Andrew's. So far that historic churchyard contains the remains of representatives of five generations of our family: it is also our son Kieran's final resting place. Resting place! Apt name for a graveyard, especially for a people conditioned to accept that death is not final, but rather a stage on the path towards eternal life.

Our son's untimely death was the one and only time in my entire life I felt totally powerless and defeated: worse again, I was *frightened*. I had a hard-fought battle with my Faith before I eventually bowed to the will of God and honestly said 'Thy Will be done.'

I never felt unduly foreign in other countries, yet only in my homeland have I felt singularly at home and at peace with myself. Every 'last time' I leave its shores, Ireland will, as it always did, tug at my very heartstrings. To paraphrase Robert Frost:

> My Irish Roots go wide and deep
> But I have promises to keep
> And words to weave before I sleep
> And miles to go before I sleep.